The Behavioral Economics of Inflation Expectations

As one of the first texts to take a behavioral approach to macro-economic expectations, this book introduces a new way of doing economics. Rötheli uses cognitive psychology in a bottom-up method of modeling macroeconomic expectations. His research is based on laboratory experiments and historical data, which he extends to real-world situations. Pattern extrapolation is shown to be the key to understanding expectations of inflation and income. The quantitative model of expectations is used to analyze the course of inflation and nominal interest rates in a range of countries and historical periods. The model of expected income is applied to the analysis of business cycle phenomena such as the great recession in the United States. Data and spreadsheets are provided for readers to do their own computations of macroeconomic expectations. This book offers new perspectives in many areas of macro and financial economics.

TOBIAS F. RÖTHELI is Professor of Macroeconomics at the University of Erfurt.

The Behavioral Economics of Inflation Expectations

Macroeconomics Meets Psychology

TOBIAS F. RÖTHELI

University of Erfurt

CAMBRIDGE
UNIVERSITY PRESS

CAMBRIDGE
UNIVERSITY PRESS

University Printing House, Cambridge CB2 8BS, United Kingdom

One Liberty Plaza, 20th Floor, New York, NY 10006, USA

477 Williamstown Road, Port Melbourne, VIC 3207, Australia

314–321, 3rd Floor, Plot 3, Splendor Forum, Jasola District Centre, New Delhi – 110025, India

79 Anson Road, #06-04/06, Singapore 079906

Cambridge University Press is part of the University of Cambridge.

It furthers the University's mission by disseminating knowledge in the pursuit of education, learning, and research at the highest international levels of excellence.

www.cambridge.org
Information on this title: www.cambridge.org/9781108482851
DOI: 10.1017/9781316987056

First published 2020

A catalogue record for this publication is available from the British Library.

Library of Congress Cataloging-in-Publication Data
Names: Rötheli, Tobias F., author.
Title: The behavioral economics of inflation expectations : macroeconomics meets psychology / Tobias F. Rötheli.
Description: Cambridge ; New York, NY : Cambridge University Press, 2020. |
    Includes bibliographical references and index.
Identifiers: LCCN 2019060122 (print) | LCCN 2019060123 (ebook) | ISBN 9781108482851
    (hardback) | ISBN 9781108447065 (paperback) | ISBN 9781316987056 (ebook)
Subjects: LCSH: Rational expectations (Economic theory) | Rational expectations
    (Economic theory)–Mathematical models. | Inflation (Finance) |
    Economics–Psychological aspects. | Extrapolation.
Classification: LCC HB3731 .R67 2020 (print) | LCC HB3731 (ebook) | DDC 332.4/1019–dc23
LC record available at https://lccn.loc.gov/2019060122
LC ebook record available at https://lccn.loc.gov/2019060123

ISBN 978-1-108-48285-1 Hardback
ISBN 978-1-108-44706-5 Paperback

To my family

Contents

List of Figures	*page* xii
List of Tables	xiv
Preface	xvii
1	**Patterns and Expectations**	**1**
	1.1 Introduction	1
	1.2 Pattern-Based Expectations and Variants of Rational Expectations	4
	1.3 Relation to Survey- and Market-Based Measures of Expectations	9
	1.4 Pattern-Based Expectations and Issues of Method	11
	1.5 The Outline of the Book	13
2	**Extrapolation and Expectations**	**16**
	2.1 Introduction	16
	2.2 Extrapolation in Economics	17
	2.3 Extrapolation in Psychology	17
	2.4 Extrapolation in Forecasting	20
	2.5 Summary and Conclusions	21
3	**Eliciting Expectations under Laboratory Conditions**	**22**
	3.1 Introduction	22
	3.2 Basic Elicitation Procedures and Data	22
	3.3 Expectations of Central Tendency and Probability Ranges	34
	3.4 Summary and Conclusions	41

Appendix 3.1 Instructions for the Basic Treatment (i),
            Translated from German   41
Appendix 3.2 The Instructions for the Probabilistic
            Treatment (iii), Translated from German   43

4   Features of the Laboratory Data   47
    4.1 Introduction   47
    4.2 The Role of Economic Context   47
    4.3 Comparison of Elicited Expectations across Treatments   49
    4.4 Pattern-Based versus Linear Extrapolation   50
    4.5 Summary and Conclusions   52

5   Similarity Matching and Scaling the
    Experimental Data   53
    5.1 Introduction   53
    5.2 Experimental Evidence on Similarity Matching 54
    5.3 Modeling Similarity Matching   56
    5.4 Scaling the Laboratory Data to Historical Data   57
    5.5 Computing Historical Time Series of Expected Inflation   62
    5.6 Summary and Conclusions   65
Appendix 5.1 Instructions for the Similarity Matching
            Experiment, Translated from German   65
Appendix 5.2 A Routine for the Computation of Pattern-
            Based Expectations   66

6   Pattern Extrapolation and Expectations Measured by
    Consumer Surveys   69
    6.1 Introduction   69
    6.2 Forecast Performance of Different Measures of Inflation
        Expectations   69
    6.3 Competing Explanations of How Consumers Form
        Expectations   71
    6.4 Summary and Conclusions   77

7   Heterogeneity and Uncertainty of Inflation
     Expectations   78
     7.1 Introduction   78
     7.2 Modeling Heterogeneity of Inflation Expectations   79
     7.3 Modeling Uncertainty of Expected Inflation   82
     7.4 Summary and Conclusions   83

8   Inflation Dynamics   85
     8.1 Introduction   85
     8.2 The New Keynesian Phillips Curve   85
     8.3 Long-Term Inflation Expectations and the Issue of
         Anchoring   89
     8.4 Summary and Conclusions   91
     Appendix 8.1 New Keynesian Phillips Curve Estimates for
                   Germany   92

9   Explaining the Course of Interest Rates   94
     9.1 Introduction   94
     9.2 Effects of the Heterogeneity of Expected Inflation   97
     9.3 Effects of the Uncertainty of Expected Inflation   101
     9.4 Estimating Interest Rate Equations   103
     9.5 Summary and Conclusions   109

10 Generalizing the Pattern-Based Approach   110
     10.1 Introduction   110
     10.2 Expectations Data   111
     10.3 Econometric Analysis of Expectations Data   115
     10.4 Inflation Expectations Based on the Generalized
          Approach   117
     10.5 Applications to Historical Data of the United Kingdom   120
     10.6 Summary and Conclusions   129
     Appendix 10.1 Comparing Expectations across
                    Subject Pools   129
     Appendix 10.2 Limitations of an Econometric Representation
                    of the Laboratory Data   131

11 A Detour to Income Expectations   133
   11.1 Introduction   133
   11.2 Expectations Data   133
   11.3 Income Expectations and the Course of the Great
        Recession   137
   11.4 Summary and Conclusions   140
   Appendix 11.1 What Goes Up Must Come Down   141

12 The Fisher Effect in Historical Times   143
   12.1 Introduction   143
   12.2 Around the World with Irving Fisher   145
   12.3 The Fisher Effect in the USA Prior to World War I   151
   12.4 Summary and Conclusions   156

13 Expectations of High Inflation   157
   13.1 Introduction   157
   13.2 Expectations Data for Different Ranges of Inflation   157
   13.3 Tests of Range Consistency and Scaling   158
   13.4 Applications to High-Inflation Economies   162
   13.5 Summary and Conclusions   168
   Appendix 13.1 Computing Elasticities of Expectations for
                 Different Rates of Inflation   169

14 The Fisher Effect in Asian Economies   170
   14.1 Introduction   170
   14.2 Estimating Interest Rate Equations   171
   14.3 Summary and Conclusions   175
   Appendix 14.1 Expected One-Year-Ahead CPI-Inflation (Exp),
                 Its Heterogeneity (Het), and Uncertainty (Unc)
                 for Six Asian Economies   175

15 The Fisher Effect in African Economies   179
   15.1 Introduction   179
   15.2 Estimating Interest Rate Equations   180

15.3 Summary and Conclusions   183

Appendix 15.1 Expected One-Year-Ahead CPI-Inflation (Exp),
Its Heterogeneity (Het), and Uncertainty (Unc)
for Six African Economies   184

16 Estimates of Expected Inflation for Major Economies   188

16.1 Introduction   188

16.2 Expected Inflation Series   188

17 Estimates of Expected Real Interest Rates for Major
Economies   199

17.1 Introduction   199

17.2 Real Interest Rate Series   199

Epilogue   206

References   207

Index   220

Figures

1.1 What people look at when forming inflation expectations *page* 5

1.2 Pattern-dependent extrapolation (patterns 13 and 3) 7

5.1 Example of display shown in the similarity assessment experiment 55

5.2 Experimental data and data based on estimated model of similarity matching 58

5.3 Estimated scaling relationship for the case of one-year expectations (treatment iii) 61

5.4 One-year-ahead expected inflation from three versions of the pattern-based model 64

5.5 One-year-ahead and five-year-ahead expected inflation 64

A5.1 Routine for the computation of the 1978M01 expectation for the CPI (in logs) for 1979M01 67

7.1 Pattern-based heterogeneity of one-year and five-year US inflation expectations 80

7.2 Heterogeneity of one-year US inflation expectations from different measures 81

7.3 Pattern-based uncertainty for one-year and five-year US inflation expectations 83

8.1 Long-term expected inflation for the United Kingdom and the USA 91

9.1 Effect of heterogeneous inflation expectations on the demand for loanable funds 98

9.2 Effect of heterogeneous inflation expectations on the supply of loanable funds 100

9.3 Effect of the risk of expected inflation on the interest rate 102

9.4	US nominal interest rates (Treasury bond yields)	103
9.5	Real interest rates based on pattern-based inflation expectations	108
9.6	Real interest rates based on Michigan measures of inflation expectations	108
10.1	US inflation expectations based on various approaches	120
10.2	Measures of the short-term real interest rate for the United Kingdom	127
11.1	US GDP growth and contributions of consumption and investment	138
11.2	Expectations of short-term US real GDP growth with uncertainty band	139
12.1	Nominal interest rates in financial centers of six countries	145
12.2	Short-run nominal interest rate and inflation expectations for the USA	152
A13.1	Elasticity of expectations for different inflation rates from different models	169

Tables

3.1   Relevant patterns for the CPI and for real GDP   *page* 26

3.2   CPI expectations for periods 5 and 9 for treatment (i)   28

3.3   CPI expectations for periods 5 and 9 for treatment (ii)   29

3.4   Real GDP expectations for periods 5 and 9 for treatment (i)   30

3.5   Real GDP expectations for periods 5 and 9 for treatment (ii)   32

3.6   CPI expectations for periods 5 and 9 for treatment (iii)   35

3.7   Measures of uncertainty of CPI expectations for periods 5 and 9 from treatment (iii)   36

3.8   GDP expectations for periods 5 and 9 for treatment (iii)   37

3.9   Measures of uncertainty of GDP expectations for periods 5 and 9 from treatment (iii)   39

6.1   Regressions relating actual annual inflation to various measures of expected inflation, sample period 1978M12–2016M12   70

6.2   Regression results for specifications explaining household inflation expectations, sample period 1981Q3–2000Q2   73

6.3   Regression results for specifications explaining household inflation expectations, sample period 1981Q3–2016Q4   75

6.4   Regression results for unrestricted adaptive-extrapolative expectations   76

8.1   Regression results for various NKPC specifications   87

8.2   Regression results for NKPC with PB measures for both expected inflation and marginal cost   88

9.1   Regression results for the one-year nominal interest rate   104

9.2	Regression results for the five-year nominal interest rate	106
10.1	CPI expectations for periods 4 (one-year-ahead) and 8 (five-year-ahead)	113
10.2	Measures of one-year- and five-year-ahead uncertainty of CPI expectations	114
10.3	The shortened set of patterns and corresponding short-term CPI expectations	119
10.4	Tabulated series of pattern-based expectations for the United Kingdom	122
11.1	Real GDP expectations for periods 4 (one-year-ahead) and 8 (five-year-ahead)	134
11.2	Measures of one-year- and five-year-ahead uncertainty of real GDP expectations	135
11.3	The shortened set of patterns and corresponding short-term GDP expectations	136
A11.1	Deviations of one-year- and five-year-ahead expected GDP from its actual course	142
12.1	OLS estimates of interest rate equations for six countries	148
12.2	Instrumental variables estimates (first differences) with pattern-based expectations	150
12.3	Pattern-based measures of expected inflation for the USA	153
12.4	Instrumental variables estimates of the interest rate equation in levels	155
13.1	CPI-expectations for four treatments with different ranges of inflation	159
13.2	The shortened set of patterns and corresponding one-year-ahead CPI-expectations	162
13.3	Money demand equations for four high-inflation countries	165
13.4	Fisher equations for four high-inflation countries	167
14.1	Interest rate equations estimated in first differences	172

14.2   Interest rate equations allowing for effects of
        heterogeneity and uncertainty   173
14.3   Instrumental variables estimates of interest rate
        equations   174
15.1   Interest rate equation in first differences   181
15.2   Interest rate equations allowing for effects of
        heterogeneity and uncertainty   182
15.3   Instrumental variables estimates of interest rate
        equations   183
16.1   Expected one-year-ahead CPI inflation, its heterogeneity,
        and uncertainty for the USA, China, Japan, Germany,
        and the United Kingdom   190
16.2   Expected one-year-ahead CPI inflation, its heterogeneity,
        and uncertainty for India, France, Brazil, Italy, and
        Canada   193
16.3   Expected five-year-ahead CPI inflation for the USA,
        China, Japan, Germany, the United Kingdom, India,
        France, Brazil, Italy, and Canada   196
17.1   Statistics for the pattern-based and World Bank measures
        of the real interest rate   201
17.2   Real interest rates based on the pattern approach for
        the USA, China, Japan, Germany, the United Kingdom,
        India, France, Brazil, Italy, and Canada   202

Preface

The notion that expectations play a key role in economic decision-making is a very old one. Over the past 100 years, major advances in the application of this insight in the formulation of economic models have been made in various subfields of economics. The concept of extrapolation – the idea that past observations of a series are the basis for making projections into the future – was present from the start of the modeling of dynamic economic processes. Forms of extrapolative expectations dominated microeconomic, financial, and macroeconomic models until the early 1960s. Then a fundamental shift occurred. Rational expectations as introduced by John Muth (1960, 1961) became the new paradigm. There appeared to be no alternative to the underlying view that optimization should be seen to rule all aspects of economic behavior. Hence, expectations were conceived to be optimal in the sense of being informed by all relevant data (not just the history of the series to be forecast) and by knowledge of causal relationships. The previously popular hypothesis of extrapolative expectations was dismissed as simplistic.

In this book, I argue that the recent resurgence of interest in extrapolation as a descriptive theory of expectations is well founded in empirical evidence. It is argued that an important reason for extrapolation to have been discarded lies in the weakness of the popular version of this theory. This book outlines a theory of pattern-based extrapolation that departs from older versions of extrapolative expectations. The new model of pattern-based expectations is rooted in cognitive psychology and empirical observation. The modeling starts with the elicitation of data in the laboratory and proceeds by clarifying the central issues of similarity matching and scaling of expectations. Its final version builds on all these elements and leads to the computation of short- and long-term expectations based on the historical series of the underlying variable. The prominent variable for which expectations are modeled in this book is inflation. The essential building blocks of the model are developed in the first few chapters of the book. This is followed by empirical analyses of the three dimensions – the mean, the heterogeneity, and the uncertainty – of these expectations and by comparisons with other models of expectations. Finally, applications of the pattern-based model of expectations in econometric analyses illustrate the empirical usefulness of this new hypothesis for explaining important macroeconomic phenomena.

In the course of writing this book, I have benefited from the many inputs of teachers and colleagues. At my alma mater, the University of Berne, debates between two prominent monetary economists, Jürg Niehans and Karl Brunner, set the stage for this work. The most important support for developing a behavioral theory of expectations was afforded to me in the early 1990s when I was a visiting scholar at the departments of economics of Harvard University and Stanford University. It was then that I started to formulate an expectations model using insights gained from psychology. Scholars from the departments of psychology, Sheldon White at Harvard and David Rumelhart at Stanford University, generously helped me become oriented in experimental psychology and learn about models of cognition. When I returned to Berne as a lecturer, Marina and Rudolf Groner further continued to guide my endeavors in this direction.

The procedures and models outlined in this book are thus the result of a process that has spanned a quarter of a century. The final steps necessary to formulate a general model applicable to empirical research were made possible by a grant from the German Research Foundation (DFG). The Deutsche Bundesbank financially supported the laboratory work presented in Chapters 10, 11, and 13. The procedures and results developed in this project were presented in many research seminars. I have thus benefited from comments of colleagues at the Claremont Graduate University, Delhi School of

Economics, Deutsche Bundesbank, Federal Reserve Banks of Boston and Atlanta, Florida State University, Georgia State University, San Francisco State University, Simon Fraser University, University of Alicante, University of Missouri-St. Louis, University of South Florida, New York University, Santa Clara University, Swiss National Bank, Western Economic Association International conference (WEAI) conference in Seattle, and Leibniz-Zentrum für Europäische Wirtschaftsforschung (Leibniz Centre for European Economic Research; ZEW) in Mannheim. In particular, I would like to thank Monica Capra, Jim Cox, Jerry Dwyer, Max Gillman, Peter Katuscak, Huston McCulloch, Luba Petersen, Christian Rojas, Kurt Schnier, Elizabeth Searing, John Spraggon, Bob Triest, Larry Wall, and Tom Willett for comments on different parts of this project.

I am very grateful to Dave Rose, Mary Burke, David Leiser, and Dick Sylla for appreciating the potential of this book project at an early stage. Christoph Mölleken and Jannick Plaasch read all of the chapters and gave detailed comments. Time and again Ruth Parham has offered helpful remarks for improving the style. Susann Storz gave organizational support and Lennard Sund checked for errors.
A succession of committed research assistants helped with the laboratory work. My particular thanks go to Phil Good who believed in this book from the very beginning. Last but not least, my gratitude for continuous support of all my endeavors goes to Sylke.

I   Patterns and Expectations

This book is a contribution to a new way of doing economics. It will show that when taking fundamental insights from psychology into account, we can develop a bottom-up approach to the understanding of economic behavior. Instead of making a priori assumptions on human rationality, we draw on insights from cognitive psychology to elicit such behavior in the laboratory. The concrete behavior thus studied and modeled is the formation of expectations. The book will explain in detail how a model of expectations is built, starting from measurement of expectations under experimental conditions and then proceeding to apply the data thus elicited to real-world situations. With its focus on expectations regarding inflation, this text is a contribution to behavioral macroeconomics. It will appeal to readers who demand more from behavioral economics than just a critique of mainstream economics, thanks to its emphasis on bottom-up quantification and modeling.

Expectations have long been recognized to be important in economics. With the advent of formal and quantitative models in the 1920s, researchers had to make explicit their views on how people process information to form expectations. Irving Fisher (1930) was one of the first to propose a clearly articulated model of such a process. Tellingly, the variable he was most concerned with – expected inflation – is also the central topic of this book and is a key macroeconomic variable. Fisher proposed that inflation expectations could be understood as a weighted average of past inflation rates. This was his notion of how humans extrapolate from past events to predict future outcomes. Further, he thought it plausible that the weights economic

I

agents give to recent inflation rates are higher than the weights given to inflation in the more distant past. The most prominent use that Fisher made of his theory of inflation expectations concerned the relationship between the nominal interest rate and the rate of anticipated inflation. Fisher proposed that nominal rates would move in tandem with expected inflation. This occurs because lenders demand compensation from borrowers for the loss of purchasing power caused by a generalized increase of prices. Fisher saw expected inflation as a weighted sum of lagged rates of inflation. The weighting that maximized the fit of his model of nominal interest rates suggested that the tail end of these lags reach about two decades into the past.

Variants of the model of extrapolative expectations were developed in the 1940s and 1950s. Cagan (1956) and Nerlove (1958) popularized the idea of adaptive expectations. This hypothesis is a variant of Fisher's extrapolative expectations where the weights given to past rates of inflation follow a geometric distribution.[1] Although the modeling of human extrapolation did indeed see some further refinements in the 1950s and 1960s, this process was stalled by the introduction and the rising popularity of the concept of rational expectations by John Muth (1960, 1961).

For many economists, rational expectations offered the definitive answer to the question of how to model expectations, since this approach presented a straightforward extension of the optimization principle to the issue of foresight. Economic decision-makers – according to this view – should form optimal statistical forecasts. As a result, the rational expectations hypothesis spread to macroeconomics and finance from its early applications in agricultural economics.[2] Reservations and opposition to this perspective were, however,

---

[1] Interestingly, based on a detailed study of cases of hyperinflation from the 1920s, Cagan (1956) contradicted Irving Fisher regarding the weights given to past inflation rates. Cagan found that the weights people give to lagged inflation tend to decrease very rapidly with the length of the lag.

[2] Early applications of rational expectations in macroeconomics can be found in Lucas (1972) and Sargent (1973).

quickly raised by researchers with an affinity to psychology. Given
that information processing takes time and energy, human behavior is
guided by heuristics which do not typically maximize utility but
merely satisfice. Herbert Simon (1959, 1972) was the first researcher
to offer a criticism of what he called substantive rationality along
these lines. Today his view is shared by many behavioral economists.

From this perspective, the study of rationality has to be an
investigation of the procedures and techniques that humans use.
Among these techniques, some are based on reasoning and conscious
thinking while others belong to the realm of automatic behavior. This
view has been outlined by Daniel Kahneman (2003). He proposed a
distinction of human cognition into a "System 1" that is automated
and fast, and a "System 2" that is analytic and slow. We will build on
this distinction for modeling everyday expectations. During most
times, the mental resources for reasoning are absorbed by other
human tasks rather than for the forming of expectations of variables
like future inflation. For a concrete model of everyday expectations,
we make use of more specific insights from cognitive psychology. In
particular, research shows that neural networks can learn and generate quick responses to a vast number of patterns (shapes, forms), and it
documents the merits of pattern recognition as a positive theory.[3]
The ability to see patterns and recognize situational similarities has
a very high survival value: It helps to make quick inferences.[4] Accordingly, pattern recognition plays a central role in our story about the
formation of expectations.[5] Expectations, according to the view
developed here, consist of extrapolating simple time series patterns
for the variable to be forecast. Muthian rational expectations, according

[3] See Puccetti (1974), Rumelhart et al. (1986), Posner (1989), and Lund (2001).
[4] See Edelman and Reeke (1990) on the issue of fitness. Not surprisingly, pattern
recognition and pattern completion are part of IQ testing and research on child
development. Jones (2012) treats intelligence testing while Bhatt et al. (2006) and
Collins and Laski (2015) treat issues of pattern recognition in cognitive development.
[5] Early experimental contributions in this area came from Feldman (1963) and
Eggleton (1982).

to our perspective, are the System 2 complement of the pattern-using System 1. Hence, in times of a major policy shift, decision-makers may well use their reasoning capacities to infer the consequences of, for example, a policy package intended to end a period of hyperinflation.[6]

I.2 PATTERN-BASED EXPECTATIONS AND VARIANTS OF RATIONAL EXPECTATIONS

The hypothesis of rational expectations suggests that people first identify and then quantify structural causal relationships that tie the variable to be forecast to data of driving variables. In this process, agents are assumed to use economic theory and a host of macroeconomic data. This strict, Muthian form of the rational expectations hypothesis has been tested in a variety of ways. By and large, the rational expectations hypothesis has failed these tests. Various types of tests using data from surveys of expectations and experimental assessments, as well as econometric analyses of macroeconomic and financial variables that are influenced by expectations have largely come out negative.[7] Substantive rationality of expectations is simply not an adequate description of reality. Weaker forms of rational expectations are more behaviorally and empirically plausible. They see people as either following the advice of experts or as engaging in

---

[6] Thus, substantively rational expectations (System 2 thinking) may rule expectations in the type of situations described by Sargent (1983).

[7] Testing using survey data started with Figlewski and Wachtel (1981), Zarnowitz (1985), and Lovell (1986). More recent contributions in this field still mostly reject rational expectations (Sosvilla-Rivero and Ramos-Herrera, 2018, Cavallo et al., 2017). In terms of experimental works that study tasks of expectations formation, Williams (1987), Bolle (1988a, 1988b), and Hey (1994) reject the hypothesis of rational expectations whereas, e.g., Plott and Sunder (1988) find some empirical support. Further studies have investigated the possibility that some subjects form rational expectations while others extrapolate (Haruvy et al., 2007, Pfajfar & Zakelj, 2014). Examples of econometric studies of historical data that reject the rational expectations hypothesis are Chow (1989) and Fair (1991). See also Rötheli (2007) for a survey of older empirical tests and Landier et al. (2017) and D'Haultfoeuille et al. (2018) for recent contributions.

Data	Theory	Expert opinion
Long time series of price level	Quantity theory	Professional forecaster
Long time series of income	Phillips curve	Monetary authority
Long time series of money supply	Cost-push theory	Newspapers
Long time series of unemployment	.	Colleagues, friends, family
Long time series of oil prices	.	.
Long time series of labor productivity	.	.
.	.	.

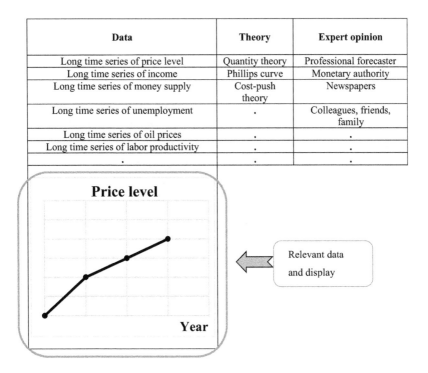

FIGURE 1.1 What people look at when forming inflation expectations

the costly analysis of updating expectations only at certain times.[8] These views of rationality are treated here as hypotheses that compete with our perspective that humans merely extrapolate univariate patterns.

For a specification of a modern extrapolative view of expectations, the question that has to be addressed is what people do when they project a time series into the future. The evidence indicates that humans in this situation tend to rely on a visualization of the time series. The commonly used expression "getting a picture of something" conveys this idea. Our view of everyday formation of expectations is highlighted in Figure 1.1. Among all the information,

---

[8] Variants of this approach have been proposed by Mankiw and Reis (2002), Carroll (2003), and Sims (2003) under the headings of "sticky information," "sticky expectations," and "rational inattention," respectively.

theories, and opinions that are potentially available, it is argued that the decision-maker focuses on the visual display of the recent history of the variable to be forecast.

In order to learn how specifically people extrapolate, we make use of procedures administered in the laboratory. More concretely, subjects are shown cases of how the price level can proceed over the course of four years and they are asked for their one-year and five-year-ahead forecasts. With this, we build on evidence indicating that it takes people just a few observations – typically not more than three or four – of a series to assess whether they see a trend.[9] Importantly, these episodes of the time series are visualized in the form of charts.[10] Thus, a key element of the hypothesis laid out here is that the extrapolations by humans are based on visualization. In the process of assessing a pattern display, subjects may come to different conclusions. Hence, we see the heterogeneity of expectations as a reflection of the diverse ways of extrapolation prevalent in the population. A further dimension of expectations, namely the uncertainty attached to it, can also be measured. For this purpose, a probabilistic version of the laboratory procedure is developed.

The notion of a fixed-pattern response is of particular importance for the expectations model developed here. A fixed-pattern response means that when facing the same sequence of events (pattern) at different times, the representative subject will show the same response (Rötheli, 2007). Given this aspect of behavior, it becomes possible to model expectations by showing subjects an encompassing set of circumstances to elicit their responses. Specifically, the patterns shown in the laboratory are stylized, representative displays of how the price level moves over the course of four years. However, even

---

[9] See, e.g., Rötheli (1998) and Carlson and Shu (2007) on these findings regarding the relevant number of past observations.

[10] Here we follow earlier studies like that by Bloomfield and Hales (2002) by presenting the graphs in level form and not in the form of changes. For the importance of visualization of information, see, for example, Chaomei and Czerwinski (2000).

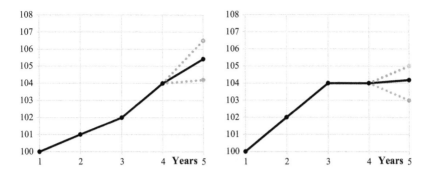

FIGURE I.2 Pattern-dependent extrapolation

with a stylized representation, the possible cases are too numerous for subjects to assess in a laboratory session. This leads us to study only the subset of patterns that are empirically relevant for countries like the USA and Germany. In Chapter 10, the conditions for further generalization are explored and developed.

A key laboratory finding from earlier studies is that the weighting of past observations varies with the shape of the curve of the time series over the recent past. Figure 1.2 gives a first impression of these behavioral tendencies that will be explored in detail in the coming chapters. Here we see two patterns that are presented to the subjects among other cases. The case presented in the left-hand panel is an example of a pattern with a clearly trending time series. By contrast, the right-hand panel shows a case where the price level plateaus. The displays for the two cases show the average of the one-year-ahead expectation elicited as well as the upper 95 percent and the lower 5 percent of the distribution of responses. Note that subjects' responses to the two patterns are impossible to square with the linear model of extrapolation. Such a model represents expectations as a simple weighted sum of past observations. In the left-hand panel it appears that the last two changes in the series have about equal weight, while in the plateau case the last observed change receives almost all the weight. Such a pattern-dependent weighting scheme is not compatible with the idea that a standard linear model of extrapolation can explain the laboratory expectations data.

If a linear model is inappropriate, how should we then proceed to formulate an operational model of expectations? How can the data gathered in the laboratory be used to generate quantitative models of expectations of such variables as inflation? The key here is to work with an encompassing set of patterns to elicit expectations. Building on the elicited data, a method is proposed that fits subjects' responses to historical courses of time series of the price level. The outcome computed thus is a behavioral model of expected inflation. This approach preserves a maximum of the information gained in the laboratory when using it to compute time series of expectations. Although "inflation expectations" is the central topic of this book, expectations of the course of real aggregate income (gross domestic product [GDP]) are also covered and similarities and differences between expectations for these variables are documented.

The use of cognitive psychology and the measurement of behavior in the laboratory distinguish the approach developed here from older models of extrapolative expectations. It should be seen as a bottom-up model of rationality. The model is sufficiently rich in detail yet parsimonious enough to be useful in a variety of applications. Central elements of the approach outlined have already proven to be successful when modeling expectations for financial variables. Rötheli (2011) documents that pattern-based expectations outperform other variants of expectations in econometric models explaining stock prices and exchange rates. Furthermore, pattern extrapolation appears not to be affected by the culture and the history of subjects. The fact that experimentally elicited subjective expectations in Germany and Japan concerning financial variables are essentially the same suggests that there are human generalities in the reliance on patterns for forecasting (Rötheli, 2011). The reliance on pattern for extrapolation may indeed be among the psychological universals.[11] This finding is of central importance when a laboratory-based model

---

[11] See Norenzayan and Heine (2005) for a discussion of universals in psychology and anthropology.

of expectations is proposed for use for a wide set of circumstances and countries. However, the universal tendency of relying on patterns in subjective forecasting does not preclude that the context of the forecast can play an important role. Clearly, differences regarding the type of variable concerned may affect pattern-based expectations. This justifies the detailed study of extrapolation of different macroeconomic variables described in this book.

I.3 RELATION TO SURVEY- AND MARKET-BASED MEASURES OF EXPECTATIONS

The modeling of pattern-based expectations begins with inviting subjects to the laboratory. Subjects are shown a comprehensive set of time series patterns (called cases) and their assessment of short- and long-term expectations is obtained. This sort of laboratory-based survey is novel. Clearly, there are key differences between our procedure and the well-known periodic surveys of expectations. Such surveys are, for example, the consumer survey conducted by the University of Michigan or the survey of professional forecasters conducted by the Federal Reserve Bank of Philadelphia.[12] The distinguishing feature of the approach proposed here is the notion that one can conduct a once-only survey and thereby cover all aspects of expectations.

When evaluating the time series of expectations computed with our procedure, we will turn to survey data of expectations. If one accepts expectations data from surveys as a manifestation of actual behavior, then such data must be explicable by any proposed hypothesis of expectations formation. This is a well-established procedure used for evaluating expectation models.[13] In one version of such an evaluation, Carroll (2003) tests the hypothesis that the agents surveyed

---

[12] See Clements (2019) and Curtin (2019) for comprehensive treatments of the survey approach to measuring expectations.
[13] See Nerlove (1983) and Manski (2004) for work both with aggregate and individual data.

show a delayed updating of expectations to experts' forecasts.[14] We will present estimates and tests that contradict this view. In fact the econometric evidence indicates that variations of survey expectations over time can be best explained by the hypothesis that agents merely extrapolate univariate patterns.

Consider a final comparison of the new approach with surveys of expectations. The procedure described in this book offers a much more general approach than any regular survey. By extracting time-invariant characteristics of human subjective forecasting, the model of pattern-based expectations can be used both to study historical periods for which no survey data exist and to make predictions in what-if scenarios. Hence, it is not primarily a measurement of expectations but a theory of expectations.

Another popular way of measuring inflation expectations is based on data of inflation-indexed bonds. The difference between the interest rate on a bond offering a nominal return and the rate of a bond with the same maturity and issuer but with compensation offered for changes in purchasing power can be seen as the market's estimate of expected inflation over that maturity. On the basis of this approach, researchers have measured and analyzed inflation expectations over various horizons. The weakness of this approach is the possible presence of a premium for inflation uncertainty. If the market demands a compensation for the uncertainty of inflation, this premium becomes part of the nominal interest rate. This premium is not paid on indexed bonds since the holder does not bear this risk. Likewise, heterogeneity of inflation expectations can affect the nominal interest rate. Consequently, the difference between the nominal interest rate and an interest rate on an inflation-indexed bond will misrepresent inflation expectations. More importantly, as uncertainty and heterogeneity of expectations vary, so will the difference between these rates.[15] Hence,

---

[14] Carroll's (2003) work is a key contribution here.

[15] This has been known since the early contributions on the use of inflation indexed bonds for the measurement of inflation expectations (Paunio & Suvanto, 1977). However, the argument set out here has only recently come to be more fully

such market measures of inflation expectations cannot replace a direct measurement and modeling of inflation expectations.

1.4   PATTERN-BASED EXPECTATIONS AND ISSUES OF METHOD

Findings from earlier experimental studies are used to structure the tasks given to subjects in this study. However, in the procedures developed for this study, there is no testing of hypotheses in the laboratory. Instead, the laboratory is used to conduct a survey in which the data available to subjects and the form of the data presentation is controlled. This is clearly an uncommon use of the laboratory. The data obtained in the experimental setup yields a distillate of behavior that we judge to be time invariant and thus transferable to different historical settings and economic relationships. Empirical tests of these conjectures are conducted when pattern-based expectations are used in econometric analyses to explain variables like nominal interest rates. Readers doubtful of the behavioral foundation of expectations proposed here may remain skeptical until the empirical results are presented. Judgment concerning the merits of pattern-based expectations should be made on the basis of the model's ability to shed light on interesting economic phenomena where expectations play an important role. This is essentially Milton Friedman's (1953) position on the scientific method, and it can and should be applied to evaluate models with behavioral foundation as it is applied to standard economic models.

In most of the treatments used in the laboratory, subjects are paid a flat fee as a compensation for their involvement. This choice is empirically plausible: individuals and households hardly keep track of their views of future prices for a comparison with factual outcomes. With an expectations horizon of one to five years, the feedback of realizations on expectations is extremely loose. In this light, the

appreciated (Bauer & McCarthy, 2015). It supports the notion that survey measures of inflation expectations may be more accurate than market-based measures.

argument that subjects in the laboratory should receive immediate feedback regarding their expectations errors and financial incentives to reduce them is not plausible.[16] Our stance on financial incentives is similar to the measurement approach for surveys. In surveys of expectations of inflation and other indicators conducted, for example, by the University of Michigan, there is no compensation for participants as a function of accuracy of their prediction. Nevertheless, many analysts, researchers, and policy makers consider these data to merit attention.

A final point concerns the question of theory building in economics. Some readers may demand from an economic theory that it is derived in mathematical form starting from first principles. While concepts from cognitive psychology and insights from experiments are the building blocks of the model of pattern-based expectations, we do not offer a formal derivation from basic principles. This process of theory building is very common in science. Hong (2013) provides an insightful description of the development of mathematical models in biology and a range of other fields. He further describes how visual thinking and pattern recognition typically guide the creative process leading up to theoretical developments. In this sense, patterns and pattern recognition are not only key concepts in our approach but also act as guides for its very development. This brings us to a detailed outline of the book.

---

[16] Experimental economists regularly raise the objection that a flat rate compensation is not incentive compatible, meaning that subjects have no incentive to truthfully reveal their views. Given the laboratory tasks used in this project, it is hard to see any validity of this argument. If asked about one's forecast of a macroeconomic series, there is clearly no incentive to distort one's view. Furthermore, an approach that treats subjects with respect and inquires about their personal assessment for the purpose of scientific research may arguably be the best way to motivate participants. It is indeed questionable whether making payments to subjects depending on forecast performance yields reliable data. Consider experimentally studying saving for retirement. Arguably, fewer people would show empirically well-known forms of suboptimal savings if their retirement hardship could be fed back to their younger selves as suggested and practiced in much of experimental economics.

I.5   THE OUTLINE OF THE BOOK

Chapter 2 puts the concept of pattern-based extrapolation in the context of a range of research on extrapolation coming from the fields of economics, psychology, and forecasting. Chapter 3 outlines the procedures used in the laboratory to elicit macroeconomic expectations. Chapter 4 documents properties of these expectations data and – by comparing inflation expectations with expectations for real GDP – shows that pattern extrapolation is indeed context dependent. In Chapter 5 we explain how the elicited data is used to compute historical series of inflation expectations. For this transformation of laboratory data to historical time series, the concepts of human similarity matching and scaling as they relate to pattern-extrapolation need to be addressed. These elements are essential ingredients to modeling pattern-based expectations. Chapter 6 compares the new series of expected inflation with expectations from the Michigan survey of consumers, and it documents that pattern extrapolation offers a sensible explanation of the Michigan survey data. The pattern-based approach also leads to a time series measure of the heterogeneity of expectations. Chapter 7 compares this new measure with the corresponding series from the Michigan survey.

Chapter 8 is the first in a series of econometric investigations that documents the explanatory power of the pattern-based theory of expectations. This chapter studies the role of expectations in the dynamics of inflation. It is well known that expected inflation is an important driving force of inflation. Within the context of the New Keynesian Phillips curve, we demonstrate that pattern-based expectations is an important addition to the toolbox of economic modelers. Chapter 9 presents an investigation of the so-called Fisher effect. Here, the role of expected inflation in the determination of nominal interest rates is econometrically estimated with short- and long-term US government bond rates from the 1960s to 2016. The empirical analysis of the Fisher effect is continued in later chapters where a wide range of countries and historical episodes is covered.

Chapter 10 marks the transition to a more streamlined and at the same time more general approach to modeling pattern-based expectations. This generalized approach is based on its own set of elicited laboratory data. While retaining the essential elements used previously, the data elicited here are based on an even simpler description of extrapolation. This further simplification allows the computation of inflation expectations in a more general way than before. In particular, the generalized approach allows the computation of expected inflation for any geographical and historical context. Chapter 11 extends this approach to the modeling of expectations concerning aggregate real income. An analysis of the experience of the great recession in the USA shows how pattern-based expectations for real GDP can be put to use in business cycle analysis. The general model of expected inflation is again applied in Chapter 12 where the role of inflation expectations as a determinant of US interest rates before the First World War is studied.[17]

Chapter 13 embarks on a risky journey. The expectations models developed before use laboratory data where subjects are shown stylized courses of the price level with inflation rates in the range between +2 and −2 percent. The modeling of inflation expectations outside this range is based on an estimated scaling relationship. This approach is put to a severe test when modeling expectations in countries with high inflation. In order to check the reliability of the approach, a new set of expectations data is experimentally elicited. In this new setting, subjects assess situations with inflation rates reaching up to 80 percent annually. The new laboratory data confirm the scaling relationship documented before. Indeed, when researching countries and episodes with high inflation, the model of Chapter 10

---

[17] When applying the new paradigm of pattern-based expectations to earlier times, it may be helpful to indicate that time series plots of economic phenomenon have already been popular in the nineteenth century. William Playfair is credited for having introduced and popularized time series plots for a variety of applications including economics at the beginning of the nineteenth century (see Spence, 2006 and Symanzik et al., 2009, for historical accounts on Playfair).

holds up well against the more specific version based on laboratory data elicited for high rates of inflation. In conclusion, the model of Chapter 10 should be considered the workhorse for empirical studies.

Chapters 14 and 15 turn the reader's attention to the international arena by investigating the link between inflation expectations and interest rates in Asian and African economies, respectively. The empirical findings support the conclusion that the model of pattern-based expectations has the potential to outperform alternative notions and measures of inflation expectations. The two final chapters round off the book by presenting and discussing data computed with the pattern-based approach for the world's 10 largest economies. While Chapter 16 provides estimates of expected inflation, Chapter 17 presents data of real interest rates and compares them to measures published by the World Bank. This new data promises to be helpful for researchers, policy makers, and practitioners looking for an alternative to simple measures of expected inflation and real interest rates.

The text describes in detail all of the procedures introduced. Furthermore, the experimentally elicited data are tabulated. Computer programs that readily help to calculate time series of expectations can be downloaded from the book's website at Cambridge University Press. Hence, readers will be able to use the approach outlined in the text to address their own research questions. With these tools, interested researchers in macroeconomics and financial economics are given a new modeling instrument that can immediately be put to work and checked against competing approaches.

2 Extrapolation and Expectations

2.I INTRODUCTION

This book builds on a long tradition of research on the role of extrapolation in various fields. To make it clear, extrapolation means that the future course of a time series is seen as depending only on past observations of this series. It seems reasonable to begin the discussion of earlier contributions on this topic with research from the field of economics. Here we can connect with the material already discussed in Chapter 1. Clearly, Irving Fisher (1930) stands out for initiating the explicit mathematical modeling of extrapolative expectations in his work on inflation expectations. Variations of this theme were proposed in the form of adaptive and regressive expectations. While the hypothesis of adaptive expectations is a special variant of extrapolative expectations, the notion of regressive expectations brings in the element of a long-term anchor for predicted values.[1] Expectations are said to be regressive when they show a tendency to revert to a fixed value. In a more general use of this term, we will speak of a regressive tendency if expectations increase in an under-proportional way in response to an increase in the underlying variable (e.g., inflation). Clearly, expectations can combine the elements of extrapolation and regressiveness, and we will pursue this topic in the chapters to come.

---

[1] Cagan (1956) and Nerlove (1958) proposed the concept of adaptive expectations which is a special form (with geometrically declining weights) of extrapolative expectations. Bossons and Modigliani (1960) analyze regressiveness in producers' expectations and Frenkel (1975) formalized the concept of regressive expectations further. This concept can be traced back to Keynes general theory (Keynes, 1936).

2.2 EXTRAPOLATION IN ECONOMICS

In applied work as well as in economic theory, the notion of extrapolation was sidelined for more than 30 years. The theory of rational expectations proposed by John Muth (1960, 1961) holds that economic agents make use of economic theory and a wide array of data – not just the history of a variable – to judge a variable's likely continuation. However, as the evidence against this notion of substantive rationality accumulated, researchers turned to behaviorally more plausible notions regarding expectations. In no subfield of economics is this more salient than in financial economics. In this field of inquiry, researchers have an abundance of high-quality data available for the testing of theories. Robert Shiller stands out as a pioneer in the documentation of contradictions of rational expectations theory as applied to asset pricing. His finding of excess volatility of stock prices relative to the rational expectations solutions (Shiller, 1981), although amply challenged, has stood the test of time. Looking for explanations for such deviations from the rational expectations theory, researchers began to explore notions of simpler forecasting schemes on the side of financial market participants (Barsky & De Long, 1993, De Bondt, 1993). Yet, it was the financial crisis that erupted in 2007 that led to a spurt of research in this direction and recent years have seen studies on stock price booms, overpriced real estate, and a variety of phenomena relating to interest rates and exchange rates all building on the notion that financial decision-makers form extrapolative expectations.[2]

2.3 EXTRAPOLATION IN PSYCHOLOGY

Important insights into issues pertaining to the prediction of time series have also emerged from the field of psychology. Experimental

---

[2] Contributions on the relationship between asset pricing and consumption have been proposed by Hirshleifer et al. (2015). Work on real estate price booms come from Granziera and Kozicki (2015) and Zheng et al. (2017). Greenwood and Shleifer (2014), Gennaioli et al. (2015) and Andonov and Rauh (2018) have studied investors' expectations and Cozzi and Davenport (2017) investigate the influence of extrapolation on international capital flows.

psychologists in particular have documented interesting behavioral elements concerning expectations formation. Here we focus on that part of the psychological literature that pertains to the project of this book, that is, we discuss the findings reported by scientific psychologists regarding the projection of time sequences. Notably, this research is not primarily concerned with economic variables, but it still yields insights pertinent to economic modeling.

One relevant line of research comes from the so-called heuristics and biases research program initiated by Amos Tversky and Daniel Kahneman (1974). In a contribution pertinent to extrapolation, Gilovich et al. (1985) documented that when it comes to assessing the likelihood of a successful shot in basketball, both players and spectators tend to see the chances of a further score after a player has just scored as overly elevated relative to factual frequencies. The documented tendency of seeing a positive autocorrelation in random sequences which leads to the judgment of streaks in scores (the so-called hot hand phenomenon) was buttressed by subsequent work in the laboratory as well as by naturalistic data from sports, consumption decisions, and gambling. However, several researchers have suggested a critical view of these results and have questioned whether the hot hand phenomenon is in fact a fallacy. Studies such as those by Yaari and Eisenmann (2011) and Raab et al. (2012) document that there are indeed elements of autocorrelation in successful throws in basketball that in principle validate a belief in streaks of success. In terms of explanations for the perception of runs, a number of different approaches have been proposed.[3] For the purpose of this book, key concepts that have been suggested in explanations are the availability heuristic introduced by Tversky and Kahneman (1973) and the documented tendency of decision makers to rely on patterns in the data (Oskarsson, 2009). Both approaches suggest that recent observations of the series to be forecast are of key importance and that the weighting tends to depend on the trending behavior in the data.

---

[3] See Alter and Oppenheimer (2006) and Rabin and Vayanos (2010) for surveys.

We also need to mention the so called gambler's fallacy that some decision-maker's show. This phenomenon describes the expectation of a reversal of outcomes following a run of one particular outcome (Tversky & Kahneman, 1974, Rabin & Vayanos, 2010). This tendency has been attributed to a small-sample bias in statistical reasoning. As before with the hot hand phenomenon, this behavioral tendency, when documented under experimentally randomized conditions, is a clear violation of correct statistical reasoning. However, the notion that streaks tend to end or the tendency of growth processes to slow down may well be in line with practical experiences and hence can be functional in real life.

Another line of relevant psychological experiments was pioneered by Willem Wagenaar and coauthors. In a sequence of papers, they documented that subjects tend to underestimate the future path of an exponentially growing variable (Wagenaar & Sagaria, 1975). Interestingly, the tendency to underestimate future growth was shown to be invariant of whether a variable was visualized in the form of a time series or with the intuitive paradigm of duckweed growth on a pond (Wagenaar & Timmers, 1978). This work is also pertinent to this study because the findings document that showing fewer observations to subjects tends to improve their forecasting precision. Wagenaar and Timmers (1979) document that the best forecasting performance is reported when subjects are shown between three to five previous observations. This finding is compatible with findings from other studies to be discussed in Chapter 3 and supports the choice of short time-series patterns to be shown in our laboratory sessions.[4]

As with the previously discussed psychological literature, the reader should be on guard against taking the just-described experimental findings as documenting a systematic (and potentially correctable) flaw in human forecasting behavior. While it seems innocuous to

---

[4] Ebersbach et al. (2008) and Christandl and Fetchenhauer (2009) document newer findings in this research tradition.

show subjects continuously and exponentially trending series in the laboratory, many real-life growth processes eventually slow down or are even reversed. Hence, the experimentally documented tendency toward a regressiveness of expectations may be adaptive under real-life circumstances. This point is in effect particularly important for the understanding of inflation expectations as will be detailed in later chapters.

We finish this section by pointing toward a psychological contribution that is particularly close to the methodological approach taken by economists. Harvey et al. (1994) present experimental work comparing various expectations theories. Their findings reject rationality of expectations by showing that information from sources other than the series to be forecast is of no help for predictions. Furthermore, extrapolative expectations dominate adaptive expectations when compared as explanations of human behavior. In fact, contrary to the scheme of adaptive expectations, subjects relied only on the most recent realizations of the series to form their forecast.[5] Again, this is in line with the approach outlined in the following chapters.

2.4 EXTRAPOLATION IN FORECASTING

It should not be surprising that the field of economic forecasting, as opposed to the theorizing about agents' expectations formation, is replete with variants of extrapolation. Fildes (1979) and Armstrong (2001) offer good surveys. Petropoulos et al. (2018) and Han et al. (2018) report newer findings. Besides formal models (including autoregressive integrated moving average [ARIMA] time-series algorithms), forecast researchers have also delved into the question of how intuitive forecasters adjust projections that are based on formal

---

[5] Yet another piece of evidence comes from the study of consumer surveys of expectations. As documented by Simmons and Weiserbs (1992) survey respondents tend to take the most recent past of prices into account when forming expectations. Trehan (2015) replicates the result of a high weight on very recent observations with newer data of consumers' inflation expectations.

statistical methods. The term used for the type of forecasting that does not follow statistically more sophisticated procedures is "judgmental forecasting." In this field again the weighting of past observations of a time series, that is, extrapolation, has been shown to be of prime importance (Lawrence et al., 2006).

2.5   SUMMARY AND CONCLUSIONS

We have covered a wide range of contributions that bear on the issue of extrapolation in expectations formation. While some of the studies surveyed do not concern the prediction of economic phenomena, the findings across applications tend to be very similar. Particularly, psychological studies suggest that the very recent past of a series of observations is the basis of forecasts. Many researchers inquire whether documented forms of expectations conform to correct statistical reasoning or whether they represent a fallacy. This tendency parallels the discussion in behavioral economics where for many years researchers predominantly focused on documenting deviations from rational and optimal behavior. As the discussion on the hot hand phenomenon and the gambler's fallacy illustrate, this view is changing. An up-to-date perspective on a topic like human extrapolation has to start with an understanding of the functional and adaptive part of the documented behavior while still acknowledging the possible deficiencies of such heuristics. This approach is in the process of becoming the new paradigm in behavioral economics. It uses terms like "adaptive rationality" (Smith, 2003) or "smart decision-making" (Altman, 2017) to highlight the human tendency to find simple yet practical ways to move about in a complex and uncertain world.

3 Eliciting Expectations under Laboratory Conditions

3.1 INTRODUCTION

This chapter details the procedures used for eliciting expectations in the laboratory as well as the data gathered. The expectations hypothesis set out here builds on the idea that people extrapolate univariate patterns in time series. The task, therefore, is to capture the general tendencies of extrapolation across different patterns or shapes of the time series. In the following, a pattern will be defined as an ordered sequence of observations over the recent past of an economic time series. The reliance on simple patterns by ordinary people should not be confused with the so-called technical analysis used by professional chartists. If anything, we could refer to humans under everyday conditions as "natural born" chartists.

3.2 BASIC ELICITATION PROCEDURES AND DATA

The procedure introduced here is best described as a survey under laboratory conditions. Data are elicited using a design used previously in the elicitation of expectations of financial variables (Rötheli, 2011). Appendix 3.1 provides the instructions for the basic treatment. Subjects are shown short sequences of a time series they are told to consider as a particular macroeconomic series. The concrete series to be considered are the consumer price index (CPI) and real gross domestic product (GDP). Importantly, the stylized episodes of the time series are visualized in the form of charts.[1] The aim is to make

---

[1] As in Bloomfield and Hales (2002), visualized data is presented in level form and not in the form of changes. For a discussion on the significance of visualization of information, see, for example, Chaomei and Czerwinski (2000).

sure that what we get out of this exercise are the various forms of agents' extrapolation of visual patterns and their relative importance.

Subjects are informed that they are going to see different possible cases of how the series evolves over the course of four years and that it is their task to assess the likely continuation of this series. For each of the sequences shown, subjects are asked for their expectations one and five years ahead. Note that the described framework proceeds on the notion of fixed-pattern responses. That is, we abstract from possible modifications of pattern use over time and experience. This simplification is justified based on earlier research.[2] As will be shown, this assumption is helpful in designing laboratory tasks that in terms of time use are feasible for subjects. In the laboratory, the neutral term "case" is used for the short sequences shown. In this text, we will synonymously use the term "pattern."

To make it clear – there is no testing of hypotheses in the laboratory. The laboratory is only used to administer different versions of a highly stylized one-time survey. The evaluation of this approach comes later when the thus quantified expectations are used in econometric analyses. As in the related study by Bloomfield and Hales (2002), subjects do not receive any feedback regarding the realizations of the series. For expectations of macroeconomic variables one or more years into the future, this seems all the more appropriate. It reflects the notion that when it comes to such expectations, we make predictions by seeing and completing patterns without typically keeping track of how well we are doing.

---

[2] In a binary time series extrapolation task (Rötheli, 1998) where modification of pattern use was studied, the following was found: (a) there is a significant number of subjects who do not alter pattern use over repeated showings of the same pattern (e.g., a run of 1s or 0s). Among the subjects who do modify their behavior, there are two groups of roughly equal size. These different responses can best be explained for run patterns. The first group shows a tendency to increase their expectation of a continuation of a run the more often, in the past, the run was followed by a run-extending outcome. By contrast, the second group tends to judge a break in the run to become more probable. Overall, the behavioral modification in these two groups tend to neutralize. Hence, the assumption of fixed-pattern response appears appropriate for modeling the behavior of the average subject.

The length of the data window shown is chosen based on earlier research indicating that in a similar task, few subjects rely on information that reaches farther back than the last four observations of a time series. In Rötheli (1998), subjects are shown a binary series that develops over the course of the experiment (50 periods). Beginning in period 4, subjects form a one-period-ahead expectation. On relating subjects' responses in individual regression models to the past of the series, it is found that few subjects rely on information farther back than the last four periods. Further, empirical research reported by Carlson and Shu (2007) considering a variety of circumstances finds that it typically takes people just three observations to conclude that a series of outcomes forms a streak. Our present procedure simplifies the course of time series shown to subjects to sequences that proceed in steps of +2, +1, 0, −1, −2. With this restriction, there is a total of 125 cases of how the series advances over four periods.[3] This opens the opportunity to show subjects an encompassing set of cases and not just a few prominent courses of history (like in Bloomfield & Hales, 2002). However, even the reduction to 125 patterns poses a problem. It is simply not feasible to have subjects assess 125 patterns during a laboratory session.

Thus, when working with patterns of length four, we further limit the number of cases.[4] In order to present a manageable task to subjects, they are only shown cases that are historically relevant. More concretely, we study the course of annual CPI data from 1950 to 2010 from the USA and Germany. By investigating all data windows covering four consecutive years, it is found that only a relatively small number of possible sequences (patterns) among the 125 cases are relevant. Only relatively few patterns are ever selected when searching for the pattern that has the highest correlation with the historical sequence. When looking at CPI data for the USA

---

[3] With the four observations shown in the laboratory treatments, there are three changes involved. Given that these changes come in five possible steps of ±2, ±1, and 0, there is a total of $5^3 = 125$ patterns.

[4] In Chapter 10, when working with patterns of three periods, subjects will be shown all (i.e., a total of 25) possible patterns.

(Germany), we find in fact that only 15 (21) different patterns are ever selected. Based on this finding, subjects are shown a set of 22 different patterns covering all of the cases relevant for both the USA and Germany. A similar reasoning leads to the selection of 32 different patterns for real GDP based on applying the maximum correlation criterion which selects 30 and 27 (largely overlapping) patterns for the USA and Germany, respectively. Table 3.1 lists these two sets of patterns for the CPI and for GDP.

In the laboratory, each case is presented separately. The fact that each display shows the series starting at the value of 100 clearly sets apart the different cases shown. This favors the type of behavior we want to elicit, that is, the reliance on visual patterns. Further, the chosen form of display makes it possible to interpret the given responses as percentage changes. Subjects (after 15 minutes of instructions) had to allocate a minimum of 40 minutes to complete the task. The maximum time allowed was 90 minutes. During that time, participants were allowed to make changes to any of their answers.[5]

The laboratory survey was run in three different versions with 45 subjects, respectively: treatment (i) asks for subjective point predictions for a one-year horizon and for a five-year horizon for a total of 22 CPI patterns as well as for 32 GDP patterns. Treatment (ii) elicits higher-order expectations for the same set of patterns. Specifically, for each of the patterns, subjects are asked to predict the median of the answers over all of the subjects taking part in this treatment. Hence, subjects in the two treatments, (i) and (ii), assessed CPI as well as GDP patterns. The sequential order here was that first subjects assessed the 22 CPI

---

[5] We pay a flat participation fee and thus do not offer a financial incentive for learning to make better predictions during the laboratory session. This approximates reality outside the laboratory where there exists only a very loose and delayed feedback of forecast errors concerning macroeconomic variables to the personal financial situation of the typical agent who forms expectations. Incidentally, regular surveys like the Michigan survey of expectations give no financial incentives at all. In the treatment asking for higher-order expectations, where participants judge the average subject's response, a remuneration for the overall accuracy over all cases shown is offered.

Table 3.1 *Relevant patterns for the CPI and for real GDP*

	Patterns for the CPI					Patterns for the real GDP			
	Time					Time			
Pattern	1	2	3	4	Pattern	1	2	3	4
1	100	102	104	106	1	100	102	104	106
2	100	102	104	105	2	100	102	104	105
3	100	102	104	104	3	100	102	104	104
4	100	102	103	105	4	100	102	104	103
5	100	102	103	104	5	100	102	103	105
6	100	102	103	103	6	100	102	103	104
7	100	102	103	102	7	100	102	103	103
8	100	102	102	103	8	100	102	103	102
9	100	102	102	102	9	100	102	102	104
10	100	102	100	100	10	100	102	102	102
11	100	101	103	105	11	100	102	101	103
12	100	101	103	104	12	100	101	103	105
13	100	101	102	104	13	100	101	103	104
14	100	101	102	103	14	100	101	102	104
15	100	101	102	102	15	100	101	102	103
16	100	101	101	101	16	100	101	102	102
17	100	101	100	100	17	100	101	101	103
18	100	100	101	103	18	100	101	101	102
19	100	100	100	102	19	100	101	101	101
20	100	100	100	101	20	100	101	101	99
21	100	99	99	100	21	100	101	100	102
22	100	98	98	100	22	100	100	102	104
					23	100	100	102	103
					24	100	100	102	100
					25	100	100	101	103
					26	100	100	101	102
					27	100	100	101	100
					28	100	100	100	102
					29	100	100	100	101
					30	100	100	99	100
					31	100	100	98	100
					32	100	99	101	103

patterns followed by the 32 GDP patterns. Treatment (iii) extends treatment (i) by asking subjects for point predictions as well as probability ranges for all patterns presented. For treatment (iii), one group of 45 subjects assessed CPI patterns and a separate group assessed GDP patterns. Since the instructions for this probabilistic treatment differ considerably from how earlier approaches elicit probability ranges, we will describe it in detail in the next section.[6] Given that treatment (iii) is rather time consuming, subjects are only presented either the CPI or the GDP patterns. Thus, for each of the two runs with treatment (iii), a separate group of subjects was invited to the laboratory.

The subjects participating in this study were all undergraduate students from the University of Erfurt who had completed at least one principal course of macroeconomics. Subjects earned a participation fee of 12 Euros. In the treatments asking for higher-order expectations, the three highest performing subjects received 20, 15, and 10 Euros in addition to the participation fee. The elicited answers of subjects for different treatments and horizons are presented in the tables that follow. Specifically, Table 3.2 shows the results for treatment (i) for CPI patterns. The data are presented in terms of the mean of individual expectations as well as the values that mark the upper 95 percent and the lower 5 percent quantile of the distribution as an indication of the heterogeneity of expectations. There are two sets of results, respectively. The first applies to the one-year-ahead forecast (year 5) and the second to the five-year-ahead forecast (year 9). Table 3.3 presents the corresponding data for treatment (ii) again for the CPI.

The elicited expectations based on treatment (i) for the real GDP are presented in Table 3.4 and for treatment (ii) in Table 3.5. Again, the tables report the means over 45 subjects as well as the upper 95 percent and the lower 5 percent quantile of the distribution. As with the CPI data, expectations for the one- and five-year horizon are tabulated.

---

[6] A pilot study showed that an extension of the probabilistic questions to a version asking for higher-order expectations could not be clearly communicated to subjects.

Table 3.2 CPI expectations for periods 5 and 9 for treatment (i)

Pattern	Time 1	2	3	4	Mean 5	Upper 95%	Lower 5%	Mean 9	Upper 95%	Lower 5%
1	100	102	104	106	107.7467	108.00	106.92	113.3778	116.00	107.30
2	100	102	104	105	105.8822	106.50	105.32	107.4395	112.45	102.00
3	100	102	104	104	104.2455	106.00	103.00	106.4409	111.85	100.15
4	100	102	103	105	106.5533	108.00	105.68	110.8311	114.80	106.10
5	100	102	103	104	105.0444	106.00	104.00	107.8045	111.00	102.27
6	100	102	103	103	102.9356	104.00	102.00	104.2422	108.00	98.40
7	100	102	103	102	101.2756	103.00	100.00	102.6489	106.36	98.06
8	100	102	102	103	103.8556	105.00	103.00	106.2911	110.00	101.06
9	100	102	102	102	102.1222	103.16	100.00	103.4556	106.32	99.60
10	100	102	100	100	99.8311	102.00	98.00	101.5568	105.43	97.00
11	100	101	103	105	106.6400	108.00	105.20	110.3533	118.80	102.20
12	100	101	103	104	105.0318	106.00	103.15	107.9489	112.00	102.20
13	100	101	102	104	105.6244	107.00	104.80	109.0644	114.00	103.20
14	100	101	102	103	103.9667	104.84	103.00	107.0822	108.98	103.54
15	100	101	102	102	102.0778	103.00	101.00	103.1533	106.40	98.20
16	100	101	101	101	101.1089	102.58	100.00	102.2022	104.80	99.80
17	100	101	100	100	99.8705	101.00	99.00	101.0289	104.80	97.20
18	100	100	101	103	104.5545	106.00	103.06	108.3533	116.80	102.04
19	100	100	100	102	102.7156	104.24	101.00	104.9778	111.44	100.50
20	100	100	100	101	101.7178	103.48	101.00	103.1614	106.00	100.24
21	100	99	99	100	100.8289	102.00	99.28	101.9311	105.74	99.00
22	100	98	98	100	101.2244	102.94	100.00	103.0956	109.60	99.00

Table 3.3 CPI expectations for periods 5 and 9 for treatment (ii)

Pattern	Time 1	2	3	4	Mean 5	Upper 95%	Lower 5%	Mean 9	Upper 95%	Lower 5%
1	100	102	104	106	107.7023	108.17	106.83	114.2800	116.08	109.20
2	100	102	104	105	105.8535	106.59	105.32	108.7911	112.50	104.40
3	100	102	104	104	104.3023	105.19	103.20	106.9795	110.26	102.23
4	100	102	103	105	106.2932	107.00	105.83	110.8156	113.00	107.60
5	100	102	103	104	104.8556	105.92	104.00	108.1122	110.94	104.20
6	100	102	103	103	103.1907	104.27	102.02	104.6525	108.00	101.12
7	100	102	103	102	101.6386	103.00	100.08	102.3000	105.97	97.26
8	100	102	102	103	103.7686	104.95	103.00	106.4070	108.90	104.50
9	100	102	102	102	102.4818	103.37	101.75	103.3868	105.84	100.00
10	100	102	100	100	100.3727	102.00	99.00	101.3943	104.43	98.27
11	100	101	103	105	106.6341	107.29	106.00	111.8705	115.34	108.00
12	100	101	103	104	105.1628	106.00	104.02	108.8093	112.00	105.10
13	100	101	102	104	105.4837	106.49	105.00	110.2012	114.62	107.00
14	100	101	102	103	103.8622	104.08	103.10	107.3511	108.46	102.60
15	100	101	102	102	102.2045	103.00	101.50	103.5477	105.84	100.59
16	100	101	101	101	101.2318	102.00	100.53	102.0749	104.60	100.00
17	100	101	100	100	100.3568	101.17	99.11	100.7864	102.79	98.15
18	100	100	101	103	104.6111	105.96	103.16	109.0022	114.16	102.76
19	100	100	100	102	102.9591	104.00	102.00	105.3830	108.87	103.00
20	100	100	100	101	101.6953	102.96	100.82	103.4512	107.29	100.11
21	100	99	99	100	100.4089	101.50	99.08	101.3844	106.14	99.00
22	100	98	98	100	100.5523	102.00	99.00	101.7705	107.75	98.28

Table 3.4 Real GDP expectations for periods 5 and 9 for treatment (i)

Pattern	Time				Mean 5	Upper 95%	Lower 5%	Mean 9	Upper 95%	Lower 5%
	1	2	3	4						
1	100	102	104	106	107.7489	108.16	107.00	112.4822	116.00	106.88
2	100	102	104	105	105.8289	106.96	105.00	107.8600	112.40	101.00
3	100	102	104	104	104.1200	105.28	102.00	107.0378	110.00	104.00
4	100	102	104	103	102.4956	104.00	101.00	104.6844	110.00	99.20
5	100	102	103	105	106.6356	108.00	106.00	110.1911	115.56	105.00
6	100	102	103	104	104.6333	105.46	104.00	107.0156	110.24	102.40
7	100	102	103	103	103.0756	104.00	102.00	104.8455	108.00	101.00
8	100	102	103	102	101.1667	103.00	100.00	102.8500	107.85	97.81
9	100	102	102	104	105.0955	106.00	104.00	108.0778	111.00	104.00
10	100	102	102	102	102.1756	103.00	101.00	104.2000	108.52	100.26
11	100	102	101	103	103.3356	105.08	102.00	105.7089	110.00	102.12
12	100	101	103	105	106.8333	108.00	105.12	110.6956	118.00	103.10
13	100	101	103	104	104.9222	106.00	104.00	107.2356	111.64	102.36
14	100	101	102	104	105.7136	107.00	104.50	109.2133	113.80	104.76
15	100	101	102	103	104.0600	104.46	103.00	106.7956	109.24	103.74
16	100	101	102	102	101.8956	103.00	101.00	103.7822	106.80	100.20
17	100	101	101	103	104.1489	106.00	103.00	106.5444	110.00	102.42
18	100	101	101	102	102.5886	104.00	101.12	104.4844	107.00	101.10

19	100	101	101	101	101.0133	102.00	100.00	101.9556	104.94	99.00
20	100	101	101	99	98.1644	99.96	96.20	99.7600	104.00	95.00
21	100	101	100	102	102.5200	104.00	101.00	104.5600	107.90	101.00
22	100	100	102	104	105.4318	106.97	104.56	108.1682	112.00	102.11
23	100	100	102	103	103.6000	104.82	102.24	105.6045	109.00	101.70
24	100	100	102	100	99.5244	101.40	98.00	101.3711	103.94	98.20
25	100	100	101	103	104.7533	106.00	103.68	108.0222	113.00	102.20
26	100	100	101	102	102.8227	104.00	102.00	105.3533	109.00	101.28
27	100	100	101	100	99.9067	101.38	98.00	101.3091	104.85	98.75
28	100	100	100	102	103.0800	104.00	101.20	105.0511	109.40	100.36
29	100	100	100	101	101.6156	103.00	100.00	103.1889	106.46	100.16
30	100	100	99	100	100.4400	102.00	99.08	101.6600	105.00	99.00
31	100	100	98	100	100.6200	102.08	99.00	101.7067	106.82	97.20
32	100	99	101	103	104.2444	105.82	102.00	106.6273	110.34	101.39

Table 3.5 *Real GDP expectations for periods 5 and 9 for treatment (ii)*

Pattern	Time 1	2	3	4	Mean 5	Upper 95%	Lower 5%	Mean 9	Upper 95%	Lower 5%
1	100	102	104	106	107.6711	108.00	106.84	113.6600	116.00	109.00
2	100	102	104	105	105.8633	106.54	105.06	108.9078	112.66	104.28
3	100	102	104	104	104.5023	106.00	103.00	106.5395	110.74	100.05
4	100	102	104	103	102.6512	104.00	102.00	105.0644	108.00	100.40
5	100	102	103	105	106.1395	106.90	105.50	110.3930	113.27	107.00
6	100	102	103	104	104.9452	105.69	104.02	107.7644	110.00	104.60
7	100	102	103	103	103.2326	104.28	102.00	104.9978	108.32	101.50
8	100	102	103	102	101.5045	102.67	100.42	103.2705	106.77	99.12
9	100	102	102	104	104.7140	105.69	104.00	108.0023	110.69	104.10
10	100	102	102	102	102.3233	103.48	101.51	103.9698	107.18	101.05
11	100	102	101	103	102.9978	104.60	102.00	105.5864	109.53	102.27
12	100	101	103	105	106.3465	107.09	105.21	111.7500	115.17	106.18
13	100	101	103	104	105.1093	106.00	104.30	108.9500	112.17	105.02
14	100	101	102	104	105.2932	106.17	104.32	109.9778	115.88	105.28
15	100	101	102	103	103.9720	104.38	103.40	107.5773	109.49	105.05
16	100	101	102	102	102.2047	102.80	101.23	104.0296	106.26	101.04
17	100	101	101	103	103.9477	105.17	103.00	107.0682	110.79	102.36
18	100	101	101	102	102.3860	103.40	101.10	104.4867	107.60	102.76

19	100	100	101	101	101.1326	102.00	100.50	101.8568	104.00	100.00
20	100	101	101	99	98.3455	99.94	97.03	98.2341	102.00	94.06
21	100	101	100	102	102.7022	103.96	101.16	104.6133	107.72	101.14
22	100	100	102	104	105.3535	106.28	104.03	109.4733	113.96	105.02
23	100	100	102	103	103.64419	104.77	103.00	106.25	108.00	104.00
24	100	100	102	100	99.855814	101.48	98.41	100.46163	102.97	96.72
25	100	100	101	103	104.49186	105.98	103.01	108.51977	113.91	102.13
26	100	100	101	102	102.83256	103.89	102.00	105.37889	108.90	103.00
27	100	100	101	100	100.14	101.86	99.00	100.93864	103.91	98.15
28	100	100	100	102	103.075	104.17	101.15	105.51556	109.50	101.20
29	100	100	100	101	101.4907	102.46	100.53	102.79091	104.96	100.03
30	100	100	99	100	100.34773	101.78	99.50	101.36591	103.34	99.11
31	100	100	98	100	100.57273	102.00	99.50	101.72791	106.48	98.08
32	100	99	101	103	104.28721	105.94	102.10	107.83667	111.08	101.40

3.3 EXPECTATIONS OF CENTRAL TENDENCY AND PROBABILITY RANGES

Here we outline the procedure of eliciting point expectations as well as probability ranges. This procedure is of particular relevance when addressing uncertainty of expected inflation. The new treatment for eliciting probability ranges differs from survey methods used, for example, by De Bruin et al. (2011) where participants of the survey are asked a total of eight questions regarding what changes in prices are likely to happen over the next 12 months. In that setting, subjects are asked about the probability that prices will go up between 0 and 2 percent, 2 and 4 percent, etc.[7] With this approach, a distributional assumption is necessary to estimate the median and the interquartile range of the inflation outlook. By contrast, the questions used in our instructions ask for only three numerical values which then permit the identification of the median as well as the interquartile range without any further assumptions.

The procedure developed here starts with the same setup as in the treatment (i). Subjects are first asked to think about their point forecasts for a one-year and a five-year-ahead horizon. Then comes the new part where subjects are encouraged to think about uncertainty by describing bands or ranges of possible developments around their central projection. In two steps, subjects are instructed to mark the upper and lower limits of the interquartile range for the two expectations horizons. Appendix 3.2 provides the detailed instructions for the case of the CPI. Table 3.6 presents the results for the CPI concerning the two dimensions of the mean and the heterogeneity for this treatment. Table 3.7, again for the CPI, documents the additional dimension of the uncertainty of expectations that treatment (iii) measures. Here, the mean of expectations for each pattern as well as the means of subjects' answers pertaining to the upper 75 percent and the lower 25 percent quartile are reported. In later chapters, these data on the uncertainty of expectations will be the basis for work investigating the effects of inflation uncertainty on variables

---

[7] See also Manski (2017) for a survey of newer developments in the measurement of macroeconomic uncertainty.

Table 3.6 CPI expectations for periods 5 and 9 for treatment (iii)

Pattern	Time 1	2	3	4	Mean 5	Upper 95%	Lower 5%	Mean 9	Upper 95%	Lower 5%
1	100	102	104	106	107.7422	108.00	106.20	113.1244	116.00	105.96
2	100	102	104	105	105.8067	107.00	104.60	108.0778	111.80	102.40
3	100	102	104	104	104.1911	105.00	103.00	106.5222	111.60	102.00
4	100	102	103	105	106.4489	107.80	106.00	110.9022	114.80	106.24
5	100	102	103	104	104.8067	105.00	104.00	107.4333	110.00	104.36
6	100	102	103	103	103.0356	104.00	102.00	104.1200	107.80	99.20
7	100	102	103	102	101.4622	103.00	100.56	102.3067	106.00	98.60
8	100	102	102	103	103.8867	105.00	103.00	106.2733	108.00	104.10
9	100	102	102	102	102.3178	103.80	101.00	103.6067	106.00	101.00
10	100	102	100	100	100.2778	101.80	98.10	101.7422	105.00	98.00
11	100	101	103	105	106.7667	108.00	105.20	117.7356	116.80	107.00
12	100	101	103	104	104.9667	106.00	104.00	108.2067	112.00	105.00
13	100	101	102	104	105.4244	106.50	104.20	109.3867	113.80	104.00
14	100	101	102	103	103.9533	104.16	104.00	107.0067	109.00	104.60
15	100	101	102	102	102.0578	103.00	101.00	103.5511	106.00	101.00
16	100	101	101	101	101.1578	102.00	100.00	102.5000	105.80	99.20
17	100	101	100	100	100.0000	101.00	99.00	101.0956	104.00	98.00
18	100	100	101	103	104.8556	106.00	103.20	109.9200	116.00	104.20
19	100	100	100	102	103.0333	104.00	101.00	105.7600	110.40	100.20
20	100	100	100	101	101.7489	102.00	101.00	103.5511	106.00	100.20
21	100	99	99	100	100.8467	102.00	100.00	102.7622	108.00	100.00
22	100	98	98	100	100.9800	102.00	99.60	102.8044	107.00	99.00

Table 3.7 Measures of uncertainty of CPI expectations for periods 5 and 9 from treatment (iii)

Pattern	Time 1	2	3	4	Mean 5	Mean of upper 75%	Mean of lower 25%	Mean 9	Mean of upper 75%	Mean of lower 25%
1	100	102	104	106	107.74	109.05	106.68	113.12	115.91	110.27
2	100	102	104	105	105.81	107.12	104.54	108.08	110.62	105.42
3	100	102	104	104	104.19	105.60	102.79	106.52	109.18	103.09
4	100	102	103	105	106.45	107.83	105.18	110.90	113.60	108.04
5	100	102	103	104	104.81	105.98	103.49	107.43	109.90	104.80
6	100	102	103	103	103.04	104.69	101.66	104.12	107.12	100.99
7	100	102	103	102	101.46	103.18	99.97	102.31	104.68	99.15
8	100	102	102	103	103.89	105.26	102.40	106.27	108.83	103.50
9	100	102	102	102	102.32	103.62	100.78	103.61	106.08	100.62
10	100	102	100	100	100.28	101.76	98.76	101.74	104.33	98.85
11	100	101	103	105	106.77	108.13	105.37	111.74	114.82	108.07
12	100	101	103	104	104.97	106.48	103.59	108.21	111.00	104.86
13	100	101	102	104	105.42	106.81	104.20	109.39	112.32	106.57
14	100	101	102	103	103.95	104.95	102.95	107.01	108.95	104.51
15	100	101	102	102	102.06	103.28	100.86	103.55	105.66	100.80
16	100	101	101	101	101.16	102.22	100.08	102.50	104.45	100.01
17	100	101	100	100	100.00	101.30	98.94	101.10	102.88	98.71
18	100	100	101	103	104.86	106.24	103.51	109.92	112.98	106.60
19	100	100	100	102	103.03	104.40	101.72	105.76	108.32	103.05
20	100	100	100	101	101.75	102.84	100.39	103.55	105.72	101.20
21	100	99	99	100	100.85	102.01	99.62	102.76	105.08	100.05
22	100	98	98	100	100.98	102.26	99.32	102.80	105.42	99.52

Table 3.8 GDP expectations for periods 5 and 9 for treatment (iii)

Pattern	Time				Mean 5	Upper 95%	Lower 5%	Mean 9	Upper 95%	Lower 5%
	1	2	3	4	5			9		
1	100	102	104	106	107.7867	108.00	107.00	112.7933	116.00	108.20
2	100	102	104	105	105.8089	106.66	105.08	108.1956	113.04	104.60
3	100	102	104	104	104.1889	105.00	103.00	105.9822	108.86	101.20
4	100	102	104	103	102.6578	104.00	101.00	104.1444	108.80	99.00
5	100	102	103	105	106.2867	107.00	106.00	110.6711	113.00	108.00
6	100	102	103	104	104.7356	105.40	104.00	106.9622	110.90	102.00
7	100	102	103	103	102.9378	104.00	102.00	103.9578	108.20	99.20
8	100	102	103	102	101.2444	102.66	100.00	102.1400	106.00	97.10
9	100	102	102	104	104.8622	106.00	104.00	108.1311	111.80	104.00
10	100	102	102	102	102.1689	103.00	101.00	103.3333	106.80	99.00
11	100	102	101	103	103.0822	105.00	102.00	105.6556	108.44	104.00
12	100	102	103	105	106.6311	107.88	105.20	110.8067	114.00	104.00
13	100	101	103	104	104.7000	105.90	104.00	107.7622	111.40	103.20
14	100	101	102	104	105.7133	106.90	104.76	109.5200	115.80	104.10
15	100	101	102	103	103.9956	104.00	104.00	107.0644	108.00	104.00
16	100	101	102	102	101.9622	103.00	101.00	103.7933	106.00	100.00
17	100	101	101	103	104.1867	105.00	103.00	106.8733	110.80	102.00
18	100	101	101	102	102.4133	103.00	102.00	104.4289	107.40	101.00

Table 3.8 (cont.)

Pattern	Time				Mean			Mean		
	1	2	3	4	5	Upper 95%	Lower 5%	9	Upper 95%	Lower 5%
19	100	101	101	101	100.9711	102.00	100.00	101.7133	103.40	99.00
20	100	101	101	99	97.9956	99.00	96.00	97.9533	102.00	91.30
21	100	101	100	102	102.7867	104.00	102.00	104.8022	107.80	101.18
22	100	100	102	104	105.3156	106.00	104.00	108.5200	112.00	102.20
23	100	100	102	103	103.5256	104.00	102.60	105.2111	108.00	102.00
24	100	100	102	100	99.4667	101.70	98.00	100.0133	103.00	93.40
25	100	100	101	103	104.6933	106.00	103.20	108.1200	113.00	103.00
26	100	100	101	102	102.6533	103.46	102.00	105.2956	109.00	101.92
27	100	100	101	100	99.7867	101.00	98.84	100.6467	103.80	97.60
28	100	100	100	102	103.0311	104.00	102.00	105.5689	110.00	101.60
29	100	100	100	101	101.6156	103.00	100.52	103.0511	107.60	97.60
30	100	100	99	100	100.2222	101.00	99.00	101.5689	105.00	99.00
31	100	100	98	100	100.5111	102.00	98.20	101.9267	105.00	99.00
32	100	99	101	103	104.1844	105.00	102.60	107.5222	113.00	102.00

Table 3.9 Measures of uncertainty of GDP expectations for periods 5 and 9 from treatment (iii)

Pattern	Time 1	2	3	4	Mean 5	Mean of upper 75%	Mean of lower 25%	Mean 9	Mean of upper 75%	Mean of lower 25%
1	100	102	104	106	107.79	108.79	106.69	112.7933	114.77	110.40
2	100	102	104	105	105.81	106.81	104.77	108.1956	110.16	106.00
3	100	102	104	104	104.19	105.57	102.98	105.9822	108.36	103.34
4	100	102	104	103	102.66	104.04	101.38	104.1444	106.60	101.48
5	100	102	103	105	106.29	107.38	105.21	110.6711	112.66	108.34
6	100	102	103	104	104.74	105.87	103.82	106.9622	108.96	104.93
7	100	102	103	103	102.94	104.03	101.75	103.9578	106.09	101.47
8	100	102	103	102	101.24	102.54	100.09	102.1400	104.26	99.52
9	100	102	102	104	104.86	106.16	103.77	108.1311	109.93	105.98
10	100	102	102	102	102.17	103.27	101.05	103.3333	105.39	101.22
11	100	102	101	103	103.08	104.52	101.82	105.6556	107.81	103.41
12	100	101	103	105	106.63	107.66	105.44	110.8067	112.93	108.55
13	100	101	103	104	104.70	105.79	103.61	107.7622	109.67	105.74
14	100	101	102	104	105.71	106.70	104.55	109.5200	111.53	107.25
15	100	101	102	103	104.00	104.85	103.11	107.0644	109.01	105.38
16	100	101	102	102	101.96	103.19	100.92	103.7933	105.90	101.36
17	100	101	101	103	104.19	105.33	103.00	106.8733	109.42	104.77
18	100	101	101	102	102.41	103.60	101.34	104.4289	106.42	102.70

Table 3.9 (cont.)

Pattern	Time 1	2	3	4	Mean 5	Mean of upper 75%	Mean of lower 25%	Mean 9	Mean of upper 75%	Mean of lower 25%
19	100	101	101	101	100.97	102.23	99.90	101.7133	103.54	99.98
20	100	101	101	99	98.00	99.26	96.61	97.9533	100.61	95.16
21	100	101	100	102	102.79	103.99	101.47	104.8022	107.11	102.18
22	100	100	102	104	105.32	106.56	104.10	108.5200	110.72	106.06
23	100	100	102	103	103.53	104.65	102.44	105.2111	107.25	103.18
24	100	100	102	100	99.47	100.74	98.00	100.0133	102.56	97.14
25	100	100	101	103	104.69	105.88	103.48	108.1200	110.28	105.74
26	100	100	101	102	102.65	103.82	101.62	105.2956	107.48	103.31
27	100	100	101	100	99.79	100.94	98.75	100.6467	102.66	98.61
28	100	100	100	102	103.03	104.38	101.72	105.5689	107.97	103.38
29	100	100	100	101	101.62	102.76	100.45	103.0522	105.38	100.91
30	100	100	99	100	100.22	101.35	98.92	101.5689	103.84	99.45
31	100	100	98	100	100.51	101.90	99.12	101.9267	104.35	99.10
32	100	99	101	103	104.18	105.44	102.98	107.5222	110.12	105.02

such as the interest rate. Tables 3.8 and 3.9 present the expectations data elicited with treatment (iii) for the real GDP.

3.4   SUMMARY AND CONCLUSIONS

This chapter presents the different treatments used in the laboratory to elicit expectations. In particular, the expectations data cover both a short- and a long-term horizon. The data elicited with the first and the second treatment pertain to subjective and higher-order point expectations for the CPI and real GDP. This probabilistic treatment offers a straightforward approach to the measurement of subjects' uncertainty of expectations. Two appendices detail the instructions used for the various treatments applied in the laboratory. The following chapter offers a detailed statistical analysis of this data. This analysis helps to assess whether, for example, systematic differences can be found in how subjects extrapolate different macroeconomic variables.

APPENDIX 3.1   INSTRUCTIONS FOR THE BASIC TREATMENT (i), TRANSLATED FROM GERMAN

This experiment is devised to study expectations. For this purpose, we will show you how the price level (the consumer price index as a measure of the general course of prices in an economy) and the real national income (the real gross domestic product as a measure of the total of goods produced in an economy) of a country can evolve. In concrete terms, we will present you with a number of cases that show how these economic variables develop over the course of four years. The cases shown are a selective representation of reality inasmuch as we limit the presentation to cases where the time series from one year to the next either moves up or down by one or two units, or else remains constant. However, the size of the changes over time could also take other values. This is important for the tasks given to you. We are interested in your forecast for each of the cases shown and your prediction of the size of future changes in the series can be different from the integer values shown and can also be larger than 2 or smaller than −2. We would like you to address two tasks for each of the cases shown. We are at present in period 4 and your task is to assess the future course of the variable shown that you judge the most likely.

1. What will be the value of the variable in period 5 (your forecast one year into the future)?
2. What will be the value of the variable in period 9 (your forecast five years into the future)?

Please give the numerical values with a precision of one place after the decimal point (e.g., 103.4). Financial reward: For answering all of the tasks, you will receive 12 Euros. We assure anonymity of the participants of this study. The following 22 cases show the price level (the consumer price index, CPI).

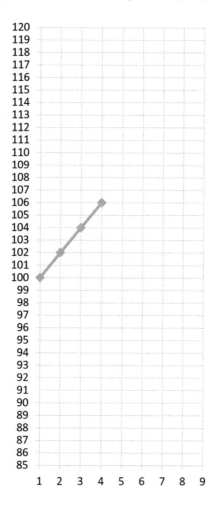

What value do you expect the consumer price index to take in period 5: ....

What value do you expect the consumer price index to take in period 9: ....

[On the next 21 pages, cases 2 to 22 follow, and thereafter follow the 32 cases for the real GDP.]

APPENDIX 3.2   THE INSTRUCTIONS FOR THE PROBABILISTIC TREATMENT (iii), TRANSLATED FROM GERMAN

This experiment is devised to study expectations. For this purpose, we will show you how the price level (the consumer price index as a measure of the general course of prices in an economy) of a country can evolve. In concrete terms, we will present you with 22 cases that show how this economic variable develops over the course of four years. The cases shown are a selective representation of reality inasmuch as we limit the presentation to cases where the time series from one year to the next either moves up or down by one or two units, or else remains constant. However, the size of the changes over time could also take other values. This is important for the tasks in the experiment. We are interested in your forecast for each of the cases shown and your prediction of how the size of future changes in the series may be different from the integer values shown and they may also be larger than 2 or smaller than -2. For each of the cases shown, we will ask the same questions. We are at present in period 4 and your task is to assess the future course of the variable shown that you judge the most likely.

1. What will be the value of the variable in period 5 (your expectation, or point prediction, one year into the future)?
2. What will be the value of the variable in period 9 (your expectation, or point prediction, five years into the future)?

The display below shows an example of a case that will not be shown again later in the experiment.

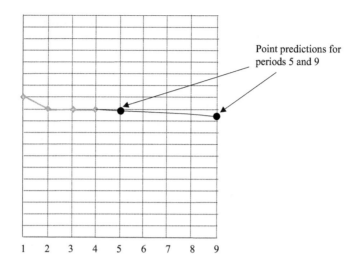

Point predictions for
periods 5 and 9

Since the future course of the price level is uncertain, the actual course may develop above or below your point predictions. Hence, we are interested in your personal assessment of the bandwidth of possible developments. For this purpose, you may think of a central cone around your point predictions (displayed in dark grey). In this central cone, you see 50 percent of the possible developments. With a probability of 25 percent, the possible course develops above the central cone and with a probability of 25 percent, it develops below the central cone (the areas displayed by the outer cone are displayed in light grey).

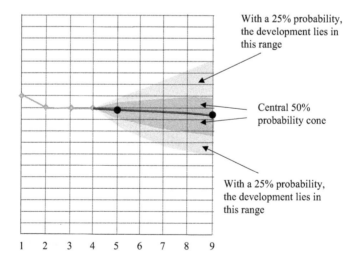

With a 25% probability,
the development lies in
this range

Central 50%
probability cone

With a 25% probability,
the development lies in
this range

What we would like to know are the upper and lower boundary values for the central 50% probability cone.

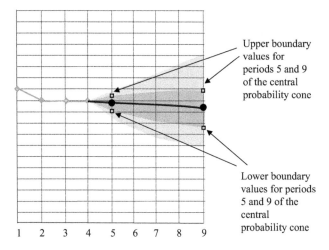

Upper boundary values for periods 5 and 9 of the central probability cone

Lower boundary values for periods 5 and 9 of the central probability cone

With your choice of upper and lower values, you may express your judgment in various ways:

(a) The more certain you are about the future development, the narrower will be the 50 percent probability cone you will choose. The more uncertain you are, the wider will be the cone you will choose.

(b) The probability cone does not have to be symmetrical around your point predictions. The following two displays illustrate this point.

If, for example, you see the possible courses above your point predictions as more widely dispersed than those below the point predictions, then your judgment could look as follows:

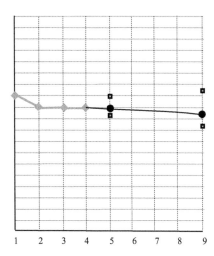

If, on the contrary, you see the possible courses above your point predictions as more narrowly dispersed than those below, then your judgment could look as follows:

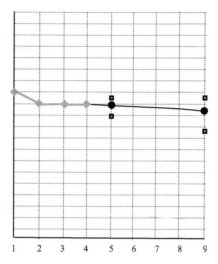

Financial reward: For answering the complete list of tasks, you will receive 12 Euros. We assure anonymity of the participants of this study.

4   Features of the Laboratory Data

This chapter analyses the data elicited in the laboratory as described in Chapter 3. More specifically, before using the expectations data for the computation of time series of expectations, we want to assess how the elicited data compare across treatments and horizons. Further, it will be demonstrated that the expectations data from the laboratory survey cannot be explained by a simple linear model of extrapolation. This finding justifies the procedures detailed in the coming chapters.

4.2   THE ROLE OF ECONOMIC CONTEXT

The issue to be addressed here is whether context matters for time-series extrapolation. More concretely, we inquire whether subjects show dissimilarities in how they extrapolate different macroeconomic variables. When statistically comparing the elicited expectations for the CPI (denoted by P) and for real GDP (denoted by Y) one year into the future, we find the following regression result:

$$P^e_{k,5} - P_{k,4} = 0.086 + 0.888\left(Y^e_{k,5} - Y_{k,4}\right)$$
$$\phantom{P^e_{k,5} - P_{k,4} = } (0.056) \ (0.051) \hspace{2cm} (4.1)$$
$$\overline{R}^2 = 0.953, \quad SEE = 0.161$$

For this regression, only the 17 patterns (and the responses) that are common to the CPI and the GDP are considered. The values in the regression are indexed by k because each of the 17 cases has a different history. Here $P_{k,4}$ and $Y_{k,4}$ stand for the value of the last (the fourth) observed value for either variable. Standard errors are shown in parentheses below the estimated coefficients. A test of the joint hypothesis that the intercept is zero and the slope parameter of the regression is one is not rejected by a Wald test (p value of 0.122). Hence, concerning short-term expectations, subjects appear to extrapolate patterns independent of which of the two macroeconomic variables is at stake. By contrast, when comparing five-year-ahead expectations, the following is found:

$$P^e_{k,9} - P_{k,4} = -0.393 + 1.289\left(Y^e_{k,9} - Y_{k,4}\right)$$
$$\quad\quad\quad (0.498)\quad (0.135) \quad\quad\quad\quad\quad\quad (4.2)$$
$$\overline{R}^2 = 0.856, \quad SEE = 0.906$$

Here, a Wald test rejects (p value of 0.021) the hypothesis that the intercept is zero and the slope is one. Hence, for long-term expectations, context does appear to matter. The finding that price level and income expectations differ when it comes to a longer term horizon is also borne out when studying the relationship between expectations for different horizons for the same variable. Specifically, we regress the expected change over five-years on the expected one-year change for both of the two macroeconomic indicators. For the CPI, the relevant regression based on 22 observations is:

$$P^e_{j,9} - P_{j,4} = 1.327 + 2.411\left(P^e_{j,5} - P_{j,4}\right)$$
$$\quad\quad\quad (0.236)\quad (0.237) \quad\quad\quad\quad\quad\quad (4.3)$$
$$\overline{R}^2 = 0.837, \quad SEE = 0.761$$

These values are indexed by j since each pattern has a different history of Ps. For the case of real GDP, the finding (here with 32 observations indexed by l) is as follows:

$$Y^e_{l,9} - Y_{l,4} = 1.804 + 1.795\left(Y^e_{l,5} - Y_{l,4}\right)$$
$$\quad\quad\quad (0.138)\quad (0.142) \quad\quad\quad\quad\quad\quad (4.4)$$
$$\overline{R}^2 = 0.840, \quad SEE = 0.594$$

Apparently, when forming expectations concerning inflation, subjects weight the short-term outlook more compared to expectations regarding output growth. By contrast, subjects consider the general drift (i.e., the constant in the regression) stronger for income than for prices.

4.3   COMPARISON OF ELICITED EXPECTATIONS
   ACROSS TREATMENTS

Next, we report tests comparing the average of the elicited expected changes under treatments (i) with those under (ii) and limit the analysis to the results concerning the CPI. Hence, it will be assessed whether subjective point expectations systematically differ from expectations concerning the expectations of the collective. In regressions, as seen in Eq. (4.5) and Eq. (4.6) the mean of subjects' responses concerning higher order expectations (denoted by $\hat{P}_5^e$ and $\hat{P}_9^e$) is related to the respective mean of subjective expectations:

$$\hat{P}_{j,5}^e - P_{j,4} = 0.232 + 0.725\left(P_{j,5}^e - P_{j,4}\right)$$
$$\quad\quad\quad\quad\,\,(0.067)\ (0.067)$$
$$\overline{R}^2 = 0.851, \quad SEE = 0.217 \tag{4.5}$$

$$\hat{P}_{j,9}^e - P_{j,4} = -0.222 + 1.16\left(P_{j,9}^e - P_{j,4}\right)$$
$$\quad\quad\quad\quad\,\,(0.247)\quad\ (0.069)$$
$$\overline{R}^2 = 0.933, \quad SEE = 0.588 \tag{4.6}$$

For the two estimates, the restriction that the intercept is zero and the slope is one is rejected at the 1 percent and the 5 percent level of significance, respectively. Apparently, subjective and higher order expectations differ systematically.

In concluding this sort of statistical assessment, let us consider comparing the point predictions of the CPI in treatment (i) with those, denoted by $\tilde{P}^e$, in the treatment (iii). The results of the regressions for the two expectations horizons are as follows:

$$\tilde{P}_{j,5}^e - X_{j,4} = 0.118 + 0.892\left(P_{j,5}^e - X_{j,4}\right)$$
$$\quad\quad\quad\quad\,\,(0.050)\ (0.051)$$
$$\overline{R}^2 = 0.938, \quad SEE = 0.163 \tag{4.7}$$

$$\tilde{P}_{j,9}^e - X_{j,4} = 0.114 + 1.050\left(P_{j,9}^e - X_{j,4}\right)$$
$$\quad\quad\quad\quad\,\,(0.217)\ (0.061)$$
$$\overline{R}^2 = 0.936, \quad SEE = 0.517 \tag{4.8}$$

Comparison of treatments documented by Eq. (4.7) and Eq. (4.8) shows that Wald tests do not reject the joint hypothesis that the intercept is zero and the slope coefficient is one at the 5 percent level of signifi-cance. Hence, there is no indication that the treatments (i) and (iii) would elicit systematically different responses. In Chapter 5, when computing time series of expected inflation and using these series in econometric analyses, we will continue to work with the three sets of data elicited with the treatments (i), (ii), and (iii).

4.4 PATTERN-BASED VERSUS LINEAR EXTRAPOLATION

If a statistical analysis of the laboratory data would indicate that elicited expectations can be well described by a linear model of trend extrapolation, much of what the following chapters of this book explore could be greatly simplified. In fact, we would be back to the standard model of trend extrapolation. As it turns out, the findings here indicate that the elicited expectations cannot be explained accur-ately by the standard model of extrapolation. This can be shown statistically by approximating the laboratory data with a model of linear trend extrapolation and comparing this to a non-linear alterna-tive. The concept of linear trend extrapolation implies that expect-ations should be explainable by a weighted average of the observed lagged changes in the series shown to subjects. Importantly, in a linear model the weights of the lagged changes should be constant over all cases shown. Accordingly, linear trend extrapolation would translate into the following regression equation:

$$P_{j,5}^e - P_{j,4} = \beta_0 + \beta_1 \left(P_{j,4} - P_{j,3} \right) + \beta_2 \left(P_{j,3} - P_{j,2} \right) + \beta_3 \left(P_{j,2} - P_{j,1} \right) + \varepsilon_j$$

$$(4.9)$$

Here, $P_{j,1}$, $P_{j,2}$, $P_{j,3}$, and $P_{j,4}$ stand for the values of the price level series shown to the subjects in periods 1, 2, 3, and 4. These values are indexed because each of the j cases has a different history of Ps. We statistically compare this standard model of trend extrapolation with a specification that allows the β coefficients to differ across two classes of patterns, namely trend patterns and no-trend patterns.[1] We conduct a specification search that leads to the estimation of Eq. (4.10). For this specification, we use the two dummy variables $D^{Trend} = 1$ if the product $(P_{j,4} - P_{j,3})(P_{j,3} - P_{j,2}) > 0$ and $D^{No\text{-}Trend} = 1 - D^{Trend}$.[2] Hence, trend patterns are cases where the series over the previous three periods changes in the same direction and no-trend patterns are all the remaining cases. The result that is obtained after using Wald tests to eliminate irrelevant regressors (i.e., lags and constant) is the following:

$$P_{j,5}^{e} - P_{j,4} = 0.839(P_{j,4} - P_{j,3})D^{Trend} + 0.584(P_{j,4} - P_{j,3})D^{No\text{-}Trend}$$
$$\qquad\quad (0.037) \qquad\qquad\qquad\qquad (0.052)$$
$$\overline{R}^{2} = 0.935, \quad SEE = 0.181$$

$$(4.10)$$

Thus, the quantitative changes $P_{j,3} - P_{j,2}$ and $P_{j,2} - P_{j,1}$ do not enter significantly once the qualitative aspect of the course of the recent past is captured in the estimate. For the estimates reported here, the mean of the responses for the data elicited in treatment (i) is used. A Wald test rejects at the 1 percent level of significance the hypothesis that the two estimated coefficients are identical across the two classes of patterns. This finding highlights a key characteristic of human time-series extrapolation: apparently, people tend to give a significantly higher weight to the recent changes in the series when it has shown a clear trend over the last three periods. A similar result is found when looking at five-year-ahead expectations. Here the specification search results in

---

[1] Clearly, a finer classification of patterns could be considered but the distinction chosen here is sufficient to document the limitations of the model of Eq. (4.9).

[2] The fact that the specification search here leads to a formulation of the dummy variables that reach back only three periods into the past already indicates what will be further explored in Chapter 10 where the patterns shown to subjects cover only three periods.

$$P^e_{j,9} - P_{j,4} = 1.465 + 2.145\left(P_{j,4} - P_{j,3}\right) \cdot D^{Trend}$$
$$(0.189)\ (0.168)$$
$$+\ 0.841\left(P_{j,4} - P_{j,3}\right) \cdot D^{No\text{-}Trend}$$
$$(0.203)$$
$$\overline{R}^2 = 0.894, \quad SEE = 0.624. \tag{4.11}$$

A Wald test again rejects the hypothesis of equal weights on the most recently observed change in the series across the two classes of patterns. Again, the result indicates that quantitatively the changes other than the most recent one in the price level are not statistically significant. Past changes tend to influence expectations only qualitatively, i.e., via the shape of the time series. Thus, the model of linear trend extrapolation fails to capture important elements of subjects' judgments and Chapter 5 will proceed to develop a model of expectations that makes full use of the information contained in the laboratory expectations data.

4.5 SUMMARY AND CONCLUSIONS

Summing up the analysis presented so far, it can be reported that context does indeed influence the extrapolation of macroeconomic data. In particular, there are significant differences between how long-term expectations are formed for the general level of prices and for aggregate output. As to the short-term horizon, subjects' formation of expectations of inflation and income growth appear to be very similar. Of particular importance for the further use of the laboratory expectations data is the finding that extrapolation cannot be captured by a simple model of linear extrapolation. Hence, a good model of extrapolative expectations needs to account for the different responses across different patterns in a time series.

5 Similarity Matching and Scaling the Experimental Data

5.1 INTRODUCTION

This chapter details how the laboratory data on expectations are used to generate historical series of expectations.[1] In essence, and proceeding on the assumption that economic agents function just like our subjects in the laboratory, we fit the responses of subjects to historical four-year sequences of the price level. In this process of fitting the laboratory expectations to historical data, two important aspects of behavior have to be addressed. The first aspect is the issue of similarity matching and the second concerns the scaling of the elicited data.

The issue of similarity matching is raised because the patterns shown in the laboratory depict stylized time series. Thus, when modeling time series expectations, it is necessary to assess which of the patterns (or which mixture of patterns) shown in the laboratory corresponds to a given historical sequence of consumer price index (CPI) values. This determines which of the elicited responses are relevant for computing expectations for a particular point in time. One way to proceed here would be to simply stipulate that the stylized pattern most similar to a given historical CPI sequence is the only relevant one. This would assume that agents are perfectly certain and accurate when making a similarity judgment. Instead of working with this assumption of perfect similarity matching, we devise an experiment that addresses this question empirically. The results of this experiment tell us how to weight the various patterns and their expectations

---

[1] Clearly, the described procedure is not only applicable to the computations of historical expectations but also to expectations in hypothetical what-if scenarios. While the text here focuses on inflation expectations, the procedures developed can and will also be applied to expectations concerning the real GDP.

at any point in time. The second crucial point is the fact that the patterns in the laboratory only show changes of 1 and 2 percent. In order to model expectations for historical inflation outside this range, we need to investigate the scaling issue. How do expectations vary when the size of the steps in the time series varies? Again, this question can be studied empirically. In the following, we first turn to the issue of similarity matching and weighting of patterns. Thereafter, the scaling relationship will be explored.

5.2 EXPERIMENTAL EVIDENCE ON SIMILARITY MATCHING

For studying how people assess similarities between stylized patterns and observed actual time series, we conduct an experiment. For this purpose, a new set of 45 subjects are given 58 matching problems where they in turn see short sequences of a time series and are instructed to judge similarity. For each of these short sequences, subjects assess correlation between this sequence and the 16 linearly independent standard sequences (the primary patterns) used in the elicitation of CPI expectations. We present only those 16 from a total of 22 patterns which in terms of changes are not collinear (e.g., 100, 101, 102, 103 is among the primary patterns while 100, 102, 104, 106 is not).[2] Subjects are instructed to find the primary pattern that has the highest correlation with the particular task sequence. Appendix 5.1 details the instructions. In this experiment, subjects are not given any economic context. Figure 5.1 presents one of the 58 different experimental tasks. In this figure, subjects see the case to be assessed in the center of the display and 16 stylized patterns above and below it.

---

[2] The index i denotes the 16 primary patterns. For completeness here is a list of these primary patterns: 100, 102, 104, 105; 100, 102, 103, 105; 100, 102, 103, 104; 100, 102, 103, 103; 100, 102, 103, 102; 100, 102, 102, 103; 100, 101, 103, 105; 100, 101, 103, 104; 100, 101, 102, 104; 100, 101, 102, 103; 100, 101, 102, 102; 100, 101, 101, 101; 100, 101, 100, 100; 100, 100, 101, 103; 100, 100, 100, 101; 100, 99, 99, 100.

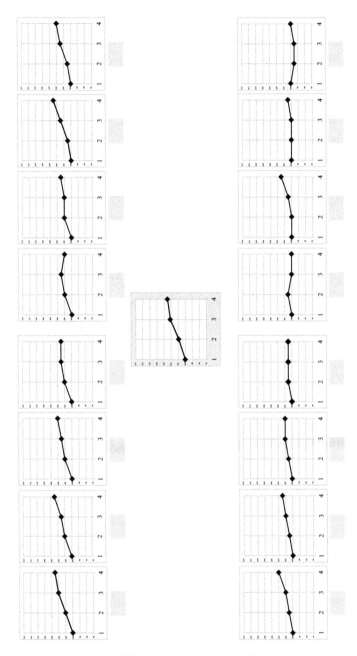

FIGURE 5.1 Example of display shown in the similarity assessment
experiment

The 58 tasks shown are taken from the historical course of the consumer price index. Each case represents one of the overlapping segments of the historical time series of the German annual CPI data, starting in 1950 and running up to 2010. At every step of the experiment, subjects can allocate a total of 10 points to the 16 cases in the list of reference patterns. More concretely, it is possible to split the 10 points on different primary patterns according to their perceived similarity with a task pattern. Subjects are compensated according to the accuracy of their judgments. In specific terms, a subject earns one unit for each point allocated to the most similar pattern, ½ of a unit for each point allocated to the second most similar pattern, ⅓ of a unit for each point allocated to the third most similar pattern, ¼ of a unit for each point allocated to the fourth most similar pattern, and so forth. At the end of the experiment, all units earned are added together and the individual's payout is twice that total in Euro cents. On average, subjects used 39 minutes to complete their tasks and earned 7.75 Euros.[3]

5.3   MODELING SIMILARITY MATCHING

For the purpose ahead, the data gathered with this experiment are used to estimate a simple model of similarity matching. This model captures various degrees of accuracy in judgment with a single parameter λ. The model describes the weight w_i (i.e., the fraction of points allocated) given to any pattern i as a function of the value of the correlation (ρ_i) of this pattern with the shown historical sequence relative to the corresponding correlations of the other patterns. In concrete terms, the model estimated with the aggregated laboratory data is[4]

---

[3] Subjects were students from the University of Erfurt. Given that the task was free of economic context, no relevant background in terms of course work was required of participants.

[4] In the calculation of weights, only patterns with a positive correlation are considered. With the exception of one period (at the beginning of the experiment) and one single subject, nobody ever allocated points to a primary pattern showing a negative correlation with the task sequence.

$$w_i = \frac{\rho_i^\lambda}{\sum_{k=1}^{16} \rho_k^\lambda} + \varepsilon_i \qquad (5.1)$$

In order to build intuition, consider various possible values of λ. If λ is very high (e.g., 1,000) the model implies that the pattern with the highest similarity receives a high weight. Consider the case where objectively the two patterns most similar to the case to be judged have correlations as similar as 0.99 and 0.98 (assuming for the sake of simplicity that all other correlations are zero). Hence, a $\lambda = 1,000$ would put a weight of 0.99996 on the first and only 0.00004 on the second pattern. By contrast, a low value of λ indicates that discrimination is poor. As an example, a value of $\lambda = 10$ would imply weights of 0.52536 and 0.47464.

Next, we turn to empirically estimating the parameter λ. For this purpose, the weights w_i implied by the model are fitted to the weights allocated by the subjects. The resulting least-square estimate of λ covering all 58 cases and 45 subjects is 125. Figure 5.2 illustrates the finding visually. Here, the weights subjects give to patterns of diminishing similarity are shown together with the weights implied by the estimated model. For this display, we consider a typical situation concerning the ranking of correlations. Hence, the weighting according to the graphed function would give the most similar pattern (and its associated expectation) a weight of approximately 0.5 followed by weights of 0.2, 0.15, etc. for the patterns next in line in terms of similarity. The computations of expectations will rely on this empirically estimated version of the model.

5.4   SCALING THE LABORATORY DATA TO HISTORICAL DATA

For the application of the laboratory data for the computation of historical series of the expected price level, one further element needs to be addressed. This element concerns the issue of scaling.[5] The focus here is on CPI expectations but clearly, the generalities of

---

[5] The routine followed here builds on the approach introduced in Rötheli (2011) and uses the average responses of subjects to the various price level patterns.

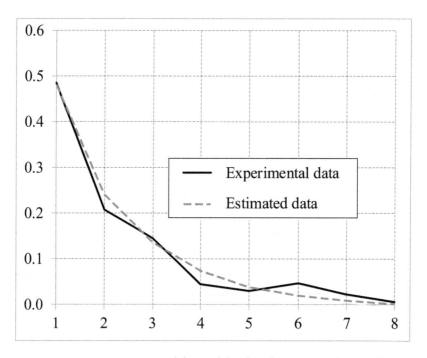

FIGURE 5.2 Experimental data and data based on estimated model of similarity matching

scaling apply to gross domestic product (GDP) expectations as well. Empirical CPI data typically show changes outside the range shown in the laboratory. Hence, the question is how the experimental expectations should be adjusted to different ranges observed empirically. The answer to the question is developed in two steps: we start with the fact that even within the set of patterns presented in the laboratory, there are cases showing inflation rates of different ranges. So the first step consists of studying the scaling tendencies in the elicited expectations data. This leads to the quantification of a scaling law. The second step then takes this scaling law to historical data.

The essential question here is how expectations differ when people face patterns that are qualitatively identical but show quantitatively different steps of change. Consider for example the pattern 100, 101, 102, 103 and the pattern 100, 102, 104, 106. Clearly, the second pattern shows qualitatively the same changes, but they are twice as large. So, how do expectations differ across such patterns? The simplest way to proceed would be to assume that this scaling is one-to-one. We reach a first rough assessment of the proportionality proposition by looking at subjects' one-year-ahead expectation for the pair of patterns considered. For the CPI sequence 100, 101, 102, 103 the one-year-ahead expectation is 103.953. Thus, it would be tempting to infer that the answer to the sequence 100, 102, 104, 106 would be 107.906, that is, simply twice the expected change compared with the previous pattern. However, empirically this regularity does not hold. Instead, the average projected value to the latter pattern is only 107.742. Thus, the scaling appears to be less than one-to-one. The parameter which will be used to capture the scaling relationship is denoted by θ. Based on the above example, it can be conjectured that the value of this parameter is less than 1.

Fortunately, we do not have to settle the scaling issue based on the single pair of observations used in the example. Clearly, there is more than one pair of patterns which, when looking at the steps of change, are perfectly collinear. There exist in total six such pairs, i.e., patterns 1-14, 3-15, 9-16, 10-17, 19-20, and 21-22. For these six pairs, the *factor of proportion*, denoted by β, is always 2. Hence, in the laboratory data, the factor of proportion is given which helps quantification of the scaling of expectations for values of β different from 2. More concretely, consider the following general specification of the scaling law:

$$P^e_{5,1} - P_4 = \left(P^e_{5,\beta} - P_4\right)/\beta^\theta \tag{5.2}$$

The subscripts 1 and β indicate patterns moving in steps of size 1 and β, respectively. We proceed to estimate the *scaling parameter* θ with the laboratory data, with the following specification[6]

---

[6] In order to estimate this scaling relationship, the empirical relevance of the described six pairs of patterns is taken into account. When looking at the primary patterns (i.e., patterns 14, 15, 16, 17, 20, 21) and taking the 1950–2010 US and German CPI data

$$\left(P^e_{m,5,1} - P_{m,4}\right) = \left(P^e_{m,5,2} - P_{m,4}\right)/2^\theta + \epsilon_m. \tag{5.3}$$

The observations are indexed by m running from 1 to 6. The number 2 in the denominator of Eq. (5.3) stands for the value of the β parameter in the laboratory data. An estimate of θ of 1 would indicate that the scaling proceeds one-to-one. Instead, for the CPI expectations elicited in treatment (i), we find an empirical θ value of 0.839 (standard error 0.018). With the data from treatment (ii, the higher-order expectations) we have a value of 0.966 (standard error 0.015) and for treatment (iii, probabilistic) we find a value for θ of 0.855 (standard error 0.016). Hence, the θ value for the two treatments asking for individuals' subjective expectations are very similar, whereas the θ estimate for the higher order expectations is much closer to unity although still significantly below the value of 1 (p value of 0.033).

Figure 5.3 shows the scaling relationship implied by the estimate for treatment (iii). The graph makes it clear that inflation expectations exhibit an element of regressivity. This does not mean that people expect inflation to regress to a specific level, but they appear to anticipate that inflation rates will lead to attenuated future inflation. Moreover, this attenuation is stronger the higher the historical inflation rate. Very similar results are found when investigating the scaling for five-year-ahead expectations. Here, the results for θ are 0.849 (i), 0.922 (ii), and 0.818 (iii). For the long-term expectations, the p values for tests of θ equal to 1 are all below 0.01. In the computations of historical expectations series in the next section, we will rely on the presented θ estimates for the various treatments.

The estimated θ coefficient is also relevant for determining subjects' expectations to those 6 of the 16 primary patterns for which there are two variants (i.e., in steps of one or two). The key concern here is to give equal weight to subjects' responses to each of the two

together, it is found that the relative occurrence of these six patterns are 0.818, 0.068, 0.023, 0.023, 0.045, and 0.023. For the estimation that follows, we thus use data where the six pairings of collinear patterns are weighted according to their historical prevalence.

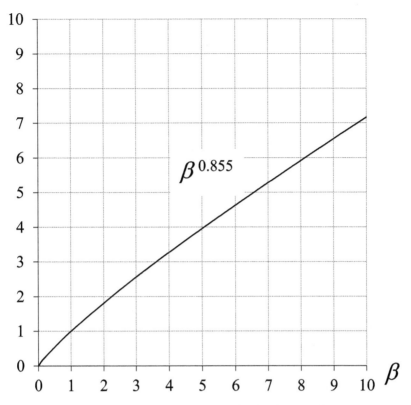

FIGURE 5.3 Estimated scaling relationship for the case of one-year
expectations (treatment iii)

patterns in a pair of collinear patterns. Take as an example the pattern
100, 101, 102, 103 where the average one-year-ahead expectation over
all subjects in treatment (iii) is 103.953 (i.e., an increase by 0.953)
whereas the response for the pattern 100, 102, 104, 106 is 107.742 (i.e.,
an increase by 1.742). For the computation of subjects' expectation to
be used in the computation of historical series the value 1.742 is
divided by 1.808 (i.e., $2^{0.855}$) resulting in 0.963, and averaged with
0.953 which gives the value 0.958. This is the value that is used for
pattern 100, 100, 100, 101 in the computations of time series of the
expected inflation. Likewise, the thus averaged expectations for the
patterns 100, 101, 102, 102 (expected change 0.082), 100, 101, 101, 101
(expected change 0.167), 100, 101, 100, 100 (expected change 0.077),

100, 100, 100, 101 (expected change 0.660), and 100, 99, 99, 100 (expected change 0.694) result.

5.5   COMPUTING HISTORICAL TIME SERIES
OF EXPECTED INFLATION

This section brings together the laboratory expectations data, the similarity matching parameter λ, and the scaling parameter θ in order to compute historical inflation expectations. For each historical data window, several steps are involved in the computation of expectations. First, correlations between the historical data and the 16 primary patterns are computed. This allows the determination of the relative weights of each pattern. Second, for a given sequence of historical data points, we estimate the factor of proportion (i.e., the β) for each of the primary patterns. Before going into more details, a simple example should help: take the primary pattern 100, 100, 100, 101. For a hypothetical empirical sequence of 100, 100, 100, 105, the value for β is clearly 5. Hence, the expected change indicated by the laboratory expectations for the primary pattern would have to be multiplied by $5^{0.855} = 3.959$. Likewise for each of the other primary patterns, a corresponding β is estimated by the least squares method and then applied in the computations.

Now all of the elements described can be put together to compute historical expectations series based on the laboratory data. For this purpose, we cut the historical CPI-series in overlapping windows of four years and find how closely each of the 16 primary patterns are correlated with the historical data. Consider as an example the computation of the (log) expected US price level one-year-ahead for the month of January 1978. The four historical data points on which we take agents to base their expectations are the December values of the CPI in 1974, 1975, 1976, and 1977 (i.e., 51.9, 55.5, 58.2, and 62.10).[7]

---

[7] The assumption here is that the public learns about the value of a period's CPI within a month. The CPI data used for computations come from the Federal Reserve Bank of St. Louis web portal https://fred.stlouisfed.org/.

Then the natural logs of these historical data are taken (i.e., 3.949, 4.016, 4.064, and 4.129). The highest correlation (with a value of 0.9981) between this sequence and our set of stylized patterns is with the pattern of 100, 102, 103, 105. For this concrete pattern, subjects expect a one-step ahead change of 1.449 percent. Minimizing the sum $(3.949 - \alpha - 1.00\beta)^2 + (4.016 - \alpha - 1.02\beta)^2 + (4.064 - \alpha - 1.03\beta)^2 + (4.129 - \alpha - 1.05\beta)^2$ and enforcing $3.949 = \alpha + 1.00\beta$ (i.e., making the actual and fitted pattern start from the same point) yields the coefficient estimates $\alpha = 0.331$ and $\beta = 3.618$.

Based on this part of the procedure assessed as of 1978M01, the computed logarithm of the expected CPI for 1979M01 would be equal to $4.1287 + (1.449/100)3.618^{0.855} = 4.172$ or an expected annual inflation of 4.35 percent. However, the matching experiment indicates that this prediction is given only a weight of 0.3518. Considering all patterns and their weighting according to similarity yields as the final result an expected value of the log of the CPI for January of 1979 of 4.1706. This means for 1978M01, an expected one-year-ahead inflation of 4.18 percent. By a step-wise application of the described procedure, we reach the expected inflation for the entire historical time series. Appendix 5.2 details how these computational steps can be organized in a worksheet routine. Such a program for the computation of a longer time series can be downloaded from the website for this book at Cambridge University Press.

Figure 5.4 shows the resulting CPI time series for the one-year-ahead inflation expectations based on the three treatments for eliciting expectations. The series capturing individuals' subjective expectations (treatments i and iii) always move very closely together (correlation of 0.997). By contrast, during the years of high inflation, the series based on the higher-order expectations is somewhat higher than the other series. In order to give an impression of how short- and long-term expectations compare, Figure 5.5 presents the one-year and the annualized five-year ahead expectations of inflation based on treatment (iii).

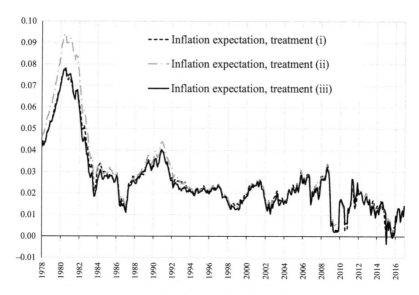

FIGURE 5.4 One-year-ahead expected inflation from three versions of the pattern-based model

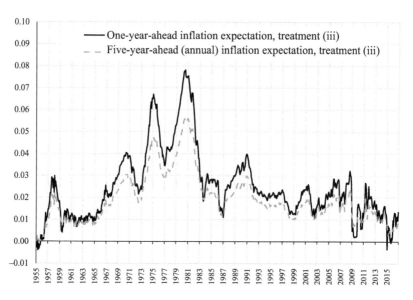

FIGURE 5.5 One-year-ahead and five-year-ahead expected inflation

5.6   SUMMARY AND CONCLUSIONS

This chapter could be considered the engine room of the book. It brings together all elements that go into the computation of pattern-based expectations. A key new element introduced concerns the weighting of the expectations elicited in the laboratory. This weighting builds on the results of an additional experiment studying similarity matching as it pertains to short sequences of a time series. The final element completing the procedure for computing expectations concerns the so-called scaling relationship. This relationship clarifies how the elicited expectations data should be scaled to the different empirically observed rates of change in the underlying variable. The interplay of the described elements is made explicit in examples and in the form of a worksheet that allows readers to make their own calculations of expectations series.

APPENDIX 5.1   INSTRUCTIONS FOR THE SIMILARITY MATCHING EXPERIMENT, TRANSLATED FROM GERMAN

In what follows, you will see a succession of 58 different cases of a short time series. With each of these cases, you will also be shown 16 standardized sequences. For each of the 58 cases, your task then is to select the one or several among the 16 cases that you judge the most similar. The display on the monitor shows you an example of what you will see during the experiment. In the center, you see the course of the time series to be assessed and above and below you see the standardized sequences to which the central display has to be compared (*here the display presented as Figure 5.1 in the main text of the book is shown*).

For each of the 58 cases shown, you have a total of 10 points to allocate. If you are sure to have correctly identified one of the 16 standardized sequences that is most similar to the case shown, you apply to this most similar sequence the full 10 points. If the assessment of similarity is not so clear, you can divide the 10 points on several of the standardized cases. Hence, you can, for example, give 5 points to one case and 5 points to another, or a combination of 6 and 4, or 5, 3, and 2. Importantly, you are only allowed to allocate full points.

The concept of correlation is the measure of similarity applied here. Correlation measures the comovement between two variables. A value of +1 indicates perfect comovement in the same direction while a value of −1 indicates a perfect comovement in the opposite direction. A value of 0 of the correlation indicates that two series move independently. In the experiment, objective similarity is assessed to be higher if correlation is higher.

The accuracy of your assessments will be measured after you have completed all 58 tasks. In any of the tasks, the points allocated to the objectively most similar case receive a value of 1. Points given to the second most similar case are weighted one half. Points given to the third most similar case are weighted by a third. Points given to the fourth most similar case are weighted by a fourth, etc.

At the end of the experiment, all your weighted points are added up. For each resulting point, you earn 2 cents. Hence, the maximum is 11.60 Euros. As a minimum compensation, we guarantee a payment of 4 Euros.

APPENDIX 5.2   A ROUTINE FOR THE COMPUTATION OF PATTERN-BASED EXPECTATIONS

This appendix details the steps involved in computing expectations in a computer program like Microsoft Excel. Clearly, we need a routine when we want to compute time series values for many periods. For this purpose, we suggest the use of a computational software that presents the steps involved in the form of a table. Figure A5.1 shows the elements that help determine for one particular observation – for the first month of 1978 – the value of the log of the one-year-ahead expectation for the CPI. On the left, we see listed the 16 non-collinear patterns. The following column displays the means of the elicited expectations data from treatment (iii) for the 16 patterns shown. This entry is termed "lab data" and the numbers represent percent changes.

The next four columns present the monthly data from the past. As indicated before, we take the most up-to date observation to be that from the month just previous to the month in which the expectations are formed. Hence, the last observation on which the expectations formed in 1978M01 is based is the observation from 1977M12. The log of that value is 4.1287. The further values come from the observation for 1976M12, 1975M12, and 1974M12. Next, we have the correlations between each of the listed patterns and the historical data window with four observations. From these correlations, we find the weights of each of the patterns in two steps: the first step consists of taking each of the positive correlations to the power of 125 (the experimentally documented λ parameter). The second step calculates the weight given to each pattern by dividing the value just described for any singular pattern with the sum of all entries in the previous column. Clearly, the weights over all patterns sum to one.

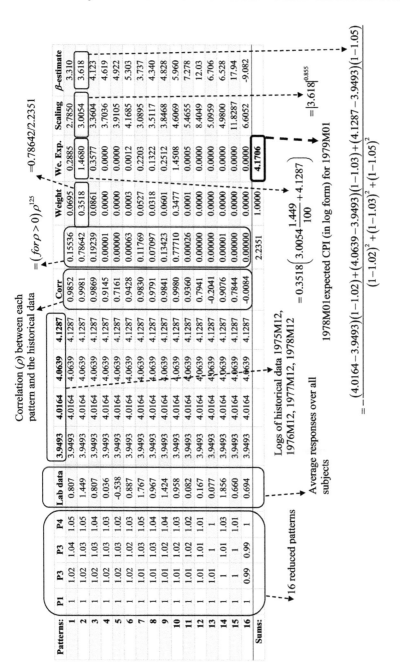

FIGURE A5.I Routine for the computation of the 1978M01 expectation for the CPI (in logs) for 1979M01

Turning now to the furthest column on right we see the regression coefficient relating the historical changes to the P1, P2, P3, and P4 data that make up any pattern. This β coefficient is the slope parameter of a regression in which the fitted first historical observation (in this case for 1975M12) is restricted to be the actual value (in the present situation 3.9493). The entries in the column to the left take this parameter to the power of θ (i.e., the scaling parameter). Hence, we come to the decisive column in which, for each pattern, the appropriately scaled expected laboratory elicited change is added to the latest observation of the log of the CPI and then multiplied by its appropriate weight. Adding up all the entries in this column leads to the final result indicated as the bold number at the bottom. The value 4.1706 is the computed log of the pattern-based CPI expectation formed in 1978M01 for 1979M01.

For a computation of additional values in the time series of CPI expectation, we simply replicate the computations shown. As a practical matter, this is most easily done by copying the range of cells already shown and pasting it below and shifted to the right by one cell. For this procedure to work, it is necessary to have the historical time series of CPI values listed at the very top of the program. Furthermore, the cells indicating the historical data must draw from this line of historical data. The online material for this book presents this worksheet in the form of an Excel program that can be readily used for new applications.

6 Pattern Extrapolation and Expectations Measured by Consumer Surveys

6.1 INTRODUCTION

An obvious question to ask is how pattern-based measures of inflation expectations compare with survey data of expectations. We start this chapter by comparing the forecast performance of pattern-based inflation expectations with the expectations available from the survey center of the University of Michigan. The second part of the chapter then presents a different way of comparing the two sets of expectations. Following the lead of earlier contributions, the Michigan survey of expectations is taken as data to be explained. We will document that survey expectations can be tracked by our model of pattern-based expectations. In fact, pattern-based expectations appear as the best among competing explanations.

6.2 FORECAST PERFORMANCE OF DIFFERENT MEASURES OF INFLATION EXPECTATIONS

The first step here is a comparison of the accuracy of inflation forecasts between the projection of the households covered by the Michigan survey and the pattern-based measures of expectations.[1] For the latter series, three measures are considered, namely the three expectations measures based on the different treatments of eliciting pattern-based expectations. Furthermore, we consider both the mean and the median of respondents' data from the survey and from our three

---

[1] The survey data from the University of Michigan are drawn from the web portal www.sca.isr.umich.edu/. CPI data come from the Federal Reserve Bank of St. Louis web portal https://fred.stlouisfed.org/.

Table 6.1 *Regressions relating actual annual inflation to various measures of expected inflation, sample period 1978M12–2016M12*

Explanatory Variable	α_0	α_1	Std. Err.
Michigan-Mean	−0.015	1.099	0.01554
	(0.002)	(0.046)	
Michigan-Median	−0.011	1.255	0.01541
	(0.002)	(0.050)	
PB-Subjective (i) Mean	0.001	1.262	0.01803
	(0.002)	(0.078)	
PB-Subjective (i) Median	0.001	0.864	0.01784
	(0.001)	(0.053)	
PB-Higher Order (ii) Mean	0.005	1.024	0.01789
	(0.001)	(0.064)	
PB-Higher Order (ii) Median	0.006	0.900	0.01785
	(0.002)	(0.062)	
PB-Probabilistic (iii) Mean	0.002	1.268	0.01782
	(0.002)	(0.076)	
PB-Probabilistic (iii) Median	0.007	0.834	0.01810
	(0.001)	(0.053)	

PB stands for pattern-based.
Numbers in parentheses are standard errors of estimated coefficients.

treatments. The data are monthly observations. The specification estimated here is

$$\pi_{t-12,t} = \alpha_0 + \alpha_1 F_{t-11}\left(\pi_{t-12,t}\right) + \varepsilon_t, \tag{6.1}$$

where F indicates one particular (survey- or laboratory-based) forecast of inflation. The timing convention for the expected series reflects the fact that at time $t-11$ the survey respondents and the pattern extrapolators base their expectations on CPI data from $t-12$ and are thus interpreted as the forecast of $\pi_{t-12,t}$ which is $\log(P_t) - \log(P_{t-12})$. The results of this regression exercise for the USA is presented in Table 6.1. The estimates indicate that the Michigan survey expectations outperform pattern-based expectations when we look at the standard error of the estimate.[2] Hence, pattern-based expectations cannot claim to be a superior predictor of inflation.

For the Michigan data, the median measure seems to perform slightly better than the mean.[3] For the various versions of pattern-based expectations, the mean of the probabilistic treatment (iii) takes the lead. Hence, in the following chapters, the point prediction from treatment (iii) is the preferred measure of expected inflation. Clearly, there is a further reason to favor this treatment in the application that follow: this data allows us to compute measures for the uncertainty of expectations. For all estimates shown in Table 6.1, the combined coefficient restriction $\alpha_0 = 0$ and $\alpha_1 = 1$ is rejected at the 1 percent level of significance.

6.3   COMPETING EXPLANATIONS OF HOW CONSUMERS FORM EXPECTATIONS

There exists a further way of comparing the new behavioral expectations data with observations from the Michigan survey expectations. The hypothesis proposed is that the systematic part of the expectations measured by surveys is made up by agents who form expectations based on pattern extrapolation. Before proceeding to empirically investigate this conjecture, we want to introduce a competing explanation of what captures behavior as measured in surveys of expectations. Carroll (2003) proposes that inflation expectations of the general public are the result of a delayed and fractional use of expert predictions of future inflation. This is a version of the sticky information explanation of expectations. It builds on the notion that economic agents most of the time are inattentive regarding information relevant for evaluating the future. In short, the idea is that every quarter, a fraction of the general public pays attention to what the experts say and assimilates it to update expectations. This expert

---

[2] This relative assessment is confirmed when calculating the root mean squared error of the various expectations measures.

[3] This has been repeatedly documented in the literature (see, e.g., Ang et al., 2007).

notion regarding future inflation is represented in empirical research by the survey of professional forecasters (SPF).[4]

The approach of pattern-based expectations presents a clear alternative to this explanation. It suggests that observed (and surveyed) expected inflation shows the pattern extrapolation of the public and that expert opinion is of negligible importance. In order to assess the merits of the two competing approaches, we start with re-estimating Carroll's specifications for his sample period of 1981Q3 to 2000Q2. We focus on the specification that captures Carroll's approach best, that is,

$$M_t(\pi_{t,t+4}) = \alpha_0 + \alpha_1 S_t(\pi_{t,t+4}) + \alpha_2 M_{t-1}(\pi_{t-1,t+3}) + \varepsilon_t. \tag{6.2}$$

Here, $M_t(\pi_{t,t+4})$ denotes the Michigan household survey measure of expected inflation in quarter t. The variable $S_t(\pi_{t,t+4})$ captures the SPF mean inflation forecast over the next year.[5] For theoretical reasons, Carroll favors a specification without a constant, and we will show estimates with and without a constant. Introducing pattern-based (PB) expectations as a potential explanation besides expert forecasts yields

$$M_t(\pi_{t,t+4}) = \alpha_0 + \alpha_1 S_t(\pi_{t,t+4}) + \alpha_2 M_{t-1}(\pi_{t-1,t+3}) + \alpha_3 PB_t(\pi_{t,t+4}) + \varepsilon_t, \tag{6.3}$$

where $PB_t(\pi_{t,t+4})$ stands for the pattern-based one-year-ahead expected inflation in quarter t. In this encompassing specification, both expert predictions and pattern extrapolation explain the course of survey data of expected inflation. For a comparison of the two approaches of modeling expectations, we also present estimates based on a specification without the expert forecasts:

$$M_t(\pi_{t,t+4}) = \alpha_0 + \alpha_2 M_{t-1}(\pi_{t-1,t+3}) + \alpha_3 PB_t(\pi_{t,t+4}) + \varepsilon_t \tag{6.4}$$

The lagged value of the survey measure is kept in this regression in order to potentially capture the fact that only a fraction of households

---

[4] For recent critical assessments of the expectations hypothesis based on the notion of sticky information, see Coibion (2010) and Pfajfar and Santoro (2013).

[5] The data from the survey of professional forecasters are drawn from the web portal www.philadelphiafed.org/research-and-data/real-time-center/survey-of-professional-forecasters/.

Table 6.2 *Regression results for specifications explaining household inflation expectations, sample period 1981Q3–2000Q2*

Specification	α_0	α_1	α_2	α_3	$\bar{R}^2$	D.W.	Std. Err.
Eq. (6.2) With const.	0.013** (0.002)	0.539** (0.063)	0.196** (0.054)		0.688	1.814	0.552
Eq. (6.2) No constant		0.502** (0.101)	0.520** (0.098)		0.584	2.010	0.633
Eq. (6.3) With const.	0.017** (0.001)	0.350** (0.240)	−0.011 (0.075)	0.464** (0.100)	0.727	1.577	0.519
Eq. (6.3) No constant		0.481** (0.100)	0.510** (0.108)	0.048 (0.074)	0.585	1.980	0.637
Eq. (6.4) With const.	0.019** (0.002)		0.126 (0.079)	0.694** (0.068)	0.691	1.673	0.549
Eq. (6.4) No constant			0.778** (0.043)	0.319** (0.063)	0.514	2.286	0.684

**, * indicate significance at the 1 percent and 5 percent level of significance, respectively.
Numbers in parentheses are White heteroskedasticity-consistent standard errors of estimated coefficients.

extrapolates patterns every quarter while the rest may be holding on to their previous projections.

Table 6.2 shows estimates of the three specifications presented (all with and without a constant) for Carroll's sample of the 1980s and 1990s. The first column in the table identifies the regression equation estimated. For Carroll's sample period, the estimate of Eq. (6.2), by and large, verifies his findings: if professional forecasts are the only variable besides lagged consumer expectations, this variable explains a significant portion of the variance of the Michigan data. The differences between the results shown and those documented by Carroll (2003) presumably are due to the convention adopted here that consumer expectations are taken as the last monthly variable (and not the average) of a quarter. This appears to be the correct approach since the Michigan survey reports data every month and the outlook of the SPF is published around the middle of the quarter. Tests for stability of the estimated coefficients over time indicate problems for the specification without a constant. Ramsey reset tests with both one and four lagged squared residuals indicate that specifications with a constant are stable over time whereas the specifications without a constant are not. The conclusion should be that the estimates including a constant term are more reliable.

Consider how introducing pattern-based expectations alters the results. When including pattern-based expectations as an additional explanatory variable, a significantly improved fit of the regression results once the estimate includes a constant term. The p value testing for exclusion of this expectations variable is lower than 0.001. Further, a specification that relies exclusively on pattern extrapolation as a model of expectations proves to be a good explanation for consumers' expectations. Interestingly, this estimate generates little evidence of a fractional updating on the side of pattern extrapolators: the coefficient of the lagged endogenous variable (α_2) is not statistically significant once a constant is included in the regression.

Table 6.3 shows these estimates with the longer sample. When extending the data set until 2016, only estimates that include constant terms are reported. In all estimates with the enlarged data set, the coefficient of the professional forecasts is smaller than in the shorter sample. Importantly, expert forecasts of inflation can be eliminated from the explanation of consumers' expectations without any significant loss in explanatory power.[6] The picture that thus emerges

---

[6] Roos and Schmidt (2011) experimentally document that when given the choice, subjects predominantly use the past of a series rather than expert input when forming expectations.

Table 6.3 *Regression results for specifications explaining household inflation expectations, sample period 1981Q3–2016Q4*

Specification	α_0	α_1	α_2	α_3	$\bar{R}^2$	D.W.	Std. Err.
Eq. (6.2)	0.016**	0.312**	0.362**		0.540	1.938	0.0064
	(0.002)	(0.070)	(0.065)				
Eq. (6.3)	0.018**	0.120	0.177*	0.477**	0.592	1.714	0.0061
	(0.002)	(0.091)	(0.089)	(0.104)			
Eq. (6.4)	0.018**		0.202*	0.589**	0.584	1.737	0.0061
	(0.002)		(0.088)	(0.092)			

**, * indicate significance at the 1 percent and 5 percent level of significance, respectively.
Numbers in parentheses are White heteroskedasticity-consistent standard errors of estimated coefficients.

is that pattern extrapolation is the key to the understanding of households' inflation expectations.[7]

To round off the analysis of the hypothesis of pattern-based expectations as an explanation of survey expectations, it is informative to further compare it with an older hypothesis of expectations formation. Figlewski and Wachtel (1981) in their study of survey data find adaptive expectations to be the best explanation of inflation expectations. Neither the hypothesis of rational nor the hypothesis of regressive expectations receives much support in their study. For the present purpose, we estimate a general specification of the model of adaptive-extrapolative expectations. More concretely, Eq. (6.5) is specified with the lag length of past rates of inflation determined by the Akaike criterion:[8]

---

[7] How does this performance square with the previously reported finding that survey expectations show superior forecast performance? One explanation is the difference in participants covered by the two methods. Keep in mind that in the Michigan survey, 10 or more times the number of agents are questioned compared to what we do in the laboratory. Furthermore, it is possible that some of the households covered by the Michigan survey form more elaborate than just extrapolative predictions.

[8] Here, lagged inflation rates are changes over the previous quarter.

$$M_t\left(\pi_{t,t+4}\right) = \alpha_0 + \alpha_1 M_{t-1}\left(\pi_{t-1,t+3}\right) + \alpha_2 M_{t-1}\left(\pi_{t-2,t+2}\right)$$
$$+ \alpha_3 M_{t-1}\left(\pi_{t-3,t+1}\right) + \alpha_4 M_{t-1}\left(\pi_{t-4,t}\right) \qquad (6.5)$$
$$+ \alpha_5 \pi_{t-1} + \alpha_6 \pi_{t-2} + \alpha_7 \pi_{t-3} + \alpha_8 \pi_{t-4} + \varepsilon_t$$

The term $M_t(\pi_{t,t+4})$ again stands for the Michigan survey measure of expected inflation. No restriction on parameter values is imposed in the estimation of this specification. Table 6.4 documents the results.

Table 6.4 *Regression results for unrestricted adaptive-extrapolative expectations*

	1981Q3–2000Q2	1981Q3–2016Q4
α_0	0.013**	0.011**
	(0.002)	(0.002)
α_1	0.175	0.292**
	(0.157)	(0.109)
α_2	0.263*	0.239*
	(0.126)	(0.107)
α_3	0.243	0.211
	(0.172)	(0.111)
α_4	−0.087	−0.065
	(0.183)	(0.086)
α_5	0.448**	0.212
	(0.116)	(0.125)
α_6	0.131	−0.071
	(0.162)	(0.055)
α_7	−0.160	−0.134
	(0.164)	(0.091)
α_8	0.010	0.119
	(0.184)	(0.064)
$\overline{R}^2$	0.650	0.531
D.W.	1.927	1.960
Std. Err.	0.0061	0.0066

**, * indicate significance at the 1 percent and 5 percent level of significance, respectively.
Numbers in parentheses are White heteroskedasticity-consistent standard errors of estimated coefficients.

The estimates show that the hypothesis of adaptive-extrapolative expectations cannot rival the hypothesis of pattern-based expectations or Carroll's hypothesis of sticky expectations. This assessment is based on standard errors reported in Tables 6.3 and 6.4. Note that it holds for both sample periods analyzed.

6.4   SUMMARY AND CONCLUSIONS

This chapter documents that pattern-based expectations are not superior predictors of historical inflation rates when compared to inflation expectations from the Michigan survey of households. This should not come as too much of a surprise, given the radically reductionist nature of our model. Simplification has its costs. However, the new behavioral model is not primarily a forecasting tool. It is a descriptive model of how people form expectations. When we empirically assess the merits of the model as an explanation of surveyed household expectations, the results are rather striking. This is documented in an exercise of econometrically explaining the data from the Michigan survey of expectations. Here, it is found that the model of pattern-based expectations dominates competing explanations drawn from the literature.

Chapter 7 studies the further dimensions of expectations elicited in the laboratory. Similar to the series of the mean of expectations, the time series for the heterogeneity and the uncertainty of expected inflation can be computed. For the measure of the heterogeneity of expectations, we will again make use of the possibility to compare the newly computed series with data from the Michigan survey of households. The measure of uncertainty will be developed particularly with the notion of using the series in econometric studies in order to explain economic data such as nominal interest rates.

7 Heterogeneity and Uncertainty of Inflation Expectations

7.1 INTRODUCTION

In previous chapters, we have focused on the mean of inflation expectations. Thus, we have answered the question, for example, where the average person sees the price level a year hence. Here we want to turn to further dimensions of expectations. In particular, it is obvious that people differ with respect to their expectations. Clearly, the standard rational expectations hypothesis is silent regarding expectations heterogeneity. It assumes that all agents use the same relevant information. The expectations model of Mankiw et al. (2003) is an interesting departure from the standard model. These authors propose that only a fraction of the public makes an informed forecast at any point in time. The rest stick to the expectations they have formed earlier. This approach is similar to the model already discussed by Carroll (2003) where experts play the role of providing informed forecasts. Again, the model of pattern-based expectations offers a clear alternative.

A further important dimension concerns the uncertainty of inflation expectations. A role for uncertainty of inflation has been suggested in the literature, for example, in the determination of bond yields, and its appropriate modeling and measurement remain important research topics (e.g., Wright, 2011). In empirical studies, the uncertainty of expected inflation is typically modeled as the variance of the unpredictable part of inflation. Hence, models with time-varying variance of the error term or varying coefficients are the approach preferred in the literature (see Grier & Perry, 1996, and Stock & Watson, 2007). An older approach to the modeling of inflation uncertainty blurs the distinction between heterogeneity and uncertainty. Accordingly, a series of publications has used measures of disagreement among forecasters as proxy for inflation uncertainty.[1]

Recent advances in the methodology of conducting surveys have offered ways to directly elicit the uncertainty of inflation expectations (see Boero et al., 2008, and De Bruin et al., 2011). These newer survey approaches are an important addition to the toolbox of researchers. The approach of measuring expectations outlined in this book provides a further alternative. The probabilistic treatment (iii) offers a straightforward method to quantify the uncertainty of expected inflation. Again, one of the advantages of the approach pursued here is that we can model measures of the uncertainty of inflation expectations for periods for which no survey measures exist. Obviously, this applies to heterogeneity as well. In order to have a consistent data basis, we are throughout using the laboratory data elicited with the probabilistic treatment (iii) that allows the quantification of both the heterogeneity and the uncertainty of expected inflation.

7.2 MODELING HETEROGENEITY OF INFLATION EXPECTATIONS

The pattern-based model explains expectations heterogeneity simply by the different ways of pattern extrapolation prevalent in the population.[2] How should we then compute a time-series measure of inflation heterogeneity? The approach followed here is quite elaborate. A key part of this procedure is the estimation of a scaling parameter for each of the 45 individual subjects. This leads to an individual expectations model for each subject that helps to compute his or her individual time path of expected inflation. This has to be done for a particular time period. For the computation presented here, the period from 1978 to 2016 for the USA is selected. Then, the interquartile range of expectations over the population of subjects is computed.

---

[1] Notable contributions come from Barnea et al. (1979), Bomberger and Frazer (1981) and Hendershott (1984).

[2] The same idea is the basis of the approach by Xu et al. (2015).

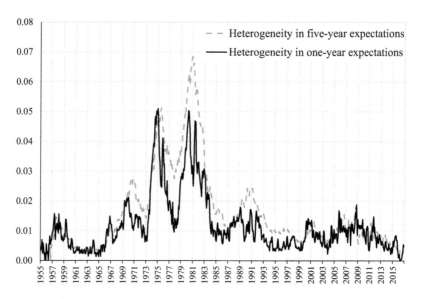

FIGURE 7.1 Pattern-based heterogeneity of one-year and five-year US inflation expectations

Obviously, computing the heterogeneity measure for any country and period requires quite some time and effort.[3] Figure 7.1 shows the monthly measures of expectations heterogeneity for the one-year and the five-year horizon. As the chart indicates, the heterogeneity of inflation expectations rose markedly in the 1970s and peaked in the early 1980s. Recent years show low levels of heterogeneity comparable with the situation of the early 1960s. Overall, the measures of expectations heterogeneity for the two expectations horizons tell very similar stories.

As before with expected inflation, our measure of inflation heterogeneity can be compared with measures of heterogeneity derived from surveys. More concretely, the pattern-based measure of heterogeneity can be compared with the interquartile range of the

---

[3] A simpler approach to the computation of a measure of heterogeneity builds on the means of the upper 95 percent and the lower 5 percent quantiles over all subjects in treatment (iii). The heterogeneity measure is then calculated as the difference between the upper projection and the lower projection at any point in time. This simpler approach will be applied in Chapters 14, 15, and 16.

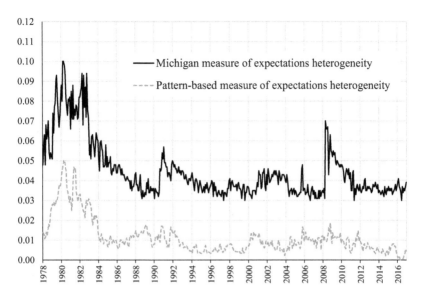

FIGURE 7.2 Heterogeneity of one-year US inflation expectations from different measures

one-year-ahead expectations elicited by the Michigan survey of consumers.[4] This is the type of check presented by Mankiw and co-authors (2003) when empirically assessing their model. For checking the power of their model to track the survey measure of heterogeneity, these authors document two measures: first, over the period 1978M01 to 2001M08 the correlation between their heterogeneity measure and the Michigan survey measure is 0.80. By comparison, the correlation of the pattern-based heterogeneity measure with the Michigan measure is 0.86. Further, Mankiw et al. (2003) report the average difference between the Michigan heterogeneity measure and their model-based measure. This difference is 4 percent while for our model it is only 3.4 percent. On both counts, the pattern-based measure performs better than the measure developed by Mankiw and his coauthors. Figure 7.2 shows the correspondence between the pattern-based

---

[4] The survey data from the University of Michigan are drawn from the web portal www.sca.isr.umich.edu/. CPI data are from the Federal Reserve Bank of St. Louis web portal https://fred.stlouisfed.org/.

heterogeneity measure and the Michigan measure. The historical period covered here is the one for which survey data are available.

7.3 MODELING UNCERTAINTY OF EXPECTED INFLATION

The measure developed here is related to measures of inflation uncertainty (Cukierman & Wachtel, 1982) and, in particular, follow the newer contributions to measuring the uncertainty of expectations (Boero et al., 2008, De Bruin et al., 2011). The uncertainty of inflation expectations is quantified here as follows: the new uncertainty series is computed based on the upper and lower quartile ranges elicited in treatment (iii). More concretely, we compute an upper-level inflation expectation with the mean of the answers to the 75 percent upper border question. Likewise, a lower-level inflation expectation based on the 25 percent lower border question is computed. In both cases, the same scaling parameter as previously applied for the mean expectation is used.[5] The resulting series for short- and long-term expectations are displayed in Figure 7.3. The two series show that uncertainty regarding future inflation has declined together with the decline in inflation since the early 1980s. The trend toward lower inflation uncertainty was temporarily reversed during the recent financial crisis. This period of turbulence – particularly regarding short-term expectations – is visible in Figure 7.3 over the period of 2009–2011.[6]

---

[5] Here we draw on data from Table 3.7. For the computations, it should be helpful to refer back to Figure A5.1. For the quantification of the uncertainty measure, we first compute, for every point in time, an upper measure by inserting the data on the upper (75 percent) border in the column "Lab data" of the worksheet. Note that this column shows the answers for the reduced set of 16 patterns. Similarly, a lower measure using the 25 percent border answers is computed. The difference between the upper and the lower measure gives the uncertainty of the inflation expectation at a particular point in time.

[6] The apparent fact that the uncertainty of short-term expectations is higher than that of long-term expectations must be seen against the background of the definition of this measure: we document the uncertainty of the expected annual inflation over the next five years. The uncertainty measure for the longer horizon is calculated by dividing the expected five-year changes by a factor of 5.

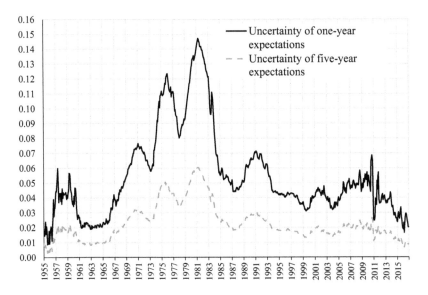

FIGURE 7.3 Pattern-based uncertainty for one-year and five-year US inflation expectations

Note again that this course of uncertainty is fully attributable to the course of the price level.[7]

7.4   SUMMARY AND CONCLUSIONS

This chapter uses the expectations data elicited for the computation of measures of the heterogeneity and the uncertainty of expected inflation. Note that these two measures are based on different elements of the laboratory data. The former dimension of expectations documents the spread of behavioral tendencies over individuals. By contrast, the high level of uncertainty indicted by the pattern-based measure reflects the high level of uncertainty of the average subject. Both measures tend to be high in times of high and variable inflation. This reflects, for example, in the historical course of the two measures for the USA: during the early 1980s, both the heterogeneity of

---

[7] The increase in uncertainty in the period noted is substantially less than suggested by some of the estimates presented by Chan and Song (2018).

inflation expectations as well as the uncertainty of expected inflation were high.

Likewise, looking at the more recent past, times of low and stable inflation imply low heterogeneity and uncertainty concerning future inflation. Later chapters will make use of the series developed here to empirically assess the relevance of expectations uncertainty and heterogeneity in the determination of interest rates. Before further pursuing heterogeneity and uncertainty, we will study the role of expected inflation in the inflation process. Hence, Chapter 8 makes the transition to using the newly computed expectations series and econometrically evaluating its ability to explain macroeconomic phenomena.

8 Inflation Dynamics

8.1 INTRODUCTION

In this chapter, we use the measure of pattern-based expectations in an econometric investigation of inflation. It is well known that expected inflation itself is an important driver of inflation. Older accounts see the inflationary expectations of workers as the central variable that explains why expectations affect the course of the aggregate price level. In more recent contributions, decision-making of firms takes central stage. The expectation of producers regarding the future course of the price level is seen as an important element in firms' price setting.[1] The empirical study here follows this newer approach.

8.2 THE NEW KEYNESIAN PHILLIPS CURVE

In this section, we investigate how pattern-based inflation expectations perform in estimates of the New Keynesian Phillips Curve (NKPC). The NKPC essentially posits that inflation is the result of price setting decisions by forward-looking firms who take into consideration future prices and marginal cost. Empirical research along these lines has been very active after the contribution of Galí and Gertler (1999). In the following, we will concentrate on what Galí and Gertler have termed the hybrid NKPC and Christiano et al. (2005) call an indexation model. In this version of the NKPC, lagged inflation enters as an additional explanatory variable because a fraction of firms does not set prices in a forward-looking manner. They either form static inflation expectations, fail to optimize prices every period, or

---

[1] Gordon (2011) offers an informative account on the history of the Phillips curve.

simply index prices to lagged inflation. This is the version of the Phillips curve estimated by Rudd and Whelan (2007), Nunes (2010), Adam and Padula (2011), Fuhrer (2012), and Coibion et al. (2018) among others. The econometric specification of this version of the NKPC of inflation (π_t) is

$$\pi_t = \gamma_0 + \gamma_1 \pi_{t-1} + \gamma_2 F_t(\pi_{t+1}) + \gamma_3 MC_t + \varepsilon_t, \qquad (8.1)$$

where $F_t(\pi_{t+1})$ stands for expected inflation. One expectations variable widely used in the literature is the one-year-ahead forecast from the survey of professional forecasters. This is called the SPF measure of expectations.[2] As a competing measure of expected inflation, we consider pattern-based expectations. This measure is identified by the acronym PB.[3] The variable MC in Eq. (8.1) stands for marginal costs which are proxied here by the deviation of log real GDP from a linear trend. The inflation series used is the annualized quarterly growth rate of the GDP deflator.[4]

When estimating Eq. (8.1) using the SPF expectations measure, the (contemporaneous) expectations term has to be instrumented to avoid simultaneity bias. When using pattern-based inflation expectations (for the GDP deflator) as an alternative measure, we make sure that the expected inflation for period t does not depend on information from that period (quarter). Table 8.1 shows the results of a first set of estimates.[5] The first line presents the result for the case where

[2] The data from the survey of professional forecasters are drawn from the web portal www.philadelphiafed.org/research-and-data/real-time-center/survey-of-professional-forecasters/. Data on the GDP deflator for the USA, United Kingdom, and Germany and the US real GDP come from the Federal Reserve Bank of St. Louis web portal https://fred.stlouisfed.org/.

[3] We do not estimate a rational expectations version of the NKPC but concentrate on behavioral measures of expectations. As indicated in Coibion et al. (2018), the behavioral modeling or measurement of expectations is widely regarded as the way forward for NKPC modeling.

[4] In the already cited empirical literature, a broad range of data is considered. Besides the various measures of inflation expectations, studies compare estimates with an array of data on marginal cost and capacity utilization.

[5] As noted the SPF variable is instrumented using its lagged value and a lagged term of the pattern-based expectations as instruments. The marginal cost variable used in the estimates is MC_{t-1}.

Table 8.1 *Regression results for various NKPC specifications*

Expectations sample period	γ_0	γ_1	γ_2	γ_3	$\overline{R}^2$	D.W.	Std. Err.
SPF	0.000	0.613**	0.346**	0.025	0.811	2.182	0.01046
1969–2016	(0.001)	(0.087)	(0.098)	(0.012)			
PB	0.000	0.570**	0.549**	0.028*	0.811	2.050	0.01045
1969–2016	(0.001)	(0.100)	(0.163)	(0.011)			
PB	0.001	0.460**	0.649**	0.042**	0.756	2.020	0.01125
1952–2016	(0.001)	(0.099)	(0.163)	(0.012)			

**, * indicate significance at the 1 percent and 5 percent level of significance, respectively.
Numbers in parentheses are White heteroskedasticity-consistent standard errors of estimated coefficients.

expected inflation is captured by the survey of professional forecasters' one-year-ahead forecast. The second line of the table shows the result – everything else unchanged – when pattern-based expectations are the choice for modeling expected inflation. It turns out that with this expectations variable, the standard error of the estimate is smaller than with the specification using the SPF measure. Interestingly, the forward-looking element in the price setting process – captured by the γ_2 parameter – is stronger in the PB version than in the SPF version. This indicates that estimates using the SPF measure reported in the literature may overstate the sluggishness of price adjustment. As noted before, a key advantage of the pattern-based measure of expectations is that it is available for a longer time span than, for example, the SPF data. Hence, the last line of Table 8.1 shows the result of estimating this hybrid NKPC with 65 years of quarterly data starting in 1952. Overall, it appears that pattern-based expectations work well as a model of producers' expectations and as an explanatory variable for the course of inflation.

Table 8.2 *Regression results for NKPC with PB measures for both expected inflation and marginal cost*

Sample	γ_0	γ_1	γ_2	γ_3	$\overline{R}^2$	D.W.	Std. Err.
1969–2016	−0.001 (0.001)	0.561** (0.101)	0.559** (0.159)	0.028** (0.010)	0.813	2.049	0.01040
1952–2016	−0.001 (0.001)	0.451** (0.101)	0.672** (0.162)	0.039** (0.010)	0.757	2.016	0.01122

**, * indicate significance at the 1 percent and 5 percent level of significance, respectively.

Numbers in parentheses are White heteroskedasticity-consistent standard errors of estimated coefficients.

Finally, consider a version of the NKPC in which the marginal cost variable is also forward looking as suggested, for example, by Mankiw and Reis (2002). Consistent with the pattern-based approach, the forward-looking *MC* variable is based on pattern-based expectations regarding real GDP. More concretely, the one-year-ahead point expectations for the 32 cases of real GDP are the basis of the computed expected GDP.[6] Table 8.2 shows the results, which are quite remarkable. For both the shorter period from 1969 to 2016 as well as for the period 1952 to 2016, the standard error of the estimate is the lowest among all NKPC specifications considered here.[7]

[6] The procedure for computing expected real GDP values is essentially the same as the one for the price level explained in Chapter 5. The θ value for the one-year-ahead GDP expectations is 0.744. Like in the modeling of inflation expectations, we make use of the empirically estimated similarity matching model. The new, forward-looking *MC* measure in our estimates then is the current log of real GDP plus the expected one-year-ahead pattern-based change minus the log of GDP one-year hence as based on the linear trend model already used in the previous *MC* estimates. It assumes an average quarterly growth rate of real GDP of 0.8 percent. As before, in the estimate the *MC* variable is lagged by one quarter.

[7] When estimating the NKPC relationship with data from higher-order expectations (treatment ii) instead of subjective expectations data (treatment iii), it is found that by and large the changes in results are minimal. In terms of fit, and considering

We further offer estimates of the New Keynesian Phillips curve for Germany to show the applicability of pattern-based expectations as a useful measure of expected inflation. Appendix 8.1 documents the estimates of the NKPC with German data. Looking over the estimates for the USA and Germany, the pattern-based measures of inflation expectations yield informative estimates regarding the role of the various factors in the inflation process. Moreover, the NKPC can be estimated and documented for historical periods for which no conventional survey measures exist.

8.3 LONG-TERM INFLATION EXPECTATIONS AND THE ISSUE OF ANCHORING

Recent years have seen a considerable amount of research on the assertion that central banks, by adopting inflation targets, should be able to manage inflation expectations. The central notion here, particularly when it comes to long-term expectations, is that agents consider information other than the information already contained in observed macroeconomic variables. The theoretical research supporting this proposition stresses the role of learning, multiplicity of equilibria, and reputation (see Persson & Tabellini, 1993 and Bullard & Mitra, 2002). Pattern-based expectations offer a competing explanation for the development of expectations. This hypothesis posits that inflation expectations can be explained based on the recent course of inflation alone. Hence, according to this view, central banks can only tame inflation expectations by delivering a track record of low and stable inflation. By itself, central bank communication is irrelevant from this perspective. In what follows, the concrete focus shall be on the concept of anchoring of expectations. Proponents of the approach of managing the public's expectations hold that central bank communication is able to bring down long-term inflation expectations and

different sample periods, either subjective or higher-order expectations interchangeably show a very slight advantage. Hence, empirically subjective expectations appear to be the relevant expectations variable for the NKPC. See Adam and Padula (2011) for a discussion.

can make it less sensitive to changes in inflation. This is what is meant with anchoring long-term inflation expectations.

How does the empirical literature document the effectiveness of policy communication in shaping expectations? The central proposition in this literature is that inflation targeting by central banks has been a decisive factor in lowering and steadying inflation expectations over the last decades. Two countries that feature prominently in this research are the USA and the United Kingdom. The gist of the literature holds that the United Kingdom, by adopting an inflation target, has been able to contain long-term inflation expectations more effectively than the USA (see Levin et al., 2004, Gürkaynak et al., 2010, and Gefang et al., 2012). More specifically, the literature sees this position supported by the marked decline of expected inflation in the United Kingdom after the adoption of an inflation target in 1992. However, when computing a times series for pattern-based inflation expectations for the United Kingdom, it is found that long-term inflation expectations according to our measure also dropped by 0.5 percent in 1992 and by another 0.5 percent in 1993. Figure 8.1 gives a graphical display of expected inflation in the two countries. The sharp drop in the UK measure of pattern-based expected inflation from 1992 to 1993 is very obvious.

Consider further aspects of the course of long-term expectations. Based on estimates of forward inflation compensation from the bond market for the USA and for the United Kingdom, Gürkaynak et al. (2010) point out that expected inflation for the United Kingdom for the period of 1998–2005 is lower than that for the USA by more than 30 basis points. Calculations based on the pattern-based model confirm this finding and indicate an average difference of 50 basis points. Furthermore, Gürkaynak et al. (2010) report that the UK measure of volatility of expectations appears to be much lower than for the USA. They report a ratio of 1–2 for the standard deviation of long-term inflation expectations. The pattern-based series for the same period also shows markedly lower volatility in the United Kingdom compared to the USA with a ratio of 1 to 1.7.

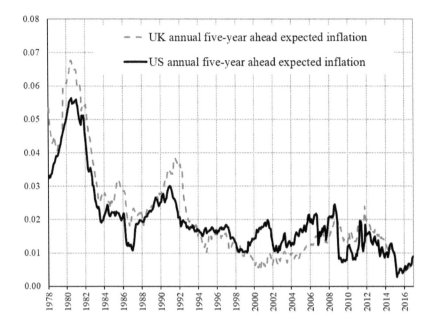

FIGURE 8.1 Long-term expected inflation for the United Kingdom and the USA

Overall, pattern-based expectations offer an explanation of relevant aspects of the historical course of long-term inflation expectations that does *not* invoke central bank communication. Hence, while inflation targeting theoretically may help to control inflation, the empirical evidence presented here suggests that the course of expected inflation can be seen as determined by the recent history of inflation and not by the announcements of central banks. Using the terminology of Kahneman (2003), it could be said that the type of central bank communication under consideration appears not to be important enough to activate decision-makers' System 2 of cognition.

8.4   SUMMARY AND CONCLUSIONS

The New Keynesian Phillips curve estimates presented in this chapter document that as a variable explaining inflation, pattern-based expected inflation performs better than expectations data from the survey of professional forecasters. Hence, the relevant expectations for pricing decisions and thus for the course of inflation appear to be well captured by the new model of expectations. The chapter also documents a further advantage of the laboratory-based expectations model over the use of survey data. Estimates of the Phillips curve based on the new approach of modeling expectations can be presented for a period going back to the early 1950s when no survey of expectations was conducted. These econometric findings confirm the relevance of the Phillips curve as a model for inflation.

The second contribution of this chapter pertains to the debate on the potential of central bank communication to influence long-run inflation expectations. We present a simpler explanation for the alleged historical successes of policy communication. The model of pattern-based expectations can explain the key differences in long-term inflation expectations between the United Kingdom, a country with inflation targeting, and the USA without such a target. In view of this result, the proposition that central banks are able to anchor long-term expectations appears questionable. Instead, expected long-run inflation is simply the result of the recent history of inflation.

APPENDIX 8.1   NEW KEYNESIAN PHILLIPS CURVE ESTIMATES FOR GERMANY

New Keynesian Phillips curves have been estimated in a number of versions for European economies (Tillmann, 2010, Mazumder, 2012, Byrne et al., 2013). This appendix focuses on Germany as the continent's largest economy. Germany is also an obvious choice because this is where the laboratory-based surveys were conducted. As previously for the US economy annualized quarterly growth rate of the GDP deflator are used to measure inflation. For Germany, there exists no survey measure of inflation pertaining to the GDP deflator. Hence, the comparisons offered in Tables 8.1 and 8.2 cannot be replicated for Germany. Instead, we directly present the estimate using pattern-based expectations of inflation. The marginal cost measure in the estimates is the residual from fitting the log of the real German GDP to a linear and a quadratic trend term. The table shown below presents the results of NKPC estimates where the marginal cost term is lagged by one quarter.

Sample	γ_0	γ_1	γ_2	γ_3	$\overline{R}^2$	D.W.	Std. Err.
1974Q1–2016Q4	0.003	0.139	0.944**	0.152*	0.446	1.827	0.0158
	(0.002)	(0.094)	(0.962)	(0.059)			
1990Q3–2016Q4	0.002	0.020	0.921**	0.157*	0.332	2.006	0.0134
	(0.002)	(0.144)	(0. 315)	(0.077)			

**, * indicate significance at the 1 percent and 5 percent level of significance, respectively.

Numbers in parentheses are standard errors of estimated coefficients.

The first line presents the results for the whole sample period from 1974 to 2016. Several authors (Fitzenberger et al., 2008) have indicated a possible break in the relationship studied here because of the German reunification in 1990. Hence, the second line of the table shows the estimate for the period after the reunification. Interestingly, we find *no* evidence of a structural break. Note that in either estimate, the inflation rate lagged by four (instead of the typical one) quarters is used. Estimates with an inflation lagged by just one quarter yield a coefficient estimate that is not significantly different from zero. This has been pointed out before (Byrne et al., 2013). The fact that there is no significant effect of lagged inflation suggests a price setting process with very little inertia, driven mostly by forward-looking behavior (see Scheufele, 2010, for a similar assessment). Overall, the findings presented here suggest a stable NKPC relationship when using the measure of pattern-based expectations.

9 Explaining the Course of Interest Rates

9.1 INTRODUCTION

Here we investigate the validity of the relationship between expected inflation and nominal interest rates proposed by Fisher (1930). Irving Fisher suggested that the nominal interest rate moves one-to-one with expected inflation. This means that an increase in *expected* inflation by one percentage point should increase the nominal interest rate by one percentage point. The basic intuition is that lenders (e.g., buyers of bonds) demand compensation from borrowers for the loss of purchasing power resulting from inflation. Formally this notion is expressed as

$$i_t = i_t^r + \pi_t^e, \tag{9.1}$$

where i_t is the nominal interest rate, i_t^r is the real interest rate, and π_t^e stands for the expected inflation over the maturity of the bond. Nothing so far is said concerning the determinants of the real interest rate. In empirical studies on the Fisher proposition, some authors assume that the real rate is a constant (or at least stationary) while others take it to follow a random walk. A key element in any attempt of testing the Fisher hypothesis concerns the measurement of inflation expectations. We first focus on the popular approach of modeling expected inflation as a weighted sum of past inflation. Fisher's (1930) original contribution as well as studies by Cagan (1956), Sargent (1973), and Friedman and Schwartz (1982) are examples of this approach. These investigations find that a significant effect of inflation on interest rates can only be documented if one accepts the notion that expected inflation depends on inflation rates from times long past. The long lags of up to 20 years documented in these studies imply that it takes expectation decades to adjust to changes in inflation. This implication has generally been judged as implausible. For the finding that nominal rates slowly, if at all, react to changes in inflation, Summers (1983) has coined the phrase of "nonadjustment of nominal interest rates."

One interpretation of the finding of a weak effect of inflation on the interest rate that is in line with Fisher's own views holds that people are afflicted by money illusion. According to this account, agents fail to perceive that a rising price level diminishes their actual return when lending money. This proposed explanation for the empirical difficulties of the Fisher proposition seems an overly strong challenge to economic rationality even for behavioral economists.[1] Instead, we pursue a line of research that focuses on the measure of expected inflation as the critical element. One popular approach to capturing inflation expectations in studies of the Fisher effect relies on survey data concerning the future course of inflation. Studies in this tradition were published, for example, by Gibson (1972), Cargill (1976), and Kaliva (2008). Many of the studies using survey data have documented a significant effect of expected inflation on nominal returns, although not typically of the form known as the strong Fisher effect, that is, not a one-to-one effect.

In the following, estimates of the Fisher effect using survey data will be compared with estimates using the pattern-based measure of expected inflation. This new behavioral model of inflation expectations differs markedly from earlier versions of extrapolative expectations with their long lags. Indeed, the pattern-based model of expected inflation suggests that people rely on inflation rates covering only a few years when forming expectations. We will compare this behavioral model of inflation expectations with the inflation expectations from the Michigan survey of households in their ability to explain the course of US nominal interest rates.

---

[1] This does not deny the possibility that money illusion is empirically relevant and can explain some economic phenomena (see Shafir et al., 1997).

For the econometric study of the Fisher effect, three dimensions of expected inflation are included as explanatory variables. Specifically, the estimates that follow are based on the following specification:

$$\Delta i_t = \alpha_0 + \alpha_1 \Delta \pi_t^e + \alpha_2 \Delta \pi_t^{e,heter} + \alpha_3 \Delta \pi_t^{e,uncer} + \varepsilon_t \qquad (9.2)$$

This equation explains the nominal rate as a function of expected inflation (π^e), the heterogeneity $(\pi^{e,heter})$, and the uncertainty $(\pi^{e,uncer})$ of inflation expectations.[2] The Fisher hypothesis states that the coefficient on the expected inflation term should be 1. Hence, attention will be particularly given to the question whether there is evidence to support the proposition that $\alpha_1 = 1$. In the literature, this is termed the strong form of the Fisher effect. A value of α_1 significantly positive but smaller than 1 is termed the weak form of the Fisher effect. The regressions that follow are estimated in first differences of all variables. The first difference specification of the Fisher relationship is all the more appropriate since we operate with an explicit model of the expectations process. Taking the Fisher hypothesis seriously means that a change in *expected* inflation should immediately influence the nominal interest rate.[3]

Estimates in first differences also alleviate potential problems of multicollinearity among the three explanatory variables in the regression equation. The correlations between the right-hand variables in Eq. (9.2) are much lower compared to the correlations between the

[2] An alternative approach found in the literature worth mentioning here studies determinants of measures of US real interest rates. A typical approach to compute real rates of interest consists of using survey measures of inflation expectations (e.g., De Bondt & Bange, 1992, Kaliva, 2008) while another approach uses returns on inflation indexed bonds (Söderlind, 2011, Haubrich et al., 2012).

[3] Hence, a possible cointegration relationship between the nominal interest rate and actual inflation is not investigated here. The concept of cointegration in the literature on the Fisher effect is typically used to avoid having to take a stance on the issue of expectations formation. The literature is replete with studies investigating the cointegration properties between nominal interest rates and inflation (Wallace & Warner, 1993, Koustas & Serletis, 1999, Westerlund, 2008). So far, the findings in this tradition present a mixed bag of evidence regarding the Fisher effect.

levels of these variables. Focusing on the pattern-based measures, we find the following regarding correlations: when going from level data to first differences and looking over the period from 1962 to 2016, the correlation between the measure of one-year- (five-year-) ahead inflation expectations and the measure of heterogeneity declines from a value of 0.87 (0.96) to 0.06 (0.55). The correlation between the one-year (five-year) heterogeneity measure and the uncertainty measure also markedly drops from 0.86 (0.97) to 0.41 (0.54) when moving to first differences of these time series.

Before presenting estimates of Eq. (9.2), it is necessary to clarify how the additional dimensions of expected inflation can potentially affect the rate of interest. Section 9.2 develops the arguments for a role of the heterogeneity of expectations in the determination of interest rates. Section 9.3 surveys the arguments for including the uncertainty of inflation expectations as an explanatory variable.

9.2 EFFECTS OF THE HETEROGENEITY OF EXPECTED INFLATION

For the discussion of possible effects of disagreement among market participants regarding future inflation, a loanable funds framework for the determination of the interest rate is applied here. Figure 9.1 outlines the various effects of heterogeneous inflation expectations on the demand for funds. The nominal interest rate is shown on the vertical axis and the quantity of loanable funds demanded on the horizontal axis. The panel at the top presents the case of a linear demand curve while the cases of convex and concave curves are shown below. Consider first the display on the upper left: the solid line marks the demand for funds in the case where everyone holds the same given inflation expectations.[4] In order to discuss the influence of heterogeneity, we first ask how the demand function is affected by

---

[4] For the purpose of the display, it is irrelevant whether the average of expected inflation is a biased or unbiased predictor of actual inflation.

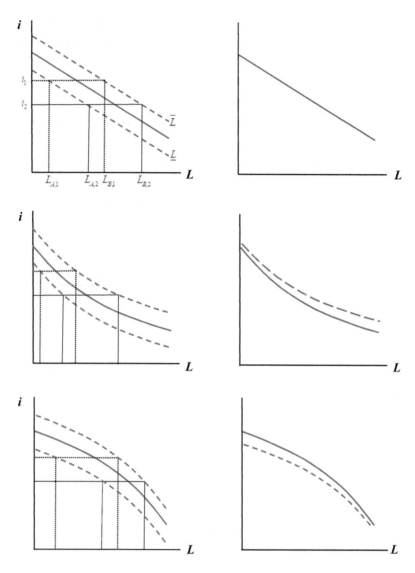

FIGURE 9.1 Effect of heterogeneous inflation expectations on the demand for loanable funds

different levels of expected inflation. In Figure 9.1, the dashed line $\bar{L}$ gives the location of the demand curve if everybody holds expectations higher than in the baseline scenario. Correspondingly, with lower inflation expectations, demand would be at $\underline{L}$.

Now think of demand as equally split in groups holding either expectations as in $\bar{L}$ or as in $\underline{L}$. This means that one half of market participants holds inflation expectations higher, and the other half lower than the average of expectations. This allows us to graphically derive the demand function for the case of heterogeneous inflation expectations. For each case considered, the display on the right-hand side of Figure 9.1 shows the resulting demand curves for the case of homogeneous and heterogeneous inflation expectations. To be clear, the curve with homogeneous expectations is always just the solid line displayed on the left. By contrast, the curve for the heterogeneous expectations needs to be derived. To make this derivation transparent, first consider the demand for loans for a given nominal interest rate i_1. Clearly, the demand for loans for agents with low-inflation expectations $(L_{A,1})$ are lower than that of agents with a high-inflation expectation $(L_{B,1})$. Total demand for funds is simply the (horizontal) average of the two demands at $\bar{L}$ and $\underline{L}$. In order to more fully illustrate the effect on total loan demand, we go through the same process of aggregation for another level of the interest rate i_2 with the corresponding demand values $L_{A,2}$ and $L_{B,2}$.

Going through this process of deriving demand, the dashed demand curves on the right-hand side of Figure 9.1 is derived. Visibly, in the case of a linear demand function, heterogeneity does not matter. Demand under heterogeneous expectations coincides with demand under homogeneous expectations.[5] In the case of a convex demand curve (the middle panel), heterogeneity increases demand in comparison to the case of expectations homogeneity. The contrary effect (a decline of demand) is the outcome with a concave demand function. The analysis here yields a further insight: with a convex demand function, the effect of heterogeneity is larger at lower levels of

---

[5] The assumption used here is that the loan demands of the two groups are equal. If instead, for example, loan demands from borrowers with above-average inflation expectations were higher than from those with below-average expectations heterogeneity has an effect even in the linear case. For more details on this point, see Cukierman (1978).

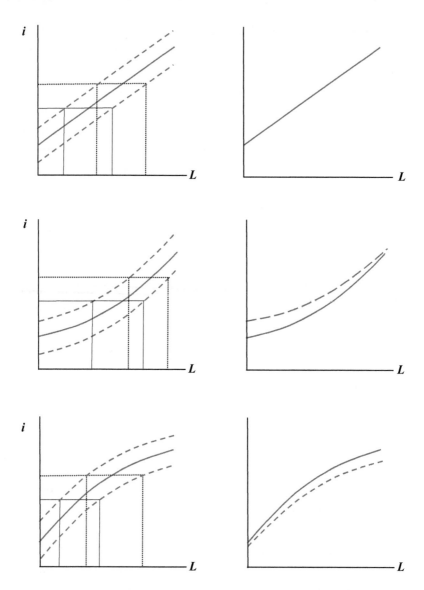

FIGURE 9.2 Effect of heterogeneous inflation expectations on the supply of
loanable funds

the interest rate while the reverse is true with a concave demand
function.

Naturally, the heterogeneity of expected inflation also has
effects on the supply of funds. Figure 9.2 presents these effects in

graphical form. Market participants who hold higher (lower) than average inflation expectations offer the same amount of funds only when the interest rate is higher (lower). The construction of the supply curves for loanable funds follows the procedure just described for demand. As before, with a linear curve, heterogeneity does not matter. With a convex curve, supply for any given interest rate is lower with heterogeneous expectations. By contrast, with a concave curve, heterogeneity increases supply. Clearly, the focus has to be placed on the resulting equilibrium interest rate since this is the variable studied in this chapter. The interaction of the effects of heterogeneity on the demand and the supply of loanable funds leads to an ambiguous outcome: the interest rate can rise, fall, or stay constant with an increase in the heterogeneity of inflation expectations. Hence, with a view to the empirical analysis, there is no prior indication as to what sign the coefficient α_2 of the heterogeneity variable should have in Eq. (9.2).[6]

9.3 EFFECTS OF THE UNCERTAINTY OF EXPECTED INFLATION

Here we outline the rationale for including a measure of the uncertainty of expected inflation into a regression model of the interest rate. In Eq. (9.2), this effect is captured by the coefficient α_3. One strand of the theoretical literature argues that uncertainty of expected inflation should induce a positive risk premium in the equilibrium interest rate.[7] An increase in the purchasing power risk of a bond induces the supplier of funds to demand compensation, that is, a

---

[6] A noteworthy point concerns the interaction of heterogeneity and the level of expected inflation. An intriguing (sign-reversing) effect can occur with a combination of a concave demand and a convex supply curve. In this case, at a low level of the equilibrium interest rate (e.g., with demand shifted to the left during a recession) an increase in expectations heterogeneity raises the interest rate while at a high level of the interest rate (e.g., during an economic upswing), an increase in heterogeneity tends to lower the interest rate.

[7] See Berument et al. (2005) for a survey of the various types of theoretical approaches and results regarding the direction of the effect of inflation uncertainty on interest rates.

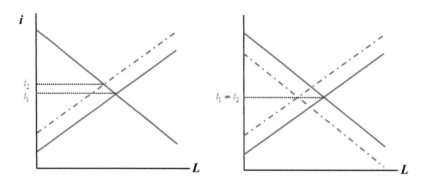

FIGURE 9.3 Effect of the risk of expected inflation on the interest rate

higher rate of interest, so the argument goes. One justification for this position states that the lenders of funds are risk averse, while borrowers are risk neutral. If lenders are households with limited options to hedge inflation risk, while borrowers, for example firms, have more sophistication in their risk management, then this argument might hold true. However, inflation risk is notoriously difficult to hedge even for professional fund managers (Moerman & van Dijk, 2010). Furthermore, loan demand also comes from households. In conclusion, the overall direction of the effect of the uncertainty of expected inflation on the rate of interest is not obvious.

In order to gauge the interest rate effect of uncertainty, again an analysis in a loanable funds framework can help. An analysis with linear demand and supply curves is sufficient to make the main points. Here we limit the displays to just two cases. The left-hand panel of Figure 9.3 shows the case typically argued in the literature. The supply of funds is diminished at any level of the interest rate if lenders bear inflation risk. The borrower side is assumed not to be affected (because of hedging or risk neutrality). The outcome then is clear: an increase in the uncertainty of expected inflation raises the equilibrium interest rate from i_1 to i_2. Compare this to the situation shown in the right-hand panel. Here suppliers and demanders of funds are both affected by inflation risk: at any given interest rate both sides are willing to reduce the amount of funds supplied or demanded.

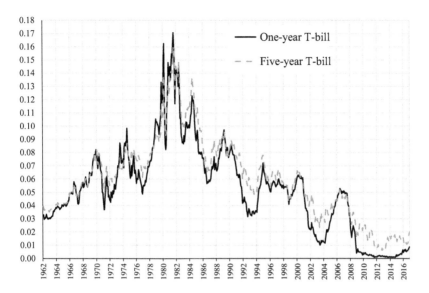

FIGURE 9.4 US nominal interest rates (Treasury bond yields)

The likely outcome is that the interest rate remains unchanged.[8] Summing up, the effect of higher inflation risk on the rate of interest is also ambiguous.

9.4 ESTIMATING INTEREST RATE EQUATIONS

Before turning to econometric estimates, graphical displays of the time series of interest rates are provided. Figure 9.4 shows US Treasury bond rates of a maturity of one and five years. The data for these nominal yields are available starting in 1962M01.[9] For these two maturities, we have measures of expected inflation, both based on the method introduced in this book as well as from the survey of consumers from the

---

[8] Common to both scenarios in Figure 9.3 is the effect of inflation risk on the quantity of funds loaned. Linked to this decrease in quantity is the reduction in investment projects realized and a corresponding loss of output.

[9] Treasury bill rates and the monthly (not seasonally adjusted) CPI data come from the Federal Reserve Bank of St. Louis web portal https://fred.stlouisfed.org/. The survey data from the University of Michigan are drawn from the web portal www.sca.isr .umich.edu/.

Table 9.1 *Regression results for the one-year nominal interest rate*

Expectations measure Sample period	α_0	α_1	α_2	α_3	$\overline{R}^2$	D.W.	Std. Err.
Michigan	−0.012	0.122	0.132		0.000	1.691	0.543
1978–2016	(0.025)	(0.355)	(0.226)				
Pattern-based	−0.010	1.018*	−1.550	−0.047	0.000	1.685	0.664
1978–2016	(0.031)	(0.514)	(1.248)	(0.469)			
Pattern-based	−0.003	1.045*	−1.355	−0.136	0.000	1.729	0.611
1962–2016	(0.023)	(0.471)	(1.156)	(0.410)			

* indicates significance at the 5 percent level of significance. Numbers in parentheses are White heteroskedasticity-consistent standard errors of estimated coefficients.

University of Michigan.[10] The Michigan survey of households also offers a measure of the heterogeneity of expected inflation. However, the Michigan poll does not ask about the uncertainty of inflation expectations. Thus, the estimates of Eq. (9.2) with survey data do not include any $\pi_t^{e,\,uncer}$ term. By contrast, the pattern-based approach of measuring inflation expectations offers measures of the mean of expectations as well as the uncertainty and the heterogeneity of expectations.

Table 9.1 documents the estimates of Eq. (9.2) for the one-year interest rate. As is obvious from the very low $\overline{R}^2$ values, the various dimensions of expected inflation are of minimal help in tracking monthly changes in nominal interest rates. Throughout, the right-hand variables are instrumented to avoid a simultaneity bias in the estimated coefficients.[11] The top line shows the findings when the

---

[10] As is common in the literature, the series of the median expectations of the Michigan survey data is used in the estimates. This choice is typically justified with the magnitude of outliers in the polled data.

[11] Lagged values of the endogenous and all exogenous variables are used as instruments with three lagged observations for all instruments. Further, the

Michigan survey measure of expected inflations is used. For the short-run inflation expectations, the polled expectations go back to 1978. With the Michigan expectations data, the findings are not at all supportive of the Fisher proportion. The estimated value for the α_1 coefficient in this specification is not significantly different from zero. The second line documents the results when using the pattern-based measure of expectations. The third line extends the estimates by lengthening the sample size back to 1962. With the pattern-based measure of expected inflation, the results with the one-year interest rate are very much in line with the Fisher proposition: for the shorter sample, the coefficient of expected inflation is 1.018. For the sample going back to 1962, the relevant coefficient estimate is 1.045.

Turning to the effects of the heterogeneity of inflation expect-ations – captured by coefficient α_2 – the evidence is mixed. As before, the survey measure of expectations does not seem to help to explain the course of the interest rate. By comparison, the pattern-based measure of heterogeneity leads to somewhat stronger results. While none of the coefficients are significantly different from zero, the estimates suggest a negative effect of heterogeneity on interest rates.[12] We will follow up on this effect in later chapters. Finally, the estimates of coefficient α_3 presented indicate that there is no statistically relevant effect of the uncertainty of expected inflation on the rate of interest. This result parallels findings by Lahiri et al. (1988). The documented finding is compatible, for example, with the

inflation rate and the growth rate of real GDP (monthly data are generated with quadratic spline functions) are among the instruments.

[12] Looking again at Figures 9.1 and 9.2, three scenarios that give rise to a clear negative effect of increasing heterogeneity can be identified. The first combination is a linear demand curve and a concave supply curve. The same outcome results with a combination of a concave demand curve and a linear supply curve. An argument for the relevance of this case can be made by referring to the very limited effect that the recent near-zero interest rate has had on investment demand. The strongest negative effect emerges when both demand and supply have concave forms. Other combinations are possible when the effect of heterogeneity on the side with a concave shape is stronger than on the side with a convex function.

Table 9.2 *Regression results for the five-year nominal interest rate*

Expectations measure Sample period	α_0	α_1	α_2	α_3	$\overline{R}^2$	D.W.	Std. Err.
Michigan	−0.018	0.121	0.076		0.001	1.640	0.262
1990–2016	(0.014)	(0.169)	(0.088)				
Pattern-based	−0.019*	0.588	0.312	−0.790	0.000	1.761	0.272
1990–2016	(0.015)	(0.437)	(0.567)	(0.666)			
Pattern-based	−0.003	1.957*	−1.619	−0.296	0.000	1.826	0.448
1962–2016	(0.017)	(0.914)	(1.380)	(0.938)			

* indicates significance at the 5 percent level. Numbers in parentheses are White heteroskedasticity-consistent standard errors of estimated coefficients.

case of symmetrical effects of uncertainty on demand and supply for loanable funds developed in Section 9.3.

Table 9.2 reports the results for the same specifications as in Table 9.1, but this time for the long-term interest rate. When Michigan survey data (available as of 1990) is used, no effect of the form suggested by Irving Fisher is apparent. The respective α_1 coefficient estimate is not statistically significantly different from zero but different from 1 (p value of less than 0.01). By contrast, the estimates for the long-term rate with the behavioral model of inflation expectations are better in line with Fisher's theory: for the shorter period from 1990 to 2016, the relevant estimated coefficient is 0.588. However, it is not significantly different from zero. For the longer period from 1962 to 2016, the coefficient is significantly different from zero.[13] For both samples, the relevant coefficient is not significantly different from 1. Again, the effects of the uncertainty and the heterogeneity

---

[13] The estimated α_1 value (of 1.957) would be closer to 1 if real GDP growth were added as an explanatory variable. A cyclical tendency of the interest rate is clearly documented in such an estimate and the estimated coefficient α_1 comes down to 1.522 (s.e. 0.530).

of inflation expectations are not significant. Yet, again the heterogeneity effect seems to be stronger than the uncertainty effect. While the coefficients of heterogeneity and uncertainty are not significant in a statistical sense it should not necessarily be concluded that the estimates imply no relevant effects. When taking, for example, the point estimate $\alpha_2 = -1.355$, we find that variations in heterogeneity in the range of ± 25 basis points (as regularly observed in recent years) can go together with induced (inverse) variations of roughly the same size of the short-term nominal rate. This is relevant for the question how the difference between nominal interest rates and rates on inflation-indexed bonds should be interpreted (Bauer & McCarthy, 2015). The present findings indicate that this rate differential can vary even without expected inflation changing and should therefore not be taken as a reliable measure of expected inflation. The effects of expectations heterogeneity and uncertainty are further investigated in Chapters 14 and 15 in econometric studies of interest rates in Asian and African economies.

In view of the results that the hypothesis of a unitary coefficient cannot be rejected for the pattern-based measure of expected inflation, we proceed to impose this very restriction. The result comes in the form of ex ante *real* rates of interest. As Homer and Sylla (1991) have aptly formulated (1991, p. 430): "Because the real rate of interest depends on the expected inflation, it cannot be directly observed." And further down p. 430: "There is thus no real rate of interest to be discovered: there are merely a variety of attempts approximately to measure it." Figure 9.5 shows real rates for the one-year and the five-year maturity. For comparison, similar measures using the Michigan survey measure of expectations are computed and presented in Figure 9.6. One distinction between the two approaches of computing real rates is evident when comparing the series in Figures 9.5 and 9.6.

Pattern-based real rates can be computed for a much longer period. For the one-year horizon, the Michigan data on expected inflation start only in 1978 and for the five-year horizon in 1990. This limits survey-based measures of the real rate of interest to these

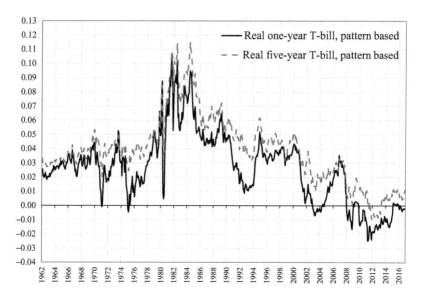

FIGURE 9.5 Real interest rates based on pattern-based inflation
expectations

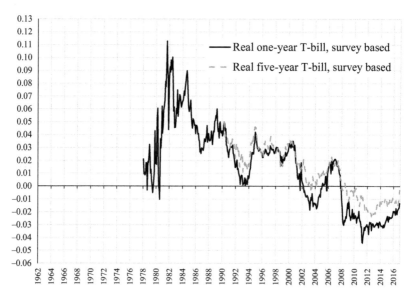

FIGURE 9.6 Real interest rates based on Michigan measures of inflation
expectations

historical periods. Furthermore, real rates of interest based on the Michigan data are more often and more strongly negative than are the pattern-based real rates. Incidentally, other measures of ex ante rates reported in the literature are also often negative. The series constructed by Dotsey et al. (2003), for example, suggests that real rates were negative over a substantial portion of the 1970s. Although negative real rates are not a logical impossibility, longer spans of negative rate appear implausible.[14]

9.5 SUMMARY AND CONCLUSIONS

This chapter applies the concept of pattern-based inflation expectations to the estimation of the Fisher effect of expected inflation on nominal interest rates. In particular, the one-year and the five-year US Treasury bill rates are examined. It is shown that the estimated effect of expected inflation on the nominal rate is in line with Fisher's theory when the pattern-based measure of expectations is applied. In particular, the estimated coefficient of the new behavioral measure of expected inflation for the one-year interest rate is very close to one. Together with the fact that this effect of inflation expectations is realized without a time lag, the findings support the strong-form Fisher effect. This contrasts with the results found with the survey measure of expected inflation from the University of Michigan. Here, the Fisher effect does not show up. Further, the econometric analysis presents some evidence for a negative effect of the heterogeneity of inflation expectations. By contrast, no evidence of an effect of the uncertainty of expected inflation on rates of return can be reported.

[14] A scenario where market equilibrium determines a negative ex ante real rate of interest is the situation with a high risk of collapse in the stock market and in consumption (see DeLong & Magin, 2009).

10 Generalizing the Pattern-Based Approach

10.1 INTRODUCTION

With this chapter, we take our approach to a wider applicability. So far, the expectations elicited in the laboratory pertained to a set of inflation patterns that was observed in countries like the USA and Germany over the years from the 1950s to the first decade of the 21st century. When we want to model expectations for a wider set of countries and historical periods, we need to generalize our approach. More concretely, it becomes necessary to consider pattern extrapolation for a wider set of possible courses of the price level. Notably, the set of 22 patterns used in the laboratory as described in Chapter 3 barely includes any cases of deflation. For the modeling of historical expectations, this can be quite limiting. Consider only the course of aggregate prices with periods of deflation in countries like the USA and the United Kingdom in the 19th century.

The logical next step in a generalization of the pattern-based approach consists of presenting the subjects with a wider range of patterns. This will include, for example, courses of downward-trending prices. If we were to simply extend the initial set of patterns with four data points, we would need to present subjects the full set of 125 possible patterns. However, this is simply not feasible in a laboratory session. At this juncture, an important finding concerning the expectations data presented in Chapter 4 turns out to be helpful: In the regression analysis of the laboratory data, it is found that the typical subject does not need more than *three* observed realizations

of the price level to form expectations.[1] In short, the last three observations of the index of aggregate prices are sufficient to explain the
experimental expectations data.

This finding opens the way to a very general approach to patterns and expectations. Specifically, it allows the simplification of
patterns from a length of four to three data points. Hence, for this
chapter, we present subjects with a set of price-level patterns that
come as sequences of consecutive observations over three years. This
shortening of the length of patterns implies that now just 25 patterns
(i.e., 5 different step sizes over 2 periods) make up a fully encompassing set of possible cases. This list of patterns is short enough to be
used in the laboratory survey. With these 25 patterns, it becomes
practicable in the laboratory to elicit expectations (including its
uncertainty) under all circumstances. The following sections describe
the laboratory procedures, the new expectations data, and the
resulting time series of expected inflation.

10.2   EXPECTATIONS DATA

The patterns shown under the generalized conditions consist of just
three data points. On the side of increases, we have the pattern 100,
102, 104 that marks the upper bound of cases and on the side of the
decreases, there is 100, 98, 96. Subjects in the laboratory are informed
that they are shown cases indicating how the price level of a country
can evolve over a period of three years. Otherwise, the exact same
instructions are used as for the treatment (iii) in Chapter 3. Hence,
subjects are asked for the point expectation one year and five years
into the future. Furthermore, subjects give their uncertainty assessment. Earlier in the book, the importance of context in the
extrapolation of economic data was emphasized. It has been shown
that an understanding of what type of variable has to be forecast is

---

[1] This is documented in the estimates of Eq. (4.10) and Eq. (4.11) where no information
(i.e., variable dated) farther back than three periods is shown to have any
explanatory power.

relevant for the task. Chapter 4 has documented differences between expectations concerning the CPI and real GDP. Thus, we assert that understanding the concepts of the variables to be forecast is relevant for subjects' behavior. To further deepen this insight, the new laboratory study is run with groups with different educational backgrounds. For this purpose, the laboratory elicitation of expectations was repeated.[2] Concretely, two runs (run I and run II) are conducted with student subjects who had a basic training in macroeconomics whereas run III is conducted with students without any training in economics.

Appendix 10.1 details the comparative analysis of the three new data sets. It turns out that the expectations elicited in the first two runs do not differ significantly while the data from run III shows notable dissimilarities. This finding suggests that in order to model expectations of macroeconomic variables from bottom-up, we should indeed work with data from subjects with a basic understanding of the concepts involved. Presumably, the real-world decision makers, whose behavior we want to model, know what the CPI measures.[3] Thus, and in line with Chapter 3, only data from economically literate subjects are considered for the computation of time series of expectations. Accordingly, the data from runs I and II are pooled for use in the computations of series of expected inflation. Tables 10.1 and 10.2 show these data in the form familiar from Chapter 3. Specifically, Table 10.1 presents the mean (now over 96 subjects) of individual expectations as well as the data on the distribution of answers. Table 10.2 in turn presents the means of the answers to the 75 percent and the 25 percent quantile questions measuring the uncertainty of expectations.

---

[2] Given the capacity of the laboratory, the number of subjects was increased to 48 as compared with the groups of 45 subjects investigated for the data of Chapter 3.

[3] This is also supported by Binder (2015) who finds that when looking at various subgroups among the participants in the Michigan survey of consumers, it turns out that the inflation expectations of educated participants appear to play a prominent role in the determination of inflation.

Table 10.1 CPI expectations for periods 4 (one-year-ahead) and 8 (five-year-ahead)

Pattern	Time 1	2	3	Mean 4	Upper 95%	Lower 5%	Mean 8	Upper 95%	Lower 5%
1	100	102	104	105.6146	106.00	104.00	109.7823	114.00	104.00
2	100	102	103	103.6750	104.13	103.00	104.8375	109.25	100.00
3	100	102	102	102.0969	104.00	101.00	103.3896	107.00	99.75
4	100	102	101	100.7365	103.00	99.00	101.7083	106.00	96.75
5	100	102	100	99.5885	102.00	97.00	100.2854	104.00	96.00
6	100	101	103	104.9188	106.55	104.00	108.5823	117.25	103.00
7	100	101	102	102.8740	103.00	102.00	105.5365	107.00	102.75
8	100	101	101	101.2031	102.00	100.00	101.8635	105.00	97.75
9	100	101	100	99.6031	101.00	98.00	100.1625	103.25	96.00
10	100	101	99	97.9010	100.00	96.00	98.0021	102.25	93.00
11	100	100	102	103.3052	105.00	101.75	105.7688	111.25	100.00
12	100	100	101	101.6292	103.00	100.00	103.1313	106.25	100.00
13	100	100	100	100.0604	101.00	99.00	100.4698	103.43	98.00
14	100	100	99	98.2365	100.00	97.00	98.0375	101.20	93.75
15	100	100	98	96.7604	98.25	95.00	96.0542	101.13	89.75
16	100	99	101	101.7156	103.00	100.00	103.7521	107.25	100.00
17	100	99	100	100.2125	101.00	99.00	101.2813	105.00	98.15
18	100	99	99	98.8656	100.00	98.00	99.3281	103.13	96.00
19	100	99	98	97.1010	98.40	96.00	95.9448	101.63	92.50
20	100	99	97	95.3500	97.00	93.80	93.5885	101.00	85.00
21	100	98	100	100.6240	102.00	98.00	101.8615	106.25	98.00
22	100	98	99	99.2354	101.00	97.00	100.1990	103.25	95.00
23	100	98	98	97.8958	99.00	96.00	97.9792	102.08	93.00
24	100	98	97	96.2214	97.00	95.00	95.8052	100.25	90.00
25	100	98	96	94.3990	96.00	93.60	92.0365	100.00	86.00

Table 10.2 *Measures of one-year- and five-year-ahead uncertainty of CPI expectations*

Pattern	Time 1	2	3	Mean 4	Mean of upper 75%	Mean of lower 25%	Mean 8	Mean of upper 75%	Mean of lower 25%
1	100	102	104	105.61	106.8385	104.4500	109.78	112.0604	107.4052
2	100	102	103	103.68	104.8063	102.4979	104.84	107.1500	102.6000
3	100	102	102	102.10	103.6031	100.3021	103.39	105.7104	100.7823
4	100	102	101	100.74	102.2125	99.1865	101.71	104.0354	99.0188
5	100	102	100	99.59	101.2167	97.8615	100.29	103.0094	97.3719
6	100	101	103	104.92	106.4188	103.3281	108.58	111.3229	105.6719
7	100	101	102	102.87	103.9865	101.6135	105.54	107.6458	103.1479
8	100	101	101	101.20	102.3375	99.8615	101.86	103.9833	99.5240
9	100	101	100	99.60	101.0677	98.2719	100.16	102.4948	97.6104
10	100	101	99	97.90	99.5969	96.3542	98.00	100.5219	95.1177
11	100	100	102	103.31	104.8823	101.7292	105.77	108.4656	103.1542
12	100	100	101	101.63	102.9896	100.2104	103.13	105.5667	100.9198
13	100	100	100	100.06	101.3000	98.7188	100.47	102.8365	97.8615
14	100	100	99	98.24	99.7771	96.8729	98.04	100.4229	95.5917
15	100	100	98	96.76	98.3896	95.2792	96.05	98.7938	93.3208
16	100	99	101	101.72	103.4635	100.1063	103.75	106.3938	100.8667
17	100	99	100	100.21	101.5698	98.8156	101.28	103.7219	98.8979
18	100	99	99	98.87	100.2646	97.5906	99.33	101.7052	96.6219
19	100	99	98	97.10	98.4333	95.6219	95.94	98.3979	93.4417
20	100	99	97	95.35	96.9646	93.8281	93.59	96.3365	90.9479
21	100	98	100	100.62	102.3281	98.7729	101.86	104.7354	98.7510
22	100	98	99	99.24	100.7115	97.8281	100.20	102.6208	97.6146
23	100	98	98	97.90	99.3115	96.4427	97.98	100.7604	95.3677
24	100	98	97	96.22	97.5865	94.9865	95.81	98.2031	93.4125
25	100	98	96	94.40	95.7885	92.9125	92.04	94.7927	89.3292

10.3   ECONOMETRIC ANALYSIS
OF EXPECTATIONS DATA

This section goes through a similar analysis of the expectations data as presented in Chapter 4. The findings again document the failure of a linear model of extrapolation to explain the laboratory data. Here, types of patterns are sorted into those showing a trend in the same direction over the last two changes and those that show no trend. This division is made clear with the dummies defined as $D^{Trend} = 1$ if $(P_{j,3} - P_{j,2})(P_{j,2} - P_{j,1}) > 0$ and $D^{no\text{-}Trend} = 1 - D^{Trend}$. These dummies correspond to those defined in Chapter 4. The central result of this specification search is the following estimate:

$$P^e_{j,4} - P_{j,3} = \underset{(0.049)}{0.839}(P_{j,3} - P_{j,2})D^{Tr} + \underset{(0.040)}{0.443}(P_{j,3} - P_{j,2})D^{no\text{-}Tr} \tag{10.1}$$

$$\overline{R}^2 = 0.946, \qquad SEE = 0.221$$

The two estimated coefficients differ significantly showing again that extrapolation differs between trending and non-trending patterns. The estimate for the case of the trending patterns replicates the exact same coefficient (i.e., 0.839) as the one in Eq. (4.10) with patterns covering four observations. In comparison, the non-trending patterns have a somewhat smaller coefficient compared to the estimate of Chapter 4. Note, however, that the set of 25 patterns shown here gives a more general representation of the course of a time series. In particular, with this set of patterns there are many more (namely eight) patterns with a reversal of the course of the price level. In the set of 22 patterns used in Chapter 3, there was just a single such case. Hence, with the richer set of patterns, it is possible to econometrically study a more elaborate classification of patterns. For this purpose, the 16 non-trending patterns (excluding 100, 100, 100) are now further grouped into (a) plateau patterns identified by $D^{Pl} = 1$ if $(P_{j,3} - P_{j,2}) = 0$, (b) take-off patterns $D^{TO} = 1$ if $(P_{j,2} - P_{j,1}) = 0$, and (c) reversal patterns noted as $D^{Re} = 1$ if $(P_{j,3} - P_{j,2})(P_{j,2} - P_{j,1}) < 0$. The parsimonious specification, resulting from applying Wald tests to eliminate nonsignificant regressors, that utilizes this partitioning of patterns is

$$P^e_{j,4} - P_{j,3} = 0.839\left(P_{j,3} - P_{j,2}\right)D^{Tr} + 0.648\left(P_{j,3} - P_{j,2}\right)D^{TO}$$

$$(0.033) \qquad\qquad\qquad (0.047)$$

$$+ 0.340\left(P_{j,3} - P_{j,2}\right)D^{Re}. \qquad\qquad (10.2)$$

$$(0.033)$$

$$\overline{R}^2 = 0.976, \quad SEE = 0.149$$

The coefficient for the plateau pattern is not significantly different from zero. Hence, for short-term expectations, plateau patterns essentially lead to static expectations.[4] The picture that thus emerges is that the weight given to the last observed change declines in value from trending patterns to take-off patterns, and further to reversal patterns. This estimated coefficient, in the terminology of Hicks (1939), is the elasticity of expectations.

For the five-year-ahead expectation, a corresponding specification search leads to the following finding:

$$P^e_{j,8} - P_{j,3} = 0.775 + 2.305\left(P_{j,3} - P_{j,2}\right)D^{Tr} + 1.452\left(P_{j,3} - P_{j,2}\right)D^{TO}$$

$$(0.096) \ (0.107) \qquad\qquad\qquad (0.152)$$

$$+ 0.613\left(P_{j,3} - P_{j,2}\right)D^{Re} + 0.335\left(P_{j,3} - P_{j,1}\right)D^{Pl}$$

$$(0.107) \qquad\qquad\qquad (0.152)$$

$$\overline{R}^2 = 0.967, \quad SEE = 0.480$$

$$(10.3)$$

The ranking of effects is the same as with short-term expectations: The patterns of clear trending imply the strongest extrapolation of recent change, followed by take-off patterns and reversal patterns. Two findings contrast the results for short-term expectations in Eq. (10.2): an intercept term and a significant effect for plateau patterns. Again, the regressive tendency of expectations is apparent: even in the case of a clearly trending price level, the five-year-ahead expectations do not move point-by-point with the general course of prices. Proportionality

---

[4] For plateau patterns, we include the variable $(P_{j,3} - P_{j,1})$ instead of $(P_{j,3} - P_{j,2})$ in the regression. The relevant coefficient does not significantly differ from zero, which is clearly in line with findings of symmetry, and is thus excluded from the final specification of Eq. (10.2).

of expectations with the actual course of inflation would require the constant to be zero and the coefficient for trending patterns to have a value of 5 rather than the empirically found value of 2.305.

Clearly, regression analysis is instructive concerning the general tendencies in the expectations data. Thus, it might be tempting to try to condense the laboratory data into an econometric model. However, the search for an econometric representation of the laboratory data is fraught with difficulties. One major problem of such an attempt is the issue of modeling expectations for inflation higher than what is shown (namely 1 or 2 percent) in the laboratory. Appendix 10.2 explains in more detail the limitations of an econometric representation of the expectations data that could be used for the computation of historical expectations. Hence, there exists no shortcut compared to the approach of using the laboratory data as outlined before. Accordingly, the computation of time series of expected inflation with the new laboratory data will proceed along the lines developed in earlier chapters. The next section presents computations of US inflation expectations based on the data presented in this chapter and compares them with the series computed in Chapter 5.[5]

10.4 INFLATION EXPECTATIONS BASED ON THE GENERALIZED APPROACH

Inflation expectations are now computed with the new data of expectations reported in Table 10.1 in combination with the procedures of similarity matching and scaling. For a comparison with the inflation expectations series modeled in Chapter 5, we compute inflation expectations for the same historical period with the new laboratory data. The starting point is 1955 and the data coverage extends to 2016. As previously, for the longer patterns a scaling parameter for the expectations data based on the three-period patterns has to be estimated. With the present 25 patterns there are eight pairs of perfectly

---

[5] The US CPI data are drawn from the Federal Reserve Bank of St. Louis web portal https://fred.stlouisfed.org/.

collinear patterns on which the estimate of the scaling parameter can be based. For the new set of data, the estimated scaling parameter turns out to be 0.861 (standard error 0.098). This value is very close to the 0.855 for the data from patterns with a length of four periods.

Among the new patterns, there are two sets of 12 symmetrical cases (e.g. 100, 101, 102 and 100, 99, 98). Hence, it is straightforward to test for symmetry of expectations. Regressing the 12 values of expectations for upward trending patterns on the corresponding expectations of downward trending patterns yields a coefficient of -1.006 (standard error 0.062) and a constant of 0.046 (standard error 0.059). These numbers and the p value of 0.458 make clear that the hypothesis of symmetry is *not* rejected. Thus, for the computations that follow, the elicited expectations data are transformed to incorporate symmetry. Accordingly, the same (average) absolute value for the expected change is used for pairs of symmetrical patterns. This data is presented in Table 10.3. Symmetry implies that for the pattern of no change (i.e., 100, 100, 100) the expected inflation should be zero. Here one further point needs clarification. The similarity matching algorithm is amended for the case where the historical series does not change over three periods. In this case, the pattern 100, 100, 100 receives a weight of one. As regards the issue of similarity matching, we continue to use the estimated model from Chapter 5.

At this point, a remark concerning the timing of the underlying series in the computations is in order. When computing monthly expectations, CPI data from the previous month (i.e., with a lag of one month) and from the months one and two years earlier (i.e., with lags of 13 and 25 months) are used. This timing does justice to the fact that consumer prices are not available in time and follows the procedure introduced in Chapter 5. This convention has the advantage that for econometric estimates with monthly data the constructed expectations series can be treated as exogenous. For the computation with annual observations, the procedure is altered. It is not plausible that the CPI of the current year (or at least an informed guess of it) should not be available when forming expectations. Accordingly, the

Table 10.3 *The shortened set of non-collinear patterns and corresponding short-term CPI expectations*[*]

Pattern	Time			Expected change
	1	2	3	
1	100	102	103	0.7268
2	100	102	101	−0.2495
3	100	101	103	1.7844
4	100	101	102	0.8857
5	100	101	101	0.1120
6	100	101	100	−0.2948
7	100	101	99	−0.9073
8	100	100	101	0.6983
9	100	100	100	0.0000
10	100	100	99	−0.6983
11	100	99	101	0.9073
12	100	99	100	0.2948
13	100	99	99	−0.1120
14	100	99	98	−0.8857
15	100	99	97	−1.7844
16	100	98	99	0.2495
17	100	98	97	−0.7268

[*] The tabulated data are first averaged over patterns with steps of 1 and their respective pattern with steps of 2 weighted by $1/(2^{0.861})$ and then averaged over symmetrical cases (expectations for declining patterns are weighted by −1).

computations of annual expectations are based on CPI values of the current year and the previous two years. When turning to econometric estimates with these annual expectations data, the instrumental variables method is the appropriate approach to deal with the simultaneity problem.

Next, the results from this generalized approach are compared with the expectations computed in Chapter 5. Both measures are based on monthly (not seasonally adjusted) CPI data for the USA. Figure 10.1 presents the new time series for one-year-ahead inflation

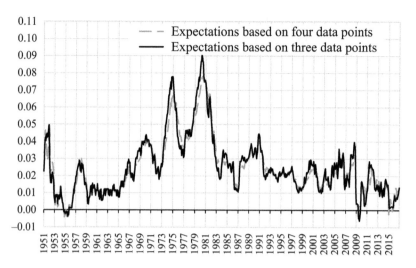

FIGURE 10.1 US inflation expectations based on various approaches

expectations from the present calculations and the corresponding series from Chapter 5. The two series are very similar (with a correlation of 0.972) and give the same general impression. Let us then turn to the particular strength of the generalized approach. The key advantage of the generalized approach is its ability to generate inflation expectations for countries and periods where the approach from Chapter 5 would be too narrow. With the generalized approach, we can study cases with periods of increasing as well as decreasing prices. This program of inquiry is started by studying inflation expectations in the United Kingdom going back as far as the early 18th century.

10.5 APPLICATIONS TO HISTORICAL DATA OF THE UNITED KINGDOM

The United Kingdom is chosen here because it is the best-documented economy when it comes to historical data. When widening the perspective to the first half of the 20th century and earlier centuries, we clearly leave the frame of the model of earlier chapters: The price level under the gold standard regularly showed downward movements. Here the application of the new expectations data is appropriate. As a start, let us focus on CPI inflation going back to the beginning of the 18th century. The computations that follow rely on a historical data set provided by the Bank of England.[6] For this data of the price level, the following measures are computed and shown in Table 10.4: the one-year-ahead expectations (column a), the uncertainty of this short-term inflation expectation (column b), and the annual five-year-ahead inflation expectation (column c). The uncertainty measure is computed based on the mean answers to the questions regarding the 75 and the 25 percent quantile for each pattern.

These long time series should be of interest for researchers in the field of economic history. Several features of these computed series are worth pointing out. First, average long-term inflation expectations have been quite stable over the centuries: the average five-year-ahead expected inflation for the 18th century is 0.70 percent; for the 19th, it is 0.34 percent; for the 20th, it rises to 1.72 percent; and in the 21st century, so far we have a value of 0.32 percent. Clearly, the 20th century stands out in historical perspective. The same general assessment holds for short-term expectations. Here, according to the present calculations, average expected inflation in the 20th century was 2.74 percent, while before and after expected inflation was lower (18th century: 0.46 percent, 19th century: −0.13 percent, 21th century so far: −0.30 percent). By contrast, the uncertainty of short-term expected inflation shows a clear downward movement over the centuries. The short-term measure of uncertainty of expected inflation was 11.07 percent in the 18th century, 8.74 percent in the 19th century, and 7.97 percent in the 20th century. Since the beginning of the new millennium, it has been merely 2.89 percent.

We now turn to a further key series, namely the real rate of interest. The Bank of England documents such a series in the already used macroeconomic data set. The nominal interest rate (a three-month rate) that is

---

[6] The data set from the Bank of England is entitled "A millennium of Macroeconomic Data," and can be found under www.bankofengland.co.uk/statistics/research-datasets.

Table 10.4 Tabulated series of pattern-based expectations for the United Kingdom
(a) one-year-ahead expected inflation; (b) the corresponding expectations uncertainty; (c) five-year-ahead expected
inflation (annualized)

	(a)	(b)	(c)		(a)	(b)	(c)		(a)	(b)	(c)
1702	-1.14	21.15	0.25	1807	-0.76	5.79	-0.13	1912	1.83	5.84	1.04
1703	-3.30	9.17	-0.97	1808	2.49	8.05	1.38	1913	0.64	3.77	0.42
1704	1.21	9.70	0.86	1809	6.16	11.06	3.56	1914	1.82	3.85	1.11
1705	-3.51	12.56	-0.69	1810	0.88	13.02	0.96	1915	6.74	16.99	3.57
1706	2.33	16.56	1.50	1811	1.39	2.63	0.96	1916	10.60	19.80	6.03
1707	-2.62	20.66	0.24	1812	5.91	18.00	3.07	1917	13.58	25.73	7.64
1708	1.35	16.15	1.14	1813	0.88	15.51	1.08	1918	11.56	25.21	6.81
1709	8.74	16.51	4.71	1814	-5.11	16.88	-1.28	1919	5.56	16.86	2.52
1710	8.05	17.71	4.87	1815	-10.07	20.19	-3.54	1920	9.43	17.35	5.35
1711	6.25	14.63	3.69	1816	1.42	16.38	1.17	1921	-1.30	15.77	0.64
1712	-9.09	32.47	-1.63	1817	0.84	13.84	0.99	1922	-9.99	18.79	-3.40
1713	-2.53	39.28	0.27	1818	-1.08	3.85	-0.23	1923	-4.08	14.48	-1.18
1714	2.32	8.64	1.30	1819	-3.33	6.20	-1.24	1924	-0.61	10.51	0.11
1715	0.74	9.24	0.73	1820	-5.40	10.01	-1.92	1925	0.10	1.20	0.11
1716	-2.28	7.55	-0.62	1821	-5.02	12.19	-2.03	1926	-0.41	1.48	-0.10
1717	-2.95	7.74	-1.22	1822	-5.34	12.67	-2.14	1927	-1.86	3.40	-0.70
1718	-1.49	5.03	-0.50	1823	0.85	9.79	0.73	1928	-0.28	4.68	0.05
1719	1.72	6.38	0.99	1824	3.06	5.98	2.01	1929	-0.79	1.45	-0.32

Year				Year				Year			
1720	3.63	7.17	2.36	**1825**	3.81	7.36	2.43	**1930**	-2.11	3.90	-0.78
1721	-0.57	6.94	0.30	**1826**	-1.23	9.65	0.12	**1931**	-3.43	6.66	-1.30
1722	-5.06	11.69	-1.59	**1827**	-3.34	8.01	-1.40	**1932**	-1.79	5.67	-0.64
1723	-2.42	8.65	-0.73	**1828**	-0.37	7.27	0.10	**1933**	-1.65	4.41	-0.71
1724	2.16	7.98	1.21	**1829**	1.78	3.11	1.12	**1934**	-0.21	4.06	0.06
1725	2.07	5.87	1.11	**1830**	-1.37	4.89	-0.29	**1935**	0.51	1.65	0.33
1726	3.87	6.99	2.34	**1831**	0.39	4.52	0.36	**1936**	0.65	1.36	0.50
1727	-1.19	9.33	0.12	**1832**	-1.50	5.37	-0.32	**1937**	2.27	5.85	1.32
1728	0.65	7.48	0.57	**1833**	-3.10	7.05	-1.29	**1938**	1.18	3.61	0.61
1729	3.80	6.87	2.30	**1834**	-1.70	5.43	-0.61	**1939**	2.32	4.12	1.45
1730	-3.33	11.91	-0.65	**1835**	-2.82	5.71	-1.12	**1940**	8.42	24.21	4.28
1731	-5.04	13.16	-2.00	**1836**	3.40	12.59	1.84	**1941**	5.93	15.44	3.19
1732	-0.61	11.49	0.15	**1837**	2.63	8.38	1.22	**1942**	4.21	10.87	2.36
1733	-2.01	6.72	-0.53	**1838**	2.96	5.95	1.98	**1943**	2.23	6.75	1.10
1734	0.99	8.20	0.72	**1839**	2.37	5.41	1.56	**1944**	2.00	4.59	1.33
1735	1.06	3.61	0.54	**1840**	-0.35	4.88	0.23	**1945**	2.13	4.40	1.48
1736	-1.01	3.62	-0.22	**1841**	-1.62	2.95	-0.64	**1946**	2.34	4.73	1.60
1737	2.56	9.47	1.42	**1842**	-3.91	7.30	-1.37	**1947**	4.84	8.46	2.79
1738	-0.73	9.05	0.39	**1843**	-5.92	11.94	-2.19	**1948**	5.01	10.18	3.21
1739	-1.77	4.27	-0.78	**1844**	0.89	10.34	0.77	**1949**	2.15	6.89	1.01
1740	4.82	15.60	2.52	**1845**	0.34	5.67	0.44	**1950**	2.99	5.61	1.91
1741	4.63	12.05	2.55	**1846**	5.74	18.54	2.95	**1951**	5.96	10.42	3.37
1742	-1.71	13.46	0.16	**1847**	4.12	11.25	2.18	**1952**	6.61	13.14	4.09

Table 10.4 (cont.)

	(a)	(b)	(c)		(a)	(b)	(c)		(a)	(b)	(c)
1743	-3.20	10.18	-1.08	1848	-5.31	18.97	-1.00	1953	2.75	9.00	1.27
1744	-7.53	13.48	-2.56	1849	-3.41	15.89	-0.85	1954	1.59	4.26	0.94
1745	-0.86	16.33	0.20	1850	-3.16	7.58	-1.33	1955	3.71	6.48	2.19
1746	5.13	16.05	2.68	1851	-1.51	5.17	-0.50	1956	3.57	7.42	2.37
1747	-0.95	11.56	0.48	1852	0.25	2.89	0.24	1957	2.64	6.29	1.66
1748	0.98	6.55	0.67	1853	7.56	24.21	3.80	1958	2.07	4.92	1.33
1749	1.50	4.55	0.76	1854	4.45	13.18	2.12	1959	0.57	4.15	0.42
1750	-0.26	3.17	0.15	1855	1.75	8.08	0.95	1960	0.76	1.44	0.55
1751	1.14	4.21	0.68	1856	0.58	2.38	0.33	1961	2.23	4.85	1.33
1752	4.42	7.72	2.56	1857	-1.16	3.85	-0.33	1962	3.10	5.98	2.01
1753	0.49	8.87	0.65	1858	-6.23	15.64	-1.84	1963	1.47	4.40	0.76
1754	-1.06	2.57	-0.49	1859	-0.83	15.76	0.20	1964	2.59	4.73	1.64
1755	-3.30	7.47	-1.09	1860	4.40	13.81	2.33	1965	3.16	6.04	2.03
1756	2.81	10.47	1.54	1861	0.86	11.37	0.87	1966	2.87	6.12	1.93
1757	13.35	24.69	6.95	1862	-0.16	1.89	0.09	1967	1.53	4.38	0.84
1758	1.16	28.31	1.78	1863	-2.63	8.18	-0.73	1968	3.13	5.56	1.90
1759	-8.85	15.78	-2.95	1864	-1.13	4.86	-0.32	1969	3.72	7.16	2.37
1760	-4.85	15.35	-1.60	1865	0.80	2.96	0.49	1970	4.46	8.68	2.82
1761	-0.92	13.34	0.08	1866	3.99	7.79	2.30	1971	6.26	11.66	3.72
1762	1.55	5.73	0.90	1867	3.58	8.01	2.30	1972	4.51	10.57	2.75

Year				Year				Year			
1763	1.69	4.46	1.00	1868	−0.55	6.64	0.29	1973	6.06	11.67	3.70
1764	5.54	11.30	3.08	1869	−4.84	8.66	−1.71	1974	9.71	17.48	5.40
1765	3.24	9.15	1.69	1870	−0.57	10.78	0.14	1975	12.64	23.68	7.09
1766	0.47	8.44	0.62	1871	1.88	5.72	1.08	1976	8.26	20.42	4.54
1767	6.94	22.42	3.51	1872	3.24	5.94	2.02	1977	8.56	18.13	5.24
1768	1.01	18.33	1.25	1873	0.66	6.24	0.56	1978	4.26	12.65	2.03
1769	−8.10	23.39	−2.16	1874	−2.24	7.39	−0.60	1979	7.38	13.57	4.28
1770	0.82	17.83	0.96	1875	−1.36	5.20	−0.41	1980	9.02	17.27	5.30
1771	4.26	7.99	2.63	1876	−0.15	2.84	0.04	1981	6.85	15.81	4.07
1772	3.28	7.45	2.10	1877	−0.04	0.45	0.03	1982	4.79	11.99	2.73
1773	0.45	7.83	0.58	1878	−1.87	6.19	−0.51	1983	3.02	8.24	1.65
1774	−0.72	2.48	−0.19	1879	−3.53	6.98	−1.35	1984	3.00	6.61	1.98
1775	−0.70	2.22	−0.28	1880	0.52	6.01	0.47	1985	3.47	6.93	2.28
1776	−3.93	12.52	−1.04	1881	−0.24	2.88	0.14	1986	2.24	5.72	1.34
1777	0.66	7.65	0.58	1882	−0.13	2.44	0.04	1987	2.38	5.04	1.63
1778	1.31	4.28	0.65	1883	0.02	0.39	0.04	1988	2.77	5.51	1.85
1779	−2.10	7.41	−0.46	1884	−2.06	6.79	−0.56	1989	3.81	7.17	2.38
1780	−0.42	8.10	0.11	1885	−2.63	6.40	−1.13	1990	4.78	9.13	2.97
1781	5.25	16.68	2.73	1886	−0.90	4.59	−0.24	1991	4.92	10.03	3.16
1782	0.81	14.18	1.00	1887	−1.71	3.06	−0.66	1992	2.64	7.50	1.39
1783	0.28	0.88	0.16	1888	−0.23	4.04	0.05	1993	1.69	4.72	0.94
1784	−2.72	8.99	−0.72	1889	0.45	1.50	0.29	1994	1.53	3.53	1.04
1785	−3.19	8.22	−1.33	1890	0.36	1.09	0.21	1995	2.13	4.05	1.41

Table 10.4 (cont.)

	(a)	(b)	(c)		(a)	(b)	(c)		(a)	(b)	(c)
1786	-0.51	7.84	0.06	1891	0.79	1.40	0.54	1996	1.86	4.01	1.29
1787	0.81	3.01	0.50	1892	0.36	1.08	0.21	1997	-1.08	4.13	0.07
1788	1.26	2.78	0.90	1893	-1.00	3.32	-0.29	1998	-1.19	3.44	0.00
1789	0.14	2.65	0.21	1894	-2.21	4.52	-0.90	1999	-1.19	2.90	-0.04
1790	3.26	10.55	1.76	1895	-1.03	3.48	-0.36	2000	-1.48	2.20	-0.15
1791	0.50	9.02	0.66	1896	-0.20	2.80	0.01	2001	-0.77	1.15	-0.04
1792	-1.97	3.55	-0.76	1897	1.16	3.74	0.68	2002	-1.21	2.32	-0.08
1793	2.32	8.58	1.29	1898	1.43	3.14	1.01	2003	-1.08	2.51	-0.04
1794	2.02	6.04	1.02	1899	-0.22	2.64	0.13	2004	-1.12	2.65	-0.04
1795	8.08	20.90	4.20	1900	1.72	5.85	0.98	2005	-0.59	1.78	0.15
1796	1.61	19.75	1.47	1901	0.36	6.38	0.48	2006	-0.45	2.41	0.19
1797	-4.22	14.00	-1.07	1902	-0.04	0.75	0.01	2007	-0.38	2.60	0.20
1798	-0.80	15.24	0.19	1903	0.76	2.44	0.46	2008	0.67	3.85	1.07
1799	9.36	30.12	4.61	1904	-0.16	1.89	0.09	2009	-0.14	3.87	0.30
1800	15.61	29.38	8.63	1905	0.13	1.06	0.11	2010	0.58	3.56	0.98
1801	1.62	30.45	1.98	1906	0.02	0.81	0.07	2011	1.43	5.17	1.49
1802	-13.30	34.02	-3.65	1907	0.98	3.16	0.59	2012	0.37	4.40	0.48
1803	-1.91	35.83	0.41	1908	1.05	2.41	0.74	2013	0.08	3.22	0.40
1804	2.94	9.51	1.60	1909	0.18	2.45	0.21	2014	-0.62	4.25	0.17
1805	7.96	14.19	4.47	1910	1.42	4.56	0.83	2015	-1.17	2.18	-0.09
1806	-1.18	14.51	0.59	1911	0.26	3.86	0.32	2016	-0.35	0.31	0.02

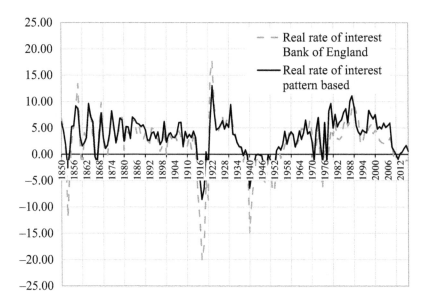

FIGURE 10.2 Measures of the short-term real interest rate for the United Kingdom

the basis of the calculations goes as far back as 1695. However, the data only show significant variations starting in the middle of the 19th century. Hence, for comparison of different ways of calculating the real rate of interest, we chose a data window from 1850 to 2016. Figure 10.2 shows the measure of the real short-term interest rate based on the generalized pattern-based approach as well as the real rate reported by the Bank of England. As it is plain to see, the series computed with the pattern-based measure of expected inflation has less variance and is rarely negative.

One remarkable aspect of the expectations series using the pattern-based approach concerns the level of real rates in recent decades: The data show a period of historically high interest rates starting in the 1980s and ending only after the financial crisis of 2007. According to our new estimates, the real short-run interest rate was 2 percentage points higher (6.53 instead of 4.46) than what the Bank of England measure suggests for the same period. In fact, the average rate according to the new measure is almost equal to the rate during an earlier period (1921–1932) of markedly elevated yields: during the interwar period of high rates, the average rate was 6.54 percent. Interestingly, the similarities regarding monetary policy during these two periods of high rates in the United Kingdom have been noted in the literature (see Eichengreen, 2004, and Dimsdale, 2015). Our present calculations further document the already known similarities. The new series for the real rate of interest should be relevant for studies of historical investment activity and international capital flows.

Finally, the constructed series of expected inflation is applied in an econometric piece of analysis of UK inflation. Concretely, the hybrid New Keynesian Phillips Curve (NKPC) in the form of

$$\pi_t = \gamma_0 + \gamma_1 \pi_{t-1} + \gamma_2 F_t(\pi_{t+1}) + \gamma_3 MC_t + \varepsilon_t, \tag{10.4}$$

is estimated for the United Kingdom. Again, in order to illustrate the possibilities of our approach, this macroeconomic relationship is estimated with annual data for the period of 1925–2016. No survey data for expected inflation is available for this period. Note, that the sample includes the years of the great depression. The result of the instrumental variable estimate (using lagged values as instruments) is

$$\pi_t = 0.007 + 0.563\pi_{t-1} + 0.438F_t(\pi_{t+1}) + 0.080MC_t + \varepsilon_t.$$
$$\quad (0.002) \quad (0.114) \qquad (0.151) \qquad\quad (0.048) \tag{10.5}$$
$$\overline{R}^2 = 0.852, \quad SEE = 0.017, \quad DW = 1.835$$

Inflation is measured by the (factor cost-based) GDP deflator, expected inflation is of the pattern-based type, and the marginal cost variable is estimated as the deviation of real GDP from a log-linear trend.[7] Lagged inflation and expected inflation contribute significantly to explaining the course of inflation in the United Kingdom. The estimated coefficients are in line with the estimates for the USA from Chapter 8. Furthermore, the estimates are in the range of coefficient values reported in the literature survey of Mavroeidis et al. (2014).

---

[7] The data for the estimates are drawn from the same Bank of England source already noted: www.bankofengland.co.uk/statistics/research-datasets.

In conclusion, our NKPC estimate with pattern-based expected inflation may go some way toward addressing the doubts concerning the relevance of this macroeconomic relationship for the United Kingdom as expressed, for example, by Nason and Smith (2008).

10.6 SUMMARY AND CONCLUSIONS

In this chapter, the hypothesis of pattern-based expectations is developed in its generalized version. For this purpose, a new set of expectations data covering all possible price-level paths is elicited. The gain in generality is made possible by documenting expectations for patterns that are shortened compared to the approach presented earlier. With the new and generalized approach, it becomes straightforward to quantify expected inflation for any country and any historical period. In particular, the approach becomes applicable to situations with increases or decreases of the general level of prices. In short, with the approach presented here, the empirical researcher does not have to scrutinize the particular history of inflation before computing pattern-based expectations.

A first application of the generalized approach is presented for the United Kingdom. Based on data published by the Bank of England, it is feasible to compute inflation expectations for as far back as the early 18th century. These data, including estimates of the uncertainty of short-term inflation expectations, are documented and discussed. Finally, the estimation of a hybrid New Keynesian Phillips curve covering more than 90 years of all data shows just one possible econometric application of our approach.

APPENDIX 10.1 COMPARING EXPECTATIONS ACROSS SUBJECT POOLS

In the following, we analyze the new data gathered for this chapter particularly with a view to deciding whether to pool data of the three different runs. Possible differences in the average responses are evaluated by estimating regressions relating the expected change for the different patterns from one run to the expected change of another run. It turns out that when comparing short-run expectations across different groups of subjects, the results are affected by the educational back-ground although not very much.[8] The two following regressions illustrate the point. The subscripts of the variables in the equations identify the pattern (with the index j running from 1 to 25), the time period, and the group of subjects (runs I, II, III). The first regression relates the short-run expectations of run III (subjects with no background in economics) to those of run I (subjects with economics background):

$$P^e_{j,4,run\,III} - P_{j,3} = -0.076 + 0.983(P^e_{j,4,run\,I} - P_{j,3})$$
$$(0.058)\quad(0.064)$$
$$\overline{R}^2 = 0.909, \quad SEE = 0.292$$
$$(A10.1)$$

The next regression relates the short-run expectations from the two runs (I and II) with the economically literate subjects.[9]

$$P^e_{j,4,run\,II} - P_{j,3} = -0.048 + 1.020(P^e_{j,4,run\,I} - P_{j,3})$$
$$(0.031)\quad(0.035)$$
$$\overline{R}^2 = 0.972, \quad SEE = 0.159$$
$$(A10.2)$$

Clearly, a common background in economics makes expectations more similar as, for example, seen by the markedly higher R^2 of Eq. (A10.2) compared to Eq. (A10.1). Differences in the way of making predictions become more apparent when comparing long-term expectations across subjects with different backgrounds. The following regression relates the five-year-ahead expectations comparing the same groups as in Eq. (A10.1):

$$P^e_{j,8,run\,III} - P_{j,3} = -10.919 + 1.104(P^e_{j,8,run\,I} - P_{j,3})$$
$$(2.392)\quad(0.023)$$
$$\overline{R}^2 = 0.989, \quad SEE = 0.501$$
$$(A10.3)$$

Here, the p value for the parameter restriction that the constant is zero and the slope coefficient is 1 turns out to be less than 0.01. Overall, economic literacy appears to affect the formation of expectations.

---

[8] The p value of the comparison of run I against run II is 0.291, for run I against run III it is 0.425, and for run II against run III it is 0.638.

[9] However, when comparing long-run expectations, it becomes clear that subjects without any economic training differ in the way they make predictions.

APPENDIX IO.2 LIMITATIONS OF AN ECONOMETRIC REPRESENTATION OF THE LABORATORY DATA

It is tempting to try to econometrically condense the expectations data into a nonlinear model that could serve as a basis for modeling expectations. Consider estimating a specification for our data with a differentiation of patterns even finer than in Eqs. (10.2) and (10.3). For the following estimate, the trending patterns are further divided into three classes. These classes differ regarding the absolute total change of the series over the last two periods. Dummy variable D^{Tr-2} identifies patterns where absolute change is two, D^{Tr-3} marks cases where this change is equal to three, and D^{Tr-4} stands for cases where this change is four. Accordingly, for example, pattern 100, 101, 102 belongs to the first class, 100, 102, 103 to the second, and 100, 102, 104 to the third class. The new estimate with the finer differentiation of trending patterns for short-run expectations is the following:

$$P^e_{j,4} - P_{j,3} = 0.886(P_{j,3} - P_{j,2})D^{Tr-2} + 0.859(P_{j,3} - P_{j,2})D^{Tr-3}$$
$$(0.108) \qquad\qquad\qquad (0.048)$$
$$+ 0.803(P_{j,3} - P_{j,2})D^{Tr-4} + 0.648(P_{j,3} - P_{j,2})D^{TO} + 0.340(P_{j,3} - P_{j,2})D^{Re}$$
$$(0.054) \qquad\qquad\qquad (0.048) \qquad\qquad\qquad (0.034)$$

$$\overline{R}^2 = 0.977, \quad SEE = 0.153 \qquad\qquad\qquad\qquad (A10.4)$$

The key finding here is the decline of the first three estimated coefficients as the trend growth of prices increases. This result indicates that the elasticity of expectations (0.886, 0.859, 0.803) tends to decrease as inflation rises. This is a sign of the regressiveness of expectations. Hence, even with the specificity of the results of Eq. (A10.4), we would have no empirical handle for modeling expectations when the underlying inflation is higher than 2 percent, for example, in the range of 5, 10, or more percentage points. This is exactly the point captured by the scaling relationship in our approach.

There exists yet another difficulty with any formulation along the lines set out in Section 10.3 and Eq. (A10.4). Applying such an equation with threshold effects for the computation of expectations could easily generate implausible outcomes. Consider 100, 100, 105, together with 100, 100.001, 105, and 100, 99.999, 105 as exemplary empirical courses of the CPI. The first case (a take-off), according to Eq. (10.2), would imply an expected change of 3.2 percent. The second case (a trend) would imply an expected change of 4.2 percent while the third case (a reversal) would set expected inflation to 1.7 percent. To an observer of the CPI trying to make up his mind, the three cases would look indistinguishable. This is exactly the point addressed with the concept of similarity matching. Independently of which of the three cases above is assessed with the similarity function introduced in Chapter 5, the take-off pattern would receive a weight of 0.9992 and only minimal weights would go to the trending and the reversal patterns. For concreteness, the expected one-year-ahead inflation calculated on the data gathered for this chapter would come out as 2.74 percent.

11 A Detour to Income Expectations

11.1 INTRODUCTION

Expected inflation is the major topic of this book. Yet, as we have noted before, the approach of pattern-based expectations can be applied to other macroeconomic variables as well. The second key variable besides inflation expectations that we have introduced and studied is the expected income. More concretely, Chapter 3 documents the laboratory data concerning subjective expectations of real GDP for patterns of length four.[1] In this chapter, the generalized approach set out in Chapter 10 is extended to the case of income expectations. Accordingly, a new group of subjects sees the 25 possible patterns of length three, together with the information that the variable in question depicts the real GDP.[2] Otherwise, the same instructions known from treatment (iii) are used again.

11.2 EXPECTATIONS DATA

Table 11.1 displays the elicited data in terms of means for the one-year and the five-year-ahead expectations as well as information on the distribution of the answers. Further, Table 11.2 gives the data on the uncertainty regarding short- and long-term expected aggregate income.

Short-run expectations for the real GDP prove to be symmetric, just as previously found for the CPI expectations. This means that the extrapolated change after a pattern like 100, 101, 102 is equal (i.e., not statistically different) to the predicted change after the pattern 100,

---

[1] Collecting separate data for income expectations is warranted given the importance of context in pattern extrapolation noted earlier.

[2] The laboratory instructions explain that the variable to be forecast is the real gross domestic product of an unknown country. Subjects had a background of at least one course of macroeconomics. A total of 48 subjects are studied under this treatment.

Table 11.1 Real GDP expectations for periods 4 (one-year-ahead) and 8 (five-year-ahead)

Pattern	Time 1	2	3	Mean 4	Upper 95%	Lower 5%	Mean 8	Upper 95%	Lower 5%
1	100	102	104	105.6917	106.00	105.00	109.2417	114.00	103.88
2	100	102	103	103.7188	104.40	103.00	105.3313	104.40	103.00
3	100	102	102	101.9813	103.00	100.94	103.2667	103.00	100.94
4	100	102	101	100.6125	102.33	99.14	101.2292	102.33	99.14
5	100	102	100	99.6708	102.00	97.68	99.8771	102.00	97.68
6	100	101	103	104.7208	106.00	103.61	108.4375	106.00	103.61
7	100	101	102	102.9042	103.10	102.00	105.4188	103.10	102.00
8	100	101	101	101.1833	102.00	100.00	102.0021	102.00	100.00
9	100	101	100	99.6438	101.00	98.32	99.7604	101.00	98.32
10	100	101	99	97.9021	100.00	96.04	97.4458	100.00	96.04
11	100	100	102	103.3167	104.83	102.00	105.9958	104.83	102.00
12	100	100	101	101.6063	102.63	101.00	103.4229	102.63	101.00
13	100	100	100	100.0875	101.00	99.00	100.4104	101.00	99.00
14	100	100	99	98.2917	99.00	97.11	97.8313	99.00	97.11
15	100	100	98	96.8042	98.00	95.14	95.8000	98.00	95.14
16	100	99	101	102.0125	103.07	100.00	103.9688	103.07	100.00
17	100	99	100	100.2667	101.70	99.00	101.3250	101.70	99.00
18	100	99	99	98.9542	100.00	98.00	99.8917	100.00	98.00
19	100	99	98	96.9813	98.00	96.00	95.4688	99.65	91.00
20	100	99	97	95.5375	96.86	94.04	93.2625	98.83	86.70
21	100	98	100	100.7333	102.00	98.35	102.1979	106.33	98.87
22	100	98	99	99.3625	100.83	97.55	100.3229	103.33	96.68
23	100	98	98	97.8417	99.00	97.00	97.8104	102.00	93.35
24	100	98	97	96.1646	97.00	95.34	95.6792	101.80	92.00
25	100	98	96	94.4604	95.65	93.44	91.7979	98.65	86.00

Table 11.2 Measures of one-year- and five-year-ahead uncertainty of real GDP expectations

Pattern	Time 1	2	3	Mean 4	Mean of upper 75%	Mean of lower 25%	Mean 8	Mean of upper 75%	Mean of lower 25%
1	100	102	104	105.6917	107.0104	104.5583	109.2417	111.9292	106.9542
2	100	102	103	103.7188	104.8792	102.5583	105.3313	107.5563	102.8333
3	100	102	102	101.9813	103.3625	100.6875	103.2667	105.5625	100.6333
4	100	102	101	100.6125	102.2104	99.1604	101.2292	103.9208	98.2833
5	100	102	100	99.6708	101.0854	97.9813	99.8771	102.5813	96.9104
6	100	101	103	104.7208	106.0208	103.3708	108.4375	110.8250	105.3333
7	100	101	102	102.9042	103.9875	101.9438	105.4188	107.5917	103.3125
8	100	101	101	101.1833	102.3729	99.8979	102.0021	103.9646	99.7313
9	100	101	100	99.6438	100.9188	98.2375	99.7604	102.2479	96.8438
10	100	101	99	97.9021	99.6000	96.3896	97.4458	100.5167	94.9500
11	100	100	102	103.3167	104.7708	101.9646	105.9958	108.1854	103.2500
12	100	100	101	101.6063	102.8792	100.5125	103.4229	105.3938	101.2979
13	100	100	100	100.0875	101.1250	99.0708	100.4104	102.5708	98.0542
14	100	100	99	98.2917	99.6729	96.9271	97.8313	100.2813	95.3896
15	100	100	98	96.8042	98.5083	95.2417	95.8000	98.6083	92.8938
16	100	99	101	102.0125	103.4521	100.4500	103.9688	106.2021	101.1167
17	100	99	100	100.2667	101.5021	98.9500	101.3250	103.6354	98.7479
18	100	99	99	98.9542	100.3646	97.8188	99.8917	102.0979	97.2000
19	100	99	98	96.9813	98.1417	95.8938	95.4688	97.9354	93.0938
20	100	99	97	95.5375	96.9417	94.0729	93.2625	96.1583	90.6146
21	100	98	100	100.7333	102.1646	98.8333	102.1979	104.8646	99.0188
22	100	98	99	99.3625	100.9208	98.0500	100.3229	102.7771	97.5792
23	100	98	98	97.8417	99.2083	96.5375	97.8104	100.2792	95.1813
24	100	98	97	96.1646	97.4854	94.8125	95.6792	98.0458	93.1271
25	100	98	96	94.4604	95.7625	93.0813	91.7979	94.9271	89.1042

Table 11.3 *The shortened set of non-collinear patterns and corresponding short-term GDP expectations*[*]

Pattern	Time 1	2	3	Expected change
1	100	102	103	0.7771
2	100	102	101	−0.3750
3	100	101	103	1.5917
4	100	101	102	0.9315
5	100	101	101	0.0768
6	100	101	100	−0.3040
7	100	101	99	−1.0552
8	100	100	101	0.6792
9	100	100	100	0.0000
10	100	100	99	−0.6792
11	100	99	101	1.0552
12	100	99	100	0.3040
13	100	99	99	−0.0768
14	100	99	98	−0.9315
15	100	99	97	−1.5917
16	100	98	99	0.3750
17	100	98	97	−0.7771

[*] The tabulated data are averaged over patterns with steps of 1 and their respective pattern with steps of 2 weighted by $1/(2^{0.841})$ and averages over symmetrical cases (expectations for declining patterns are weighted by −1).

99, 98 multiplied by −1. Table 11.3 presents the parsimonious set of expectations (reduced to 17 patterns) that takes into account the tested symmetry proposition. These are the data that go into the computation of time series of GDP expectations. Furthermore, the modeling makes use of the by now well-known elements of scaling and similarity matching.[3] In the following section, this new

[3] For short-term GDP expectations, the estimated scaling factor is 0.841. For long-term expectations, the scaling factor is estimated as 0.691. The similarity matching algorithm is amended for the case where the historical series does not change over

income expectations model is applied to an intensely debated issue of applied macroeconomics: why was the US recession after the financial crisis of 2007 so long and so deep?

11.3   INCOME EXPECTATIONS AND THE COURSE OF THE GREAT RECESSION

In several industrial countries, the recession in the wake of the financial crisis was remarkably deep and long. Because of its extraordinary proportion, this downturn has been labeled the great recession. Never since the 1930s did the world experience a similar slump in economic activity. It is not the place here to survey and assess the various explanations of the crisis.[4] Neither will we cover in any detail the various dimensions of the recession. Instead, this section pursues the notion that income expectations, and the related uncertainty, were important drivers of this downturn. Effects of this sort have already been documented empirically by several researchers: De Nardi et al. (2012), French et al. (2013), and Pistaferri (2016) focus on the effects of expectations on US consumption during the great recession. Jurado et al. (2015) and Banerjee et al. (2015) widen the scope of the analysis by studying the effect of income uncertainty on investment. For a detailed theoretical account of uncertainty effects on effective demand see Basu and Bundick (2017). The cited studies work with various measures of income expectations and its uncertainty ranging from survey data from the University of Michigan to econometric proxies. Overall, these analyses find that low expected income growth and rising uncertainty depressed consumption and investment contributing to the slow economic recovery.

Does an analysis with pattern-based measures of expected GDP and its uncertainty support these insights? In order to answer this

three periods. In this case, the pattern 100, 100, 100 (with an expected mean change of zero) receives a weight of one. As before with CPI expectations, the hypothesis of symmetry for the five-year-ahead GDP expectations is not empirically supported.

[4] The literature on the causes and forms of the great recession is multifaceted. As a start, Lo (2012) gives an overview of the mechanisms behind the financial crisis and Ng and Wright (2013) offer a review of empirical findings and the ensuing challenges for macroeconomic modeling.

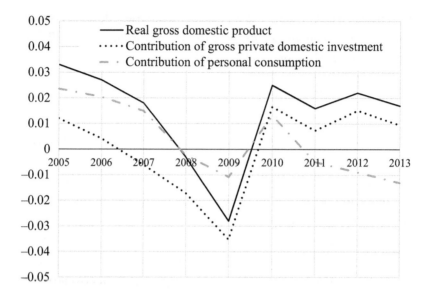

FIGURE 11.1 US GDP growth and contributions of consumption and investment

question, let us look at the course of the real GDP for the USA just before and after the great recession. Figure 11.1 depicts growth rates of GDP together with the contributions of its key components namely consumption and investment.[5] These data show that early in the recession, investment plunged sharply and it only recovered in 2010. The decline in consumption further contributed to the onset of the recession. In fact, weak consumption expenditures, after a short recovery in 2010, slowed output growth for several years.[6]

The fact that we analyze annual data here and now turn to the corresponding expectations should not be interpreted as saying that the generalized approach developed in Chapter 10 could not be

[5] The contributions of various components to GDP growth are measured by their growth rate weighted with their relative weight in GDP from the previous year. All data used in this chapter come from the Federal Reserve Bank of St. Louis web portal https://fred.stlouisfed.org/.

[6] Looking at the remaining components of aggregated demand, it becomes clear that a decline in imports (hence a substitution toward domestic goods) and government expenditures helped to moderate the recession.

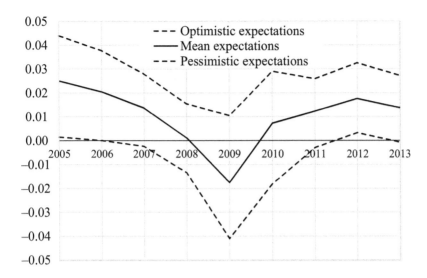

FIGURE 11.2 Expectations of short-term US real GDP growth with uncertainty band
(The upper dashed line marks the estimated growth according to the mean answers to the 75 percent quantile question in the laboratory survey. The lower dashed line is the corresponding 25 percent quantile.)

applied to monthly or quarterly data. Annual data are simply better suited here to bring out the general tendencies. When looking at the pattern-based expectations, it becomes apparent that the course of both expected income and income uncertainty contributed to the weakness of the US macroeconomy. Here, only short-term expectations shall be discussed since an assessment looking at long-run measures leads basically to the same conclusion. Growth of expected income according to the pattern approach started to slow down in 2006 as can be seen in Figure 11.2. By 2009, expected growth was negative and for almost a decade has not come back to its pre-crisis level.[7] Overall, the story told by our measure of expected income growth fits well with the findings reported in the literature.

---

[7] The five-year average of expected GDP growth for the period ending in 2006 was 2.2 percent.

Furthermore, the effect of increasing uncertainty of expected income on the course of the economy can be traced. Consider Figure 11.2 once more. The display shows the course of the mean income expectations together with the upper and lower border of the interquartile range. The lower dashed line indicates where, according to the pattern-based measure, subjects foresaw future income growth with a 25 percent probability. This can be termed the pessimistic GDP scenario, while the course of the upper dashed line would be the optimistic scenario. The numbers for the pessimistic scenario indicate that this outlook turns gloomy in 2007 and in 2008. The range of possible negative developments downright nosedives in 2009.[8] The wedge between the optimistic and the pessimistic course for future GDP is around 3 percent in 2007 and 2008 and rises to 5.2 and 4.7 percent in 2009 and 2010, respectively. Thereafter, it goes back to less than 3 percent. Thus, from this perspective, the weak recovery of the US economy in 2010 and onward *cannot* be attributed to uncertainty of income growth. Rather, the drag appears to have come from slow growth of expected income. This assessment supports the findings of De Nardi et al. (2012) and French et al. (2013) and contrasts with the position of Banerjee et al. (2015).

11.4   SUMMARY AND CONCLUSIONS

The present chapter documents expectations concerning real GDP for a general set of circumstances. These laboratory data serve the modeling of short- and long-run aggregate income expectations. The described method of computing expected GDP should be helpful for researchers in various fields. In particular, authors of historical studies of consumption will benefit from the new approach. Likewise, econometric investigations become now possible for countries where no survey measures of expected income are available. As before for expected inflation, a worksheet for computing expectations of

---

[8] Rötheli (2015) puts the theme of this analysis of expectations' role in the wider context of Keynes' hypothesis of the instability of long-term expectations.

aggregate income growth can be downloaded from the publisher's website for this book.

The great recession of recent years in the USA is studied to give an example of how the new expectations model can help to shed light on important macroeconomic phenomena. It turns out that the new measure of expected income growth and income uncertainty helps to explain the depth of the recession. By contrast, the slow recovery of expected income – and not its uncertainty – is seen here as the main reason for the shallow recovery. Hence, the use of pattern-based expectations adds to the narrative regarding the course of the US economy. The pattern-based approach should be of even greater merit when studying economies and times where no data on income expectations and uncertainty are available from surveys.

APPENDIX II.I   WHAT GOES UP MUST COME DOWN

This appendix discusses the simulated course of one-year-ahead expectations after a temporary upward deviation of real GDP from trend. The task here is to document the dynamics of expectations after a hump-shaped shock to the underlying series. This is the sort of exercise used by Beshears et al. (2013) to study elements of human expectations dynamics. Based on the analysis of experimental data, these authors conclude that, for example, after a short-lived temporary (i.e., self-correcting) shock to income, subjects tend to underestimate mean reversion even if the correction takes only 10 periods (presumably quarters) to completion. Here, we simulate a GDP process of the sort just described and look at the implied course of pattern-based expectations.

More concretely, annual one-year- and five-year-ahead expectations for a GDP series are generated for the following sequence of deviations from its long-run trend over nine years: 0, 0, 0, 0.01, 0.015, 0.01, 0, 0, 0. Thus, in year four there is a rise by 1.0 percent above trend, followed by 1.5 percent above trend and so forth. By year seven, the GDP series is back to its trend. Hence, in terms of quarterly observation, this is the sort of dynamics studied by Beshears et al. (2013). In order to find out how secular growth affects the outcome, different annual trend growth rates for GDP ranging from 0 to 3 percent are considered. The resulting numbers help to evaluate whether short- and long-run expectations indeed tend to exceed the actual development. Table A11.1 shows deviations of short- and long-run expectations (formed in period 4) from the actual course of GDP. The findings are

Table A11.1 *Deviations of one-year- and five-year-ahead expected GDP from its actual course*

Trend growth rate in percent	One-year-ahead expectations minus realization of GDP	Five-year-ahead expectations minus realization of GDP
0.0	0.18	3.44
0.5	0.12	2.48
1.0	0.08	1.25
1.5	−0.04	−0.27
2.0	−0.19	−1.94
2.5	−0.37	−3.67
3.0	−0.55	−5.43

interesting: for low trend growth, it is found that short-run expectations overshoot and five-year-ahead expectations also exceed the realized GDP value (in period 9). Yet, as the trend growth of GDP rises, these findings change. Intriguingly, for a trend growth rate of 1.5 percent (realistic for many countries) the observed expectations errors are very close to zero. Hence, pattern-based GDP expectations appear to be "ecologically rational" in the sense of Smith (2003).

12 The Fisher Effect in Historical Times

12.1 INTRODUCTION

The Fisher effect, that is, the theoretical prediction that nominal interest rates should adjust to changes in inflation expectations has been the subject of a variety of empirical studies. Chapter 9 has already presented evidence on this hypothesis with newer data. Interestingly, this theoretical proposition has not fared well for the historical data that Fisher (1930) himself studied. Irving Fisher found for the USA that the adjustment of interest rates takes about 20 years and even then is only partial. Furthermore, nominal interest rates for various countries, according to Fisher, do not adjust one-to-one to changes in inflation as witnessed by the fact that real rates of interest are lower in times of high inflation than in times of low inflation. Researchers after Fisher have largely confirmed this finding.[1] A particularly interesting historical episode – from 1869 to 1913, under the gold standard – even suggests an outright contradiction of the Fisher hypothesis as we will explain. It is to these intriguing findings that this chapter turns.

A key element in the empirical testing of the Fisher effect is the modeling of expected inflation. The early literature including Fisher's own study used lagged rates of inflation as a proxy for expected inflation. His own statistical investigation led Fisher to conclude that the interest rate takes several decades to adjust to changes in the level of inflation. For the USA, the statistical analysis suggested that the adjustment took roughly 20 years, whereas for the United Kingdom lags of up to 28 years were reported. More recent research applying the

---

[1] Examples and hints to further studies can found in Sargent (1973), Friedman and Schwartz (1982), Thies (1985), and Cooray (2003).

concept of rational expectations has not fundamentally reversed these findings. Mishkin (1992), by econometrically implementing the rational expectation hypothesis, had to concur with Fisher that the adjustment of interest rates happens only over long periods of time and confirmed the partial, that is, not one-to-one, adjustment to changes in the rate of inflation.

In the empirical study that follows, we reexamine the nexus between inflation and nominal interest rates with Fisher's original historical data using the new behavioral measure of expected inflation. The first part of this investigation covers the broad international data set Fisher used in his famous analysis. To be concrete, Section 12.2 presents an econometric study of Fisher's data on interest rates and price trends for six countries. This investigation largely replicates Fisher's results when using lagged inflation as a proxy for expected inflation. However, when working with the new behavioral model of expectations, the findings are altered remarkably: we find more evidence supporting Fisher's theoretical proposition than Fisher himself was able to report.

Section 12.3 then focuses on a particularly interesting subset of the data studied by Irving Fisher. The country studied is the USA and the period in question is between 1869 and World War I. The comovement of inflation and interest rates in the decades after the American civil war has puzzled empirical researchers since Fisher's days. Studies, for example, by Summers (1983) and Barsky and DeLong (1991) using a variety of econometric methods document that interest rates in the period prior to World War I tended to show no significant adjustment to changes in inflation. The period under investigation is divided into a first part showing a decline in the aggregate price level followed by a second, about equally long, in part characterized by rising prices. It is thus perplexing that the average nominal interest rate during the first deflationary episode is higher by more than one percentage point than in the second inflationary period. This is clearly difficult to square with Fisher's hypothesized connection between interest rates and inflation. However, as we will show, Fisher's

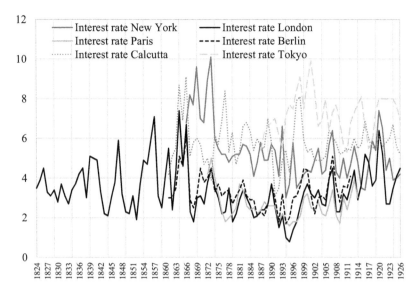

FIGURE I2.I Nominal interest rates in financial centers of six countries

hypothetical proposition gains support when the behavioral modeling of expected inflation is used in combination with newer estimates of the historical course of US consumer prices.

I2.2 AROUND THE WORLD WITH IRVING FISHER

This section bears the title of a publication by Gylfason et al. (2016) that uses Fisher's international data to econometrically study his theoretical proposition. The empirical analysis that follows likewise uses the data compiled by Irving Fisher for his study of 1930. This data set captures interest rates and inflation in six countries. More concretely, Fisher's data appendix lists interest rates and the wholesale price indices for the six financial centers New York, London, Paris, Berlin, Calcutta, and Tokyo. Figure 12.1 presents the time series of these interest rates reported by Fisher (1930). The display illustrates the wide range of international interest rates over the historical period.

Fisher's own statistical investigation proceeded by taking a weighted sum of present and past rates of inflation as a proxy for expected inflation. The weights decayed linearly (arithmetically) with the length of the lag. Further, Fisher formed various proxies for inflation expectations by varying the maximum of the lag length of inflation. The estimation procedure then consisted of searching for the expectations measure that most closely correlated with the rate of interest. For the USA, the thus estimated maximum lag was 20 years, and for the United Kingdom even longer than that. Fisher's conclusion with respect to the magnitude of the total adjustment could not come from the described search for the appropriate lag structure: his procedure would not allow for a coefficient estimate. Instead, the conclusion that the adjustment of interest rates was only partial (even after many years) was the result of comparing real rates of interest and inflation over longer spans of time. This comparison indicated that real rates were systematically lower during historical episodes with high inflation than during periods with low inflation.

The introduction of the regression method into the analysis of time series has made possible the combined estimation of the length of the adjustment process and the overall magnitude of the effect under consideration. Hence, in a first step, the following equation for each country is estimated:

$$i_t = \varphi_0 + \varphi_1 i_{t-1} + \varphi_2 \pi_t + \varepsilon_t \tag{12.1}$$

Here, the actual inflation (π_t) enters as an explanatory variable for the nominal interest rate (i_t). This specification coincides with that used by Gylfason et al. (2016). It allows the estimation of the short-run effect of inflation on the nominal interest rate as measured by the parameter φ_2, as well as the related long-run effect captured by the ratio $\varphi_2/(1-\varphi_1)$. To be clear, in this formulation, there is no separate model explaining the formation of expectations. However, similar to Fisher's (1930) approach, Eq. (12.1) implies an adjustment process of inflation expectations to the course of actual inflation. In contrast to Fisher's classic study, the dynamics captured by Eq. (12.1) imply geometrically (instead of arithmetically) declining weights.[2]

---

[2] Sargent (1973, p. 387) pointed out that Fisher's formulation of the lag structure avoids the possibly critical inclusion of the lagged endogenous variable as a regressor.

The described estimates are contrasted with a second set of regressions: the next formulation (keeping φ to identify coefficients) uses the pattern-based measure of expected inflation as an explanatory variable instead of actual inflation.

$$i_t = \varphi_0 + \varphi_1 i_{t-1} + \varphi_2 \pi_t^e + \varepsilon_t \tag{12.2}$$

The ratio $\varphi_2/(1 - \varphi_1)$ now gives the estimate of the long-run effect of *expected* inflation. The findings for the two described specifications for each country are summarized in Table 12.1. For each of the financial centers, the table first shows the results for the specification with the actual inflation rate followed by the results for the specification with expected inflation.

The present estimates with the specification using actual inflation as explanatory variable largely replicate those by Gylfason et al. (2016).[3] The results are also in agreement with the three key conclusions that Fisher draws from his study: (a) in most cases, there is a significant positive effect of inflation on interest rates, (b) in no case do we find a one-to-one effect of inflation expectations on nominal interest rates, and (c) interest rates react slowly to changes in inflation. Now to the differences in findings when using the pattern-based measure of expected inflation in the estimates: in all cases, the estimated long-run effect of expected inflation is stronger than when actual inflation is used as a regressor. This finding is in part the result of the regressive element of behavioral inflation expectations. Beyond this, the pattern-based measure of expected inflation is simply the superior explanatory variable compared to actual inflation. This is witnessed (for all countries except for Germany) by the higher $\overline{R}^2$ values of the estimates. In conclusion, the response of nominal interest rates to expected inflation is noticeably stronger than suggested by

---

[3] In most cases, the sample used here is shorter by one year in order to have comparable results with the findings using the pattern-based measure of expected inflation. Incidentally, the puzzling negative effect in the estimate for the Japanese interest rate is confirmed.

Table 12.1 *OLS estimates of interest rate equations for six countries*

Financial center / Explanatory variable associated with φ_2	φ_0	φ_1	φ_2	$\frac{\varphi_2}{1-\varphi_1}$	$\bar{R}^2$	D.W.	Std. Err.
New York (1868–1927)							
Actual Inflation	1.825*	0.642**	0.022	0.061	0.348	2.208	1.141
	(0.859)	(0.175)	(0.032)	(0.032)			
Expected Inflation	1.719	0.661**	0.056	0.168	0.357	2.204	1.133
	(0.859)	(0.175)	(0.032)	(0.164)			
London (1825–1927)							
Actual Inflation	1.437**	0.578**	0.046*	0.110*	0.325	2.142	1.032
	(0.343)	(0.114)	(0.016)	(0.053)			
Expected Inflation	(0.325)	0.556**	(0.024)	(0.092)	0.385	2.146	0.985
	1.479**	(0.108)	0.119**	0.270**			
Paris (1874–1914)							
Actual Inflation	1.054**	0.583**	0.046**	0.112*	0.427	2.040	0.457
	(0.238)	(0.092)	(0.013)	(0.043)			
Expected Inflation	1.088**	0.568*	0.086**	0.199**	0.445	2.004	0.445
	(0.233)	(0.092)	(0.020)	(0.066)			
Berlin (1863–1912)							
Actual Inflation	1.980**	0.409*	0.034*	0.058	0.230	2.001	0.784
	(0.547)	(0.173)	(0.015)	(0.034)			
Expected Inflation	2.041**	0.390*	0.056	0.092	0.219	1.960	0.790
	(0.539)	(0.171)	(0.029)	(0.058)			

Table 12.1 (cont.)

Financial center Explanatory variable associated with φ_2	φ_0	φ_1	φ_2	$\frac{\varphi_2}{1-\varphi_1}$	$\overline{R}^2$	D.W.	Std. Err.
Calcutta (1863–1926)							
Actual Inflation	3.716** (0.808)	0.349* (0.144)	0.035* (0.016)	0.054* (0.025)	0.171	1.992	0.981
Expected Inflation	3.885** (0.811)	0.319* (0.142)	0.079** (0.025)	0.116** (0.043)	0.215	1.932	0.954
Tokyo (1889–1926)							
Actual Inflation	3.517** (1.085)	0.524* (0.148)	−0.012 (0.015)	−0.026 (0.029)	0.309	1.636	0.854
Expected Inflation	3.679** (1.153)	0.505* (0.155)	−0.029 (0.032)	−0.059 (0.059)	0.311	1.630	0.854

**, * indicate significance at the 1 percent and 5 percent level of significance, respectively.
Numbers in parentheses are White heteroskedasticity-consistent standard errors of estimated coefficients.

earlier studies. Thus, estimates with the behavioral measure of expected inflation strengthen the case for the Fisher effect.

Next, we present a further set of estimates indicating that the long-term effect of expected inflation is higher than found in earlier studies and, as it happens, even higher than in the estimates presented in Table 12.1. For this purpose, the interest rate relationship Eq. (12.2) is estimated in first differences and the instrumental variables method

Table 12.2 *Instrumental variables estimates (first differences) with pattern-based expectations*

Financial center (period)	Number of lags	Sum of coefficients	$\overline{R}^2$	D.W.	Std. Err.
New York (1868–1927)	1	0.334* (0.142)	0.000	1.930	1.368
London (1827–1927)	2	0.537** (0.172)	0.000	2.088	1.341
Paris (1877–1914)	1	0.254** (0.090)	0.078	2.285	0.561

**, * indicate significance at the 1 percent and 5 percent level of significance, respectively.
Numbers in parentheses are White heteroskedasticity-consistent standard errors of estimated coefficients.

is applied to address possible problems of simultaneity. As instruments, values of the endogenous and exogenous variable lagged by one and two years are used. With this setup, significant effects of expected inflation can be documented for three of the six financial centers: when conducting estimates for New York, London, and Paris, the estimated coefficient of inflation expectations is prominently altered compared to the already reported results. In order to model the dynamics, the starting specification includes the current and two lagged terms of expected inflation as well as two lagged terms of the endogenous variable. Wald tests determine the final specifications leading to the estimates presented in Table 12.2. The first key finding is that, with the finally chosen specifications, there is no remaining evidence for a long adjustment process. In all estimates, the lagged endogenous variable has *no* significant explanatory power. Furthermore, for interest rates in New York and Paris, just one lagged term of inflation expectations has significant explanatory value. For the case of London, there are two such terms. Hence, based on this set of estimates, it becomes evident that the adjustment is different from what was suggested in previous studies: with Fisher's original data, we find a fast, although only partial, adjustment of nominal interest rates to changes in expected inflation.

Arguably, Irving Fisher would have found these results relevant since he had doubts regarding the slow adjustment of interest rates. This is witnessed by his remark regarding the findings of long lags: "[i]t seems fantastic, at first glance, to ascribe to events which occurred last century any influence affecting the rate of interest today" (Fisher, 1930, p. 137). With an analysis using the behavioral measure of expected inflation, the notion of very long delays in the adjustment of interest rates is soundly rejected. This proposition by Irving Fisher's and many others' studies should finally be put to rest. The adjustment documented here so far is still not one-to-one as the theoretical prediction would have it. Yet, compared to earlier estimates, the present results indicate a clear upward revision of the long-run effect of expected inflation. The estimated long-run effects are now in the range of 0.254 and 0.537. Clearly, the size of these effects is still significantly below the value of 1. However, the next section will document that even this empirical argument against Fisher's theoretical proposition is weaker than often thought.

12.3   THE FISHER EFFECT IN THE USA PRIOR TO WORLD WAR I

Before turning to a further set of econometric estimates, a hint at a debate in the literature regarding the quality of historical data concerning the price level is in order here. In particular, Perez and Siegler (2003) have pointed out concrete weaknesses in the measures of the aggregate price level used in earlier studies. These researchers propose different measures of the price level and find more support for the Fisher effect than in earlier studies. The two alternative measures of

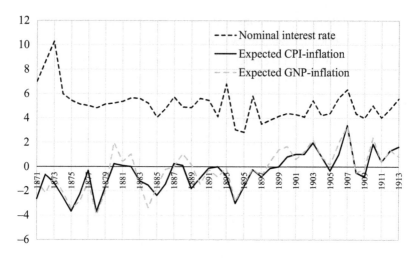

FIGURE 12.2 Short-run nominal interest rate and inflation expectations for the USA

the price level proposed are the gross national product (GNP) deflator computed by Balke and Gordon (1989) and a new CPI measure proposed by Perez and Siegler (2003) themselves. In the following, we will make use of these two measures of the price level. The data studied here cover the period from 1869 to 1913.[4] The price-level path in that period includes phases of inflation as well as deflation. With such price-level data, the general model of inflation expectations presented in Chapter 10 can prove its versatility.

Time series of pattern-based expected inflation are computed using the procedures outlined in Chapter 10. Figure 12.2 illustrates the result of this modeling exercise for the two price-level measures proposed by Perez and Siegler (2003). The chart shows expected inflation according to the two measures of the price level together with the historical series for the short-term interest rate.[5] Table 12.3 lists the

---

[4] Since it takes three observations to compute a pattern-based inflation expectations, the econometric estimates cover the years from 1871 to 1913.

[5] The interest rate studied here is the short-run interest rate reported in Homer and Sylla (1991, tables 44 and 49).

Table 12.3 *Pattern-based measures of expected inflation for the USA*

	Expected CPI Inflation	Expected GNP Inflation
1871	−2.6494	−1.1394
1872	−0.6631	−2.1747
1873	−1.3405	−0.8742
1874	−2.4784	−2.0939
1875	−3.6807	−3.4609
1876	−2.2803	−2.8519
1877	−0.3143	−1.2601
1878	−3.7141	−3.9788
1879	−1.6582	−2.0332
1880	0.2296	1.9904
1881	0.1038	0.4272
1882	0.0000	1.0401
1883	−1.1779	−1.4662
1884	−1.5222	−3.3923
1885	−2.3746	−1.6546
1886	−1.4441	−0.2402
1887	0.2451	0.0000
1888	0.1108	1.0578
1889	−1.7914	0.1809
1890	−0.9492	−1.4322
1891	−0.1137	−0.2416
1892	0.0000	−0.8408
1893	−0.7610	−0.1097
1894	−3.0092	−2.8523
1895	−1.6227	−1.4898
1896	−0.2345	−0.1552
1897	−0.8156	−0.7588
1898	−0.1311	0.3940
1899	0.0000	1.3900
1900	0.8156	1.6710
1901	1.0254	0.6126
1902	1.0151	1.2207
1903	1.9541	2.2073
1904	0.8737	0.8164
1905	−0.3275	0.1362

Table 12.3 (cont.)

	Expected CPI Inflation	Expected GNP Inflation
1906	1.0031	1.9662
1907	3.3918	3.3112
1908	−0.4880	−0.4885
1909	−0.8415	−0.2114
1910	1.8657	2.3732
1911	0.3943	0.3609
1912	1.3141	1.3704
1913	1.6391	0.8363

computed values for expected inflation for the two price-level measures.

As before, the econometric investigation starts with the Fisher equation specified in levels of the variables involved:

$$i_t = \alpha_0 + \alpha_1 \pi_t^e + \varepsilon_t \tag{12.3}$$

Unit root tests document that both the interest rate and the pattern-based measure of expected inflation are stationary.[6] Following Perez and Siegler (2003), no lagged endogenous variable is introduced. Table 12.4 presents the results of instrumental variables estimates of this specification with the two alternative measures of the price level. It turns out that the estimated coefficient for the behavioral measure of expected inflation is highly significant. Importantly, for both measures of the price level, a test for the coefficient restriction $\alpha_1 = 1$ is not rejected at the 5 percent level of significance. This suggests that the interest rate and price-level data for the historical period studied here is in accordance with the strong Fisher effect: a one-to-

[6] Tests for stationarity of the interest rate and the inflation series both in levels and first differences are reported by Perez and Siegler (2003, table 6, p. 959). Instruments are endogenous and exogenous variables and measures for industrial production and gold production all lagged by one year. For each instrumental variable, we take the log value and take first differences when necessary to assure stationarity.

Table 12.4 *Instrumental variables estimates of the interest rate equation in levels*

Price-level measure	α_0	α_1	$\overline{R}^2$	D.W.	Std. Err.
CPI	4.825**	0.757**	0.314	2.348	1.099
Perez–Siegler	(0.618)	(0.164)			
GNP Deflator	4.906**	0.723**	0.102	2.188	1.327
Balke–Gordon	(0.592)	(0.251)			

**, * indicate significance at the 1 percent and 5percent level of significance, respectively.
Numbers in parentheses are White heteroskedasticity-consistent standard errors of estimated coefficients.
Estimates include an AR(1) and AR(2) corrections.

one adjustment of nominal interest rates to changes in inflation expectations cannot be statistically rejected.

Further, the present findings are in accordance with Perez and Siegler (2003) concerning the result that a measure based on the new CPI data can explain a larger fraction of the variability of the interest rate than a GNP deflator measure. The contrast to earlier findings studying this historical period – including Fisher's own estimates – is remarkable: we find a one-to-one relation between expected inflation and the interest rate. Furthermore, this effect appears without any lagged adjustment. This strengthens the results already reported. There appears to be no long delay in the adjustment of the nominal interest rate to changing expected inflation.[7] Overall, better

[7] For completeness and for the purpose of comparison with Perez and Siegler's estimate, we also report results from a specification in the first differences of the variables. Again, expected inflation based on the CPI measure explains a larger fraction of the variation of the interest rate than the measure based on the GNP deflator. For the CPI-based measure of expected inflation, the estimated coefficient is 0.829 (standard error 0.324), while it is only 0.418 (standard error 0.170) for the GNP-deflator-based measure. These estimates are both markedly higher than estimates with competing measures of inflation expectations (e.g., the highest estimate in Perez and Siegler is 0.38). For the CPI-based measure, the estimated coefficient remains not significantly different from 1 (p value of 0.60).

price-level data and a plausible model of expectation formation go a long way to empirically document the Fisher effect in a critical historical period.

12.4   SUMMARY AND CONCLUSIONS

This chapter presents econometric investigations of the Fisher effect by focusing on historical periods and interest rate data that Irving Fisher used in his own empirical work. As before, the pattern-based measures of expected inflation is evaluated in its ability to explain interest rate movements. Two aspects of earlier findings are challenged by new results: first, the notion that the quantitative effect of inflation expectations on nominal interest is weak is not borne out. Second, the proposition that the adjustment of interest rates to changes in inflation takes several decades finds no empirical support. With respect to the first point, the econometric estimates presented here suggest that for the case of the USA between the civil war and World War I, there is evidence for a one-to-one effect of expected inflation. For interest rates of other countries and periods covering parts of the 19th century and 20th century, the effect of expected inflation is found to be only partial, but still markedly stronger than what was reported in other studies. With respect to the second point concerning the length of the adjustment process, the new evidence is even clearer. Here it becomes obvious that the reaction time of nominal interest rates to changes in inflation has been systematically overestimated. Applying the new measure of expected inflation, it is found that the adjustment of nominal interest rates occurs rather swiftly.

13 Expectations of High Inflation

13.1 INTRODUCTION

This chapter takes the pattern-based approach of modeling inflation expectations to higher levels of inflation. Remember that subjects in the generalized approach as developed in Chapter 10 were shown price-level paths with percentage changes in the range of ±2 percent. We then relied on the estimated scaling relationship to apply the elicited laboratory expectations to real-world inflation rates beyond this range. When turning to the modeling of expectations in times of high inflation, this approach is put to the test. Is it really warranted to rely on an estimated scaling relationship that was estimated with low rates of inflation when looking at annual inflation rates of 40 percent or more?

13.2 EXPECTATIONS DATA FOR DIFFERENT RANGES OF INFLATION

The appropriate way to address this question is by studying subjects' expectations in scenarios of high inflation in the laboratory. Hence, we study this question by extending the laboratory-based studies. Four new sets of expectations data are elicited based on increasingly higher inflation rates. The additional experimental treatments use the same types of price-level patterns studied before. Thus, the difference across treatments lies only in the range of percentage changes of the price level. For the present endeavor, only upward trending patterns are studied since the focus here is on documenting expectations in times of considerable price advances. The four new treatments that are presented to subjects consist of price-level patterns with the following possible rates of change:

Treatment (I): Changes of 0 percent, 5 percent, and 10 percent
Treatment (II): Changes of 0 percent, 10 percent, and 20 percent
Treatment (III): Changes of 0 percent, 20 percent, and 40 percent
Treatment (IV): Changes of 0 percent, 40 percent, and 80 percent

In terms of percentage changes, the patterns presented are perfectly collinear. Table 13.1 shows the four sets of patterns and the elicited expectations for the different ranges of inflation rates. Note that the numbering of the patterns used here accords with the numbering in Chapter 10. This should make clear that the patterns presented in the new runs of the experiment are from the list of patterns used before. The only difference between the various treatments (and the patterns from Chapter 10) concerns the scaling of the presented changes. The instructions are adapted from those used for treatment (i) as outlined in Chapters 3 and 10.[1] In each of the four treatments, 30 subjects, all students with a background in macroeconomics, were enrolled.

When looking at the patterns presented, it becomes clear that there is an overlap of patterns across treatments. For example, pattern 1 with 100, 110, 121 in treatment (I) is identical with the pattern 7 in treatment (II). Similarly, pattern 3 (11) in the treatment (I) coincides with pattern 8 (12) in treatment (II). The same pairings of identical patterns exist when comparing treatments (II) and (III), as well as treatments (III) and (IV). In total, there are nine pairs of expectations' responses for the same pattern.

13.3   TESTS OF RANGE CONSISTENCY AND SCALING

With the noted pairs of expectations, we first test the hypothesis that the same pattern generates the same expectation independent of the range of inflation rates shown. To be specific: Is the projected

---

[1] In line with treatment (i) from Chapter 3, subjects are just asked for a point forecast. However, here subjects are shown fewer, namely, eight patterns. Furthermore, we only ask for the one-year-ahead expectation. Subjects are allocated 30 minutes for their task and receive €10.

Table 13.1 *CPI-expectations for four treatments with different ranges of inflation*

Treatment	Pattern	Time 1	2	3	Mean 4	Upper 95%	Lower 5%
I	1	100	110	121	130.7857	133.00	128.70
	2	100	110	115.5	118.0909	120.00	115.00
	3	100	110	110	110.8966	118.40	102.00
	6	100	105	115.5	128.3793	139.60	117.00
	7	100	105	110.25	114.7931	117.60	111.20
	8	100	105	105	104.7778	110.00	99.30
	11	100	100	110	117.2500	130.00	101.75
	12	100	100	105	110.7308	115.75	105.00
II	1	100	120	144	168.5714	175.00	158.70
	2	100	120	132	138.6897	142.00	132.80
	3	100	120	120	120.3793	130.00	110.00
	6	100	110	132	161.0400	178.00	142.60
	7	100	110	121	131.5393	135.00	130.00
	8	100	110	110	110.1034	120.00	99.40
	11	100	100	120	134.5000	155.50	112.25
	12	100	100	110	120.1897	130.00	110.80

Table 13.1 (cont.)

Treatment	Pattern	Time			Mean	Upper 95%	Lower 5%
		1	2	3	4		
III	1	100	140	196	244.4483	276.40	160.00
	2	100	140	168	185.5333	193.20	177.25
	3	100	140	140	146.1000	160.00	120.00
	6	100	120	168	214.0333	275.50	161.75
	7	100	120	144	164.7857	179.30	140.00
	8	100	120	120	122.3333	150.00	100.00
	11	100	100	140	162.7667	217.75	120.00
	12	100	100	120	136.0667	165.50	108.90
IV	1	100	180	324	466.3333	598.75	370.00
	2	100	180	252	316.3000	338.65	294.50
	3	100	180	180	188.1000	246.50	140.00
	6	100	140	252	366.1000	463.75	290.00
	7	100	140	196	255.7667	280.00	214.50
	8	100	140	140	150.4000	180.00	120.00
	11	100	100	180	230.8000	325.50	160.00
	12	100	100	140	180.1333	240.00	140.00

continuation for a price-level path like 100, 110, 121 the same independent of whether (different) subjects see it in a group of paths with lower or with higher rates of inflation? We call the elicited expectations data "range-consistent" if this question is answered in the positive. As it turns out, the data gathered document this property: the hypothesis of consistency across treatments is not statistically rejected.[2] This is good news for the approach presented in this book. It supports the notion that we can generalize from a set of patterns presenting small changes in the underlying variable to situations with larger changes. This is what was relied on all along in earlier chapters when using the estimated scaling relationship.

Consider next a test of the scaling relationship used so far: there are 27 pairs of collinear patterns in the data from treatments (I) through (IV). In each case, one of the patterns shows changes twice as large as the changes of the related pattern. From these pairings of the data from treatments (I) through (IV), an estimate of the scaling parameter can be obtained. This new estimate of the θ parameter turns out to be 0.808 (with a standard error of 0.053). Compare this estimate to the value of the scaling parameter of 0.861 reported in Chapter 10. These two estimates from different data sets and different ranges of inflation are remarkably similar. The scaling relationship in both versions shows a clear tendency of expectations to rise less than one-by-one to changes in the rate of inflation. This has been termed the regressive tendency in the expectations data. Appendix 13.1 illustrates this tendency by computing the elasticity of expectations for different levels of inflation.

Given the communalities between the two ways of computing expectations, it is indeed questionable whether the modeling of expectations for high-inflation countries needs to be based on the special laboratory data documented in this chapter. Alternatively, we could

---

[2] The testing is conducted by running a regression of the expected percentage changes reported in the treatment with the higher (lower) roman number on the expected percentages change reported in the treatment with the lower (higher) roman number. The hypothesis that the constant is zero and the slope parameter is 1 is not rejected at the 5 percent level of significance with a p value of 0.17 (0.09).

Table 13.2 *The shortened set of patterns and corresponding one-year-ahead CPI-expectations**

Pattern	Time 1	2	3	Mean 4
1	100	102	103	0.5174
2	100	101	103	1.5990
3	100	101	102	0.8718
4	100	101	101	0.1277
5	100	100	101	0.6769

* The tabulated data are represented as positively trending patterns with steps of 1, 2, and 0 and are computed by averaging over the expectations data of this chapter applying a weighting of $1/(\beta^{0.808})$.

simply apply the general approach of Chapter 10. This issue is assessed by computing expected inflation based on the two approaches for a number of high-inflation economies. Then we study interesting macro-economic relationships involving inflation expectations: concretely, the two approaches are evaluated by assessing the explanatory power of the two alternative series of expected inflation in econometric esti-mates of the Fisher relationship and the money demand relationship. The procedure for modeling inflation expectations with the new data is just as documented in earlier chapters: the laboratory data is condensed to the expectations for a set of non-collinear patterns. Here, this means a reduction from eight to five patterns. In this process, the expectations for cases of higher inflation are downscaled using the scaling parameter reported above. The condensed expectations data are reported in Table 13.2 for the set of five non-collinear patterns. The patterns here come in changes of one and two and are numbered consecutively.

13.4 APPLICATIONS TO HIGH-INFLATION ECONOMIES

We start with a search for countries with high inflation rates that qualify for an empirical investigation of the relevance of the new expectations measures. For this purpose, countries with an experience of inflation rates similar to those covered in the laboratory are considered. This search leads to several countries with inflation rates in the range from 5 to 80 percent for which CPI data are available for 20 or more years. However, for the purpose of studying macroeconomic relationships, data on other variables are needed as well. To be concrete: the World Bank publishes comprehensive data on the CPI, lending rates, and the stock of money as a ratio to income.[3] This ratio M/Y, where M is the money supply and Y stands for nominal aggregate income, is the reciprocal of the income velocity of money. Among the other measures listed, the interest rate is the variable for which the least data are available. The interest rate variable is important since we want to study the Fisher effect in high-inflation countries. For many countries, data for the interest rate has become available only in recent years. With a requirement of at least 20 years of data, this drastically shortens the list of countries to be studied here.

Among the four countries finally selected, there are three Latin American economies and one Caribbean economy. Two of the countries thus selected experienced inflation exactly in the range given. These countries are Honduras and Jamaica (with inflation up to 34 percent and 73 percent). We further assess our approach by studying two countries with rates of inflation somewhat beyond the range covered in the laboratory. On that count, two additional countries qualify, namely Costa Rica and Venezuela with annual inflation of up to 100 percent. Among the four remaining economies – Botswana, Malawi, South Africa, and Zambia – all but one will be studied in Chapter 15.

With respect to the new relationship to be investigated here, monetary data in the form of the ratio of the money supply to income is available for most countries and for rather long periods. Furthermore, the relevant World Bank data are consistent with respect to the measurement of the money supply, which is $M2$. We will use this data

---

[3] All data used here are drawn from the World Bank's web portal under https://data .worldbank.org/indicator/.

for estimating the influence of a key determinant of money demand. In particular, the focus here is on the effect of the opportunity costs of holding liquidity denoted by C. Measuring the responsiveness of money demand with respect to a measure of the opportunity costs of holding money is difficult since measures of these costs are hard to come by. If returns on assets like savings accounts do not compensate for expected inflation (e.g., due to financial repression), their returns are not an adequate measure of the losses of holding money. In this situation, expected inflation becomes the relevant indicator of the opportunity costs of money. Following the empirical literature, the assumption of a unitary income elasticity of money demand is adopted (Goldfeld & Sichel, 1990).[4]

In the econometric study, the following relationship is estimated

$$\ln \left(V_{j,t} \right) = \alpha_0 + \alpha_1 \ln \left(V_{j,t-1} \right) + \alpha_2 \ln \left(Inf^e_{j,t} \right) + \varepsilon_t, \tag{13.1}$$

where $V \equiv Y/M$. Including a lagged term of the endogenous variable captures a partial adjustment of velocity to its long-run equilibrium. Expected inflation means a loss in the purchasing power of money. Hence, an increase in expected inflation (Inf^e) leads to a decrease in money demand. In terms of Eq. (13.1), this reflects in a positive sign of coefficient α_2: higher expected inflation increases the velocity of money. The ordinary least squares (OLS) estimates for this specification of velocity are summarized in Table 13.3. The first line for each country presents the results when using the new ("high-inflation") measure of inflation expectations specifically modeled for times of high inflation. The second line presents the results when using the measure of expected inflation based on Chapter 10. We call the latter series of expectations

---

[4] The starting point is the long-run money demand function is $M = e^{\gamma_0} Y C^{\gamma_1}$ which, transformed to natural logs and taking nominal income to the left-hand side, yields $\ln(M) - \ln(Y) = \gamma_0 + \gamma_1 \ln(C)$. M denotes the stock of money, Y is nominal income, and C stands for the opportunity cost of money holdings. The elasticity of money demand with respect to the cost of holding money (γ_1) is negative.

Table 13.3 *Money demand equations for four high-inflation countries*

Country	Pattern-based measure of expected inflation	α_0	α_1	α_2	$\bar{R}^2$	D.W.	Std. Err.
Honduras 1989–2009	High-inflation	0.329 (0.196)	0.825** (0.098)	0.067 (0.044)	0.845	1.858	0.084
	General	0.362 (0.222)	0.802** (0.114)	0.077 (0.050)	0.846	1.876	0.084
Jamaica 1976–2014	High-inflation	0.325* (0.126)	0.720** (0.117)	0.055 (0.030)	0.562	2.237	0.119
	General	0.327* (0.134)	0.717** (0.116)	0.061 (0.035)	0.567	2.231	0.118
Costa Rica 1982–2010	High-inflation	0.463** (0.181)	0.788** (0.122)	0.085 (0.043)	0.623	1.899	0.228
	General	0.494** (0.188)	0.793** (0.118)	0.107* (0.046)	0.630	1.946	0.226
Venezuela 1985–2013	High-inflation	0.276 (0.163)	0.965** (0.087)	0.115* (0.049)	0.783	2.027	0.130
	General	0.247 (0.162)	0.951** (0.109)	0.106* (0.046)	0.781	2.030	0.131

**, * indicate significance at the 1 percent and 5 percent level of significance, respectively.
Numbers in parentheses are White heteroskedasticity-consistent standard errors of estimated coefficients.

the "general" measure since its methodological basis claims to be applicable generally, that is, under all conditions. The findings suggest that for most countries (the exception is Venezuela), money demand appears to be better explained by the general version instead of the more specific, high-inflation version of expected inflation.[5]

[5] Looking at the results in more detail, the empirical estimates of long-run elasticities for Honduras (−0.38), Jamaica (−0.21), and Costa Rica (−0.66) and even Venezuela

We now turn to the estimation of the Fisher equation. The empirical literature so far suggests that rising inflation indeed leads to higher interest rates, but that particularly for high-inflation countries, this effect is less than one-to-one (Coppock & Poitras, 2000). The following specification of the Fisher equation is estimated for the four previously identified countries:[6]

$$\Delta\left(i_{j,t}\right) = \vartheta_0 + \vartheta_1\Delta\left(i_{j,t-1}\right) + \vartheta_2\Delta\left(Inf^e_{j,t}\right) + \varepsilon_t \qquad (13.2)$$

A formulation in first differences of the variables is necessary here in order to make the residuals stationary. For each country, we begin by estimating the lending rate equation by first using the pattern-based inflation expectations measure derived for high-inflation rates described in this chapter. As before, this is called the "high-inflation" measure of expected inflation. Alternatively, the expected inflation based on the model presented in Chapter 10 is applied. The relevant estimate with the "general" measure is always listed below the one with the "high-inflation" measure of expected inflation.

Table 13.4 presents the regression results. OLS is the chosen method of estimation since different choices of instruments lead to widely varying results. For all four countries studied, except for Venezuela, a one-to-one Fisher effect cannot be statistically rejected.[7] So from this perspective, there is little evidence against a strong-form Fisher effect even in cases of high inflation. Incidentally, the result is the same whether the high-inflation measure of expected inflation or the general measure is used. When comparing results across the two measures of expected inflation, it is found that the two measures have

(with a value of −2.68) are in the range reported for developing countries (Arrau et al., 1995). The long-run opportunity cost elasticity of money demand is related to coefficients of Eq. (13.1) by $\gamma_1 = \alpha_2/(1 - \alpha_1)$. Furthermore, our ordering of the three Latin American economies concerning the size of money demand sensitivities to changes in opportunity costs coincides with the findings reported by Carrera (2016).

[6] A specification with logarithms of all variables, as e.g. suggested by Phylaktis and Blake (1993), typically (with the exception of Venezuela) leads to a lower explanatory power of the estimate.

[7] This boils down to testing the coefficient restriction $\vartheta_1 + \vartheta_2 = 1$.

Table 13.4 *Fisher equations for four high-inflation countries*

Country	Pattern-based measure of expected inflation	ϑ_0	ϑ_1	ϑ_2	$\overline{R}^2$	D.W.	Std. Err.
Honduras 1989–2009	High-inflation	0.115	0.801**	0.398**	0.575	2.259	1.354
		(0.308)	(0.098)	(0.044)			
	General	0.106	0.784**	0.335**	0.586	2.310	1.337
		(0.289)	(0.140)	(0.070)			
Jamaica 1978–2014	High-inflation	0.058	0.453*	0.444**	0.262	2.341	3.083
		(0.500)	(0.174)	(0.160)			
	General	0.062	0.402*	0.351*	0.232	2.364	3.146
		(0.511)	(0.172)	(0.142)			
Costa Rica 1984–2010	High-inflation	−0.035	−0.116	0.975*	0.235	2.131	3.921
		(0.711)	(0.189)	(0.349)			
	General	0.090	−0.138	0.848**	0.273	2.006	3.822
		(0.681)	(0.183)	(0.249)			
Venezuela 1987–2013	High-inflation	0.170	−0.134	0.322	0.022	1.881	9.533
		(1.882)	(0.143)	(0.291)			
	General	0.177	−0.139	0.226	0.010	1.887	9.594
		(1.901)	(0.246)	(0.217)			

**, * indicate significance at the 1 percent and 5 percent level of significance, respectively.
Numbers in parentheses are White heteroskedasticity-consistent standard errors of estimated coefficients.

about equal explanatory power. For Venezuela and Jamaica, the measure of expected inflation computed from the data presented in this chapter explains interest rate behavior better than the general one. For Honduras and Costa Rica, the opposite holds.

Looking at the two macroeconomic relationships studied in this chapter, the general approach of modeling expected inflation appears to outperform the more specific measure for circumstances of high inflation. Yet, in all cases studied, the results with the two measures are very similar. This is not surprising given that for the countries covered here, the correlation between the two measures of expected inflation is 0.992 or higher.

13.5 SUMMARY AND CONCLUSIONS

This chapter checks the validity of the approach presented in earlier chapters when applying it to levels of inflation previously not shown in the laboratory. This test is conducted by administering a set of four new treatments in the laboratory where subjects are shown price-level paths in different brackets with increasingly higher rates of inflation. These four treatments are designed to elicit expectations for inflation rates between 5 and 80 percent. The experimental data confirm that altering the range of inflation does not significantly affect expectations for a given pattern of the price level. Subjects anticipate the same continuation for a given pattern independent of whether that pattern is presented together with cases of lower or higher rates of inflation. Furthermore, the estimate of the scaling relationship central to the present approach is in line with the findings from Chapter 10. This supports our assessment that laboratory expectations elicited from a short set of circumstances (with modest rates of inflation) can be generalized to higher rates of inflation.

The experimental data documented in this chapter is used in the computation of expected inflation for four high-inflation economies. In order to assess this more specific approach to modeling expected inflation, this series is compared with expectations computed with the approach presented in Chapter 10. The four countries covered are three Latin American economies and one Caribbean economy. For each country, the effect of expected inflation on money holdings as well as the effect on the nominal interest rate is estimated. Overall, the estimates indicate that the series of expected inflation based on the general approach is a reliable measure even for high rates of inflation. Hence, it becomes clear that for cases of high inflation, it is not necessary to base the modeling of expectations on a special model. Accordingly, the approach of Chapter 10 will be the workhorse for modeling expected inflation and real rates of interest for a wide set of countries in the next chapters.

APPENDIX 13.1 COMPUTING ELASTICITIES OF
EXPECTATIONS FOR DIFFERENT RATES OF
INFLATION

The expectations data presented in this chapter and in earlier chapters show a
regressive tendency. This means that as inflation rises, expected inflation rises
too, but less than one-to-one. This tendency can be further clarified by calculating expectations for one typical upward trending price-level pattern. For this
purpose, we select the basic pattern 100, 101, 102, and compute expected inflation for increasingly higher values of the inflation rate. Then the implied
expected inflation rate is set in proportion to the last observed inflation rate.
The result gives the elasticity of expectations. This elasticity is defined as
$Inf^e_{t+1}/Inf_t \equiv \left(\ln p^e_{t+1} - \ln p_t \right) / \left(\ln p_t - \ln p_{t-1} \right)$. Figure A13.1 presents the values
for the elasticity of expectations over a range of inflation from 1 to 80 percent.
The display presents two graphs with the dashed line indicating the measure
based on the data collected for this chapter. The solid line gives the elasticity of
expectations when building on the data presented in Chapter 10. The two measures show the same general tendency: the elasticity of expectations descends
with a rising rate of inflation.

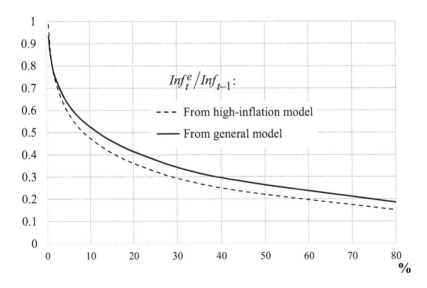

FIGURE A13.1 Elasticity of expectations for different inflation rates from
different models

14 The Fisher Effect in Asian Economies

14.1 INTRODUCTION

The research literature has investigated the validity of the Fisher effect for a number of Asian economies. Among the countries that have been studied, Indonesia, South Korea, Malaysia, the Philippines, Singapore, and Thailand figure prominently. Overall, the evidence regarding the Fisher effect is mixed. Berument and Jelassi (2002) find no statistically significant effects of expected inflation on nominal interest rates for Korea and the Philippines. Kim et al. (2018) report statistically nonsignificant effects of expected inflation for the Philippines and Singapore and a significant effect, albeit not the strong form, for Thailand. Said and Janor (2001) find signs supporting the hypothesis for Indonesia but no evidence favoring Fisher's proposition for South Korea, Malaysia, the Philippines, Singapore, and Thailand. Finally, Nusair (2008) documents a strong-form Fisher effect for South Korea and weak-form effects for Malaysia and Thailand. Summing up, the hypothesis under investigation has so far gained limited support for Asian countries.

We will study the South East Asian countries listed above since they have been repeatedly covered in the literature and since the evidence supporting the notion of an effect of inflation expectations on interest rates is rather weak. For this purpose, the approach developed in Chapter 10 for computing the series of expected inflation is applied to the Asian countries investigated. In order to have a consistent set of data, the interest rates studied here are lending rates from the World Bank. Given that this interest rate is a short-term rate, the computed series of expected inflation is made up of one-year-ahead rates.[1] The length of the data set varies from country to country. For some countries (Indonesia, Philippines, and Thailand), the data go back as far as the 1970s and 1980s. The exact estimation period will be reported in the tables showing the estimation results. For South Korea, the data only cover a little more than the past two decades. A further point is that lending rates of several Asian countries show signs of not being set by market forces.[2] We infer a politically set lending rate whenever this interest rate remains unchanged for two or more years. Such observations are deleted from our empirical study. Accordingly, for Singapore the lending series only cover the years 1978 to 2004. Finally, for Thailand the lending rate data for the first three years of the millennium are missing and the period studied is limited to the years from 1978 to 1999.

14.2 ESTIMATING INTEREST RATE EQUATIONS

The estimation of the influence of expected inflation on Asian lending rates is conducted with a first-difference specification. Concretely, the equation to be estimated is

$$\Delta i_t = \alpha_0 + \alpha_1 \Delta \pi_t^e + \varepsilon_t. \tag{14.1}$$

Table 14.1 shows the results of estimating this specification with the least squares method. For all six countries studied, we find a positive effect of expected inflation on the lending rate. In the case of Korea and Singapore, the estimate supports the view of the strong version of the Fisher effect. For Indonesia and Philippines, the relevant coefficient is significantly different from zero but less than 1. Finally, for Malaysia and Thailand, the estimated effects are not significantly different from zero, with p values of 0.105 and 0.084, respectively.

---

[1] The lending rate according to the World Bank is the bank rate that meets the short- and medium-term financing demands of the private sector. All data used here are drawn from the World Bank's web portal under https://data.worldbank.org/indicator/.

[2] See Abiad et al. (2010) for a history of financial regulation and interest rate controls.

Table 14.1 *Interest rate equations estimated in first differences*

Country Period	α_0	α_1	$\overline{R}^2$	D.W.	Std. Err.
Indonesia	−0.288	0.551**	0.574	1.905	2.054
1988–2017	(0.372)	(0.090)			
Malaysia	−0.214	0.303	0.130	1.758	0.840
1988–2016	(0.159)	(0.180)			
Philippines	−0.117	0.516**	0.373	1.717	2.485
1981–2017	(0.394)	(0.155)			
Singapore	−0.012	0.658**	0.328	1.718	1.074
1978–2004	(0.205)	(0.216)			
South Korea	−0.354	0.909**	0.672	1.615	0.929
1998–2017	(0.209)	(0.208)			
Thailand	−0.049	0.424	0.184	1.482	1.777
1977–1999	(0.358)	(0.233)			

**, * indicate significance at the 1 percent and 5 percent level of significance, respectively.
Numbers in parentheses are White heteroskedasticity-consistent standard errors of estimated coefficients.

Let us now turn to the possible effects of the uncertainty and the heterogeneity of inflation expectations. Interestingly, the study by Berument et al. (2007) shows that taking into account inflation uncertainty as a further explanatory variable is important for documenting the Fisher effect in a number of countries. The pattern-based approach makes it possible to focus on this effect and in addition to assess the role of expectations heterogeneity. This allows an assessment of what dimensions of inflation expectations are important for understanding interest rate movements. The data Appendix 14.1 lists the computed variables on inflation expectations, their heterogeneity, and uncertainty for the six countries studied here. Hence, in order to quantify the described effects, the following equation is estimated:

$$\Delta i_t = \alpha_0 + \alpha_1 \Delta \pi_t^e + \alpha_2 \Delta \pi_t^{e,\,Heter} + \alpha_3 \Delta \pi_t^{e,\,Uncer} + \varepsilon_t \tag{14.2}$$

Table 14.2 *Interest rate equations allowing for effects of heterogeneity and uncertainty*

Country Period	α_0	α_1	α_2	α_3	$\bar{R}^2$	D.W.	Std. Err.
Indonesia	−0.283	0.307*	−0.259**	0.405**	0.701	1.899	1.720
1988–2017	(0.307)	(0.126)	(0.070)	(0.089)			
Malaysia	−0.215	0.307*	−0.017	0.015	0.061	1.766	0.872
1988–2016	(0.160)	(0.139)	(0.263)	(0.254)			
Philippines	−0.077	0.394**	−0.436**	0.570**	0.624	1.654	1.922
1981–2017	(0.312)	(0.084)	(0.057)	(0.073)			
Singapore	0.030	0.183	−0.196	0.655*	0.518	1.788	0.910
1978–2004	(0.180)	(0.293)	(0.203)	(0.252)			
S. Korea	−0.321	0.913**	−0.212	0.250	0.643	1.583	0.969
1998–2017	(0.232)	(0.214)	(0.391)	(0.413)			
Thailand	0.061	0.622*	−0.553*	0.351	0.287	1.666	1.661
1977–1999	(0.349)	(0.196)	(0.230)	(0.251)			

**, * indicate significance at the 1 percent and 5 percent level of significance, respectively.
Numbers in parentheses are White heteroskedasticity-consistent standard errors of estimated coefficients.

The estimates are reported in Table 14.2. The results are in line with the findings reported by Berument et al. (2007). Typically, the Fisher effect is estimated more precisely when further dimensions of inflation expectations are taken into consideration. In Table 14.2, this is demonstrated by the fact that the α_1 coefficient is now significantly different from zero in all countries but one. Singapore is the exception to the rule. Further, uncertainty of inflation expectations generally tends to have a positively signed effect on the rate of interest. So the popular view that the uncertainty of the inflation outlook tends to reflect in an interest rate markup finds some support for the countries studied here. One key finding is new to the empirical literature of the

Fisher effect for Asian economies: the estimates indicate that the effect of the heterogeneity of inflation expectations is an important determinant of interest rates. Indeed, the results in Table 14.2 show that an increase in the heterogeneity of expectations tends to decrease interest rates in all countries studied and significantly so in three of them.

Finally, the specification of Eq. (14.2) is also estimated using the instrumental variables method. As instruments, we use the lagged terms of the endogenous and the exogenous variables for the country considered as well as from one other major Asian economy. For Indonesia, Singapore, and Thailand, the foreign variables cover Japan which is the largest Asian economy for which data for the full

Table 14.3 *Instrumental variables estimates of interest rate equations*

Country Period	α_0	α_1	α_2	α_3	$\overline{R}^2$	D.W.	Std. Err.
Indonesia 1988–2017	−0.294 (0.333)	0.435** (0.060)	−0.277** (0.053)	0.405** (0.092)	0.687	2.016	1.790
Malaysia 1988–2016	−0.165 (0.153)	0.479 (0.311)	−0.079 (0.643)	0.207 (0.548)	0.045	2.211	0.880
Philippines 1981–2017	−0.079 (0.314)	0.385* (0.148)	−0.424** (0.076)	0.558** (0.089)	0.648	1.758	1.879
Singapore 1978–2004	−0.007 (0.190)	0.296 (0.458)	−0.168 (0.203)	0.702* (0.252)	0.516	2.004	0.908
S. Korea 1998–2017	−0.313 (0.240)	0.963* (0.243)	−0.189 (0.314)	0.264 (0.387)	0.637	1.748	0.978
Thailand 1977–1999	0.154 (0.373)	0.888* (0.207)	−0.618 (0.347)	0.366 (0.327)	0.227	1.703	1.771

**, * indicate significance at the 1 percent and 5 percent level of significance, respectively.

Numbers in parentheses are White heteroskedasticity-consistent standard errors of estimated coefficients.

estimation period are available. For Korea, Malaysia, and the Philippines, the foreign instrumental variables cover Indonesia since these data explain a larger fraction of the variations of the data for the three noted countries than the Japanese data do. Table 14.3 shows that the instrumental variables method that takes care of simultaneity issues leads, in some cases, to an altered set of findings. When considering the estimated values of the key parameter α_1, the results with the instrumented explanatory variables tend to be even stronger compared to the ordinary least squares estimates. With this method of estimation, the Fisher hypothesis is found to gain significant support for several of the South East Asian economies considered here. In particular, South Korea and Thailand stand out with strong-form Fisher effects.

14.3 SUMMARY AND CONCLUSIONS

Earlier tests of the Fisher hypothesis for Asian economies have yielded limited support for this hypothesis. Estimates with the pattern-based measures of inflation expectations draw a different picture. The new estimates lend support to the notion that inflation expectations systematically affect nominal interest rates. In particular, when the elements of the heterogeneity and the uncertainty of inflation expectations are also brought to bear on the issue, it is found that the Fisher effect emerges in a clear way. Importantly, these additional dimensions of expectations are also documented to systematically affect nominal rates in Asian economies. Higher uncertainty tends to lead to higher rates while a greater dispersion of expectations tends toward lower rates.

APPENDIX 14.1 EXPECTED ONE-YEAR-AHEAD CPI-INFLATION (EXP), ITS HETEROGENEITY (HET), AND UNCERTAINTY (UNC) FOR SIX ASIAN ECONOMIES

	Indo			Mal			Phi			Sin			SKo			Tha		
	Exp	Het	Unc	Exp	Het	Unc	Exp	Het	Unc	Exp	Het	Unc	Exp	Het	Unc	Exp	Het	Unc
1962	35.56	112.9	108.2	0.03	0.49	0.35	3.70	6.35	7.21	0.42	0.52	0.86	4.28	5.39	9.73	2.37	3.52	7.07
1963	42.96	53.39	87.78	1.88	6.45	6.08	3.83	4.72	8.08	1.56	4.34	4.29	10.90	16.29	19.46	0.34	5.54	6.10
1964	35.19	44.22	79.63	0.28	4.51	4.96	5.58	7.50	10.38	1.36	1.73	3.15	15.37	20.38	28.97	−0.57	1.96	1.89
1965	67.78	95.53	119.4	−0.14	0.56	0.70	2.14	3.87	7.32	0.20	2.96	3.28	7.02	10.53	21.21	−0.08	1.37	1.58
1966	112.7	157.9	199.9	0.61	2.10	1.98	3.95	5.60	6.92	1.36	4.60	4.35	6.70	8.37	14.97	2.36	8.09	7.63
1967	39.63	86.89	151.1	2.93	7.18	7.32	4.24	5.35	8.47	2.69	3.73	4.83	6.62	8.16	13.97	3.08	3.82	6.30
1968	40.26	50.68	80.59	0.40	6.53	7.19	1.82	2.90	5.81	0.58	3.99	4.95	6.57	8.10	13.77	1.37	2.13	4.30
1969	7.73	73.54	86.14	−0.42	0.76	0.74	1.54	1.92	3.45	−0.10	1.57	1.19	7.45	9.37	14.92	2.00	2.64	3.77
1970	7.18	9.05	16.33	0.94	3.21	3.05	7.30	23.59	22.52	0.26	0.85	0.95	9.32	12.06	18.04	0.24	3.85	4.23
1971	3.12	5.17	10.19	1.32	1.63	2.89	12.16	16.35	22.57	1.34	2.46	2.73	7.80	9.71	17.26	0.31	1.08	1.01
1972	4.68	6.38	8.55	2.58	3.65	4.53	5.06	7.89	15.92	1.68	2.13	3.33	6.95	8.63	15.27	2.89	9.74	9.21
1973	13.91	30.50	32.07	6.24	9.67	11.39	10.04	14.18	17.66	9.19	30.7	29.14	2.68	5.91	10.26	8.59	13.1	15.5
1974	19.04	24.59	36.96	10.47	14.40	18.95	17.62	24.84	31.03	11.9	14.9	23.97	11.07	35.66	34.06	13.6	18.4	24.8
1975	9.16	13.59	27.26	3.56	8.70	14.47	4.63	22.04	29.58	1.74	24.5	27.35	13.00	16.07	26.85	3.96	14.9	21.3
1976	10.76	13.31	22.25	1.76	2.51	4.92	6.05	7.97	11.48	−0.53	5.73	4.55	7.76	10.75	20.79	2.86	3.64	6.64
1977	5.84	8.38	16.52	3.64	5.10	6.45	6.16	7.65	12.58	1.33	4.39	4.92	5.65	7.62	14.51	5.36	7.51	9.50
1978	4.92	6.37	11.79	3.40	4.19	7.06	4.54	5.86	10.83	3.67	5.00	6.70	8.85	11.80	16.55	5.12	6.33	10.5
1979	9.88	13.95	17.40	2.54	3.27	6.02	10.17	14.52	17.77	2.87	3.59	6.42	10.37	13.35	20.18	6.29	8.08	12.3
1980	10.03	12.52	20.32	4.81	6.74	8.52	10.06	12.44	20.78	5.79	8.21	10.16	15.38	20.88	28.23	11.5	16.3	20.3
1981	6.72	8.94	16.85	6.42	8.62	11.94	7.24	9.43	17.51	5.23	6.45	11.07	10.89	13.95	25.60	6.76	9.18	17.6
1982	5.68	7.24	13.21	3.46	4.87	9.50	6.09	7.72	14.04	2.51	3.77	7.60	4.84	7.95	15.73	3.39	5.22	10.6

1983	7.26	9.33	14.18	2.40	3.31	6.38	6.20	7.64	13.02	1.13	2.16	3.99	2.25	3.38	6.81	2.52	3.32	6.21
1984	6.37	7.88	13.85	2.82	3.50	5.81	19.83	43.27	45.56	2.11	3.00	3.69	1.61	2.18	4.16	0.84	3.29	4.65
1985	3.00	4.54	9.18	0.38	5.93	6.56	10.63	15.82	31.77	0.43	3.47	4.17	1.91	2.38	3.90	1.88	2.76	3.32
1986	4.04	5.18	7.91	0.72	1.02	1.26	1.58	25.40	27.99	-0.67	2.93	2.38	2.11	2.64	4.26	1.42	1.82	3.36
1987	6.29	8.63	11.43	0.30	0.47	0.94	2.76	4.64	5.31	0.19	3.06	2.21	2.30	2.88	4.66	2.00	2.63	3.80
1988	5.11	6.35	11.23	1.70	5.68	5.38	7.74	12.22	14.30	1.25	1.85	2.22	4.88	6.97	8.53	3.02	4.14	5.50
1989	4.16	5.25	9.51	2.15	2.68	4.36	7.24	8.96	15.76	1.97	2.70	3.60	3.77	4.76	8.62	3.88	5.15	7.30
1990	5.15	6.58	10.13	2.00	2.47	4.28	7.27	8.96	15.20	2.73	3.68	5.03	5.84	7.91	10.76	3.99	4.98	8.11
1991	6.00	7.63	11.84	3.37	4.66	6.05	11.33	15.46	20.68	2.52	3.11	5.29	5.87	7.31	11.96	3.88	4.78	8.17
1992	4.75	6.00	10.85	3.36	4.18	6.82	4.94	7.47	15.08	1.60	2.17	4.15	3.78	5.10	9.70	2.78	3.63	6.75
1993	6.21	8.05	12.01	2.45	3.18	5.87	4.29	5.45	9.95	1.79	2.21	3.73	3.23	4.12	7.52	2.38	3.01	5.45
1994	5.38	6.66	11.73	2.72	3.37	5.59	6.87	9.37	12.58	2.43	3.21	4.61	4.35	5.67	8.37	3.77	5.13	6.91
1995	5.93	7.40	12.01	2.53	3.12	5.42	4.08	5.52	10.53	1.22	1.77	3.52	2.96	3.87	7.24	3.99	5.03	7.98
1996	5.06	6.30	11.22	2.57	3.17	5.34	4.89	6.09	9.94	1.13	1.43	2.59	3.45	4.30	7.00	3.94	4.86	8.23
1997	4.03	5.12	9.33	1.95	2.50	4.58	3.63	4.67	8.62	1.71	2.29	3.17	3.12	3.86	6.76	3.83	4.72	8.08
1998	20.93	68.90	65.51	3.91	5.52	6.87	6.29	8.69	11.34	0.19	3.1	3.41	5.31	7.37	9.53	5.45	7.27	10.2
1999	10.63	16.61	33.49	1.83	2.69	5.39	3.59	4.92	9.44	-0.04	0.57	0.67	0.70	10.23	11.36	0.66	10.7	11.8
2000	2.51	18.28	22.38	1.11	1.60	3.18	2.60	3.50	6.66	0.92	3.14	2.96	1.77	2.59	3.12	1.18	3.44	3.36
2001	6.77	10.21	12.16	1.19	1.46	2.54	3.84	5.05	7.31	0.83	1.08	2.00	3.17	4.44	5.63	1.34	1.66	2.78
2002	7.15	8.84	14.77	1.51	1.96	2.93	1.82	2.70	5.42	-0.14	2.27	1.71	1.92	2.57	4.88	0.61	0.93	1.89
2003	3.89	5.57	10.99	0.76	1.11	2.21	1.76	2.20	3.93	0.14	0.94	1.05	2.66	3.44	5.15	1.48	2.14	2.60
2004	4.06	5.02	8.79	1.36	1.86	2.49	3.59	5.10	6.29	1.31	2.07	2.42	2.63	3.25	5.46	2.26	3.09	4.14
2005	6.98	9.70	12.49	2.41	3.39	4.23	4.54	5.97	8.62	0.47	1.39	2.15	2.01	2.57	4.71	3.48	4.81	6.27
2006	7.91	10.17	15.44	2.70	3.45	5.29	3.70	4.61	8.23	0.89	1.28	1.56	1.72	2.16	3.90	3.27	4.03	6.77

(cont.)

	Indo			Mal			Phi			Sin			SKo			Tha		
	Exp	Het	Unc	Exp	Het	Unc	Exp	Het	Unc	Exp	Het	Unc	Exp	Het	Unc	Exp	Het	Unc
2007	3.77	5.62	11.29	1.40	2.03	4.02	1.91	2.80	5.60	1.76	2.51	3.08	1.97	2.48	3.97	1.56	2.35	4.73
2008	6.82	9.35	12.38	3.76	5.46	6.60	5.26	7.72	9.29	4.27	6.52	7.72	3.56	5.00	6.31	3.86	5.54	6.75
2009	2.88	4.41	8.92	0.53	7.82	8.68	2.63	3.90	7.81	0.60	9.27	10.2	1.83	2.60	5.11	0.44	7.18	7.90
2010	3.60	4.55	7.17	1.37	2.05	2.45	2.73	3.38	5.92	1.95	4.81	4.90	2.23	2.76	4.56	1.41	4.76	4.85
2011	3.69	4.57	7.61	2.57	3.61	4.54	3.39	4.36	6.62	3.92	5.51	6.94	3.04	4.02	5.75	2.80	3.54	5.57
2012	2.96	3.74	6.77	1.19	1.76	3.51	2.03	2.79	5.36	3.19	3.96	7.00	1.50	2.19	4.35	2.19	2.78	5.05
2013	4.59	6.22	8.45	1.72	2.22	3.33	1.96	2.44	4.34	1.61	2.38	4.77	0.97	1.37	2.69	1.61	2.11	3.93
2014	4.27	5.27	8.93	2.52	3.41	4.64	2.78	3.69	5.22	0.84	1.28	2.60	1.09	1.34	2.28	1.51	1.87	3.32
2015	4.25	5.24	8.89	1.51	2.04	3.89	0.58	4.48	5.43	-0.14	2.23	1.69	0.57	0.83	1.64	-0.24	3.81	2.88
2016	2.25	3.26	6.46	1.66	2.05	3.47	1.16	1.63	2.05	-0.52	1.08	1.25	0.91	1.20	1.71	-0.09	1.53	1.77
2017	2.77	3.45	5.66	3.04	4.27	5.37	2.26	3.23	3.95	0.17	1.22	1.37	1.67	2.37	2.94	0.59	1.00	1.14

I 5 The Fisher Effect in African Economies

I 5 . I INTRODUCTION

The study of the effect of inflation on the nominal interest rate in African economies has already brought forth a variety of results in the research literature. For one thing, the list of countries to be discussed is rather short. Berument and Jelassi (2002) and Kasman et al. (2006) report statistical evidence for a weak-form Fisher effect for Egypt. Yet, with the interest rate data studied here, the hypothesis under consideration does not gain any support in the case of Egypt. Hence, this country is not treated any further. For Nigeria, Balparda et al. (2017) suggest that the effect under investigation only shows up for very short-term interest rates. For Malawi, Matchaya (2011) indicates that the econometric evidence is consistent with the presence of a Fisher effect. The study of short-term interest rates for Kenya by Caporale and Gil-Alana (2016) does not offer an explicit test of the Fisher hypothesis. Hence, for this country, there exists no previous finding which would permit us to make comparisons. For South Africa, the findings concerning the link between inflation expectations and interest rates are more telling: Phiri and Lusanga (2011) and Kim et al. (2018) document a significant Fisher effect for various nominal interest rates.[1]

Namibia and Mozambique are examples of African economies where only sparse data on the CPI are available. In order to study six economies like in the previous chapter, Tanzania and Zambia are added to this study. As before, we proceed with the approach developed in Chapter 10 of computing a series of one-year-ahead

---

[1] For a shorter sample (2000 to 2005), at the beginning of South Africa's experience with inflation targets, Mitchell-Innes et al. (2007) find evidence for a partial Fisher effect on long-term rates.

expected inflation for the six African countries in this investigation. In order to have a consistent set of data, the interest rates studied are lending rates from the World Bank.[2] The data sets differ with respect to the years covered. As before for the Asian economies, interest rate observations are skipped when there are signs of politically pegged lending rates. Lending rates that are pegged over a number of years are also the reason for excluding a country like Algeria from this study.

15.2   ESTIMATING INTEREST RATE EQUATIONS

We start the estimation of the influence of expected inflation on African lending rates with the following specification:

$$\Delta i_t = \alpha_0 + \alpha_1 \Delta \pi_t^e + \varepsilon_t \qquad (15.1)$$

Table 15.1 shows the results of estimating this specification with the least squares method. For all six countries investigated, a positive effect of expected inflation on the lending rate can be documented. For three countries – namely Malawi, South Africa, and Zambia – this effect is statistically significant. For Malawi and Zambia, the estimates even lend support to a strong-form Fisher effect.

For African economies as before for Asian economies, it is interesting to ask how the heterogeneity and the uncertainty of inflation expectations affect interest rates. For this purpose, we quantify these two dimensions of inflation expectations by applying the pattern-based approach from Chapter 10. The data Appendix 15.1 presents the computed variables of expected inflation, its heterogeneity, and uncertainty for the six African countries studied. The following equation including the additional explanatory variables is first estimated by ordinary least squares:

$$\Delta i_t = \alpha_0 + \alpha_1 \Delta \pi_t^e + \alpha_2 \Delta \pi_t^{e,\,Heter} + \alpha_3 \Delta \pi_t^{e,\,Uncer} + \varepsilon_t \qquad (15.2)$$

---

[2] The lending rate according to the World Bank is the bank rate that meets the short- and medium-term financing demands of the private sector. All data used here are drawn from the World Bank's web portal under https://data.worldbank.org/indicator/.

Table 15.1 *Interest rate equation in first differences*

Country	α_0	α_1	$\overline{R}^2$	D.W.	Std. Err.
Kenya	−0.011	0.207	0.034	1.979	3.381
1988–2017	(0.617)	(0.216)			
Malawi	0.650	0.629**	0.283	1.894	5.638
1982–2016	(0.971)	(0.216)			
Nigeria	0.243	0.046	0.000	2.335	3.083
1980–2017	(0.506)	(0.094)			
South Africa	0.054	0.470*	0.056	1.641	2.220
1962–2017	(0.299)	(0.191)			
Tanzania	−0.428	0.542	0.092	1.250	3.161
1993–2016	(0.671)	(0.300)			
Zambia	−1.695	1.094*	0.199	2.161	6.639
1992–2017	(1.309)	(0.514)			

**, * indicate significance at the 1 percent and 5 percent level of significance, respectively.
Numbers in parentheses are White heteroskedasticity-consistent standard errors of estimated coefficients.

The estimates are reported in Table 15.2. The results here are not quite as strong as those for the Asian economies studied in Chapter 14. In particular, a significantly positive effect of inflation uncertainty on lending rates is only found for Nigeria and in Malawi.[3] Heterogeneity of inflation expectations appears in a statistically significant way in the cases of Kenya and Malawi. Confirming the findings already reported for other countries, a higher heterogeneity of expectations tends to lower lending rates while higher expectations uncertainty tends to raise rates. For African economies, taking into consideration the role of the heterogeneity and uncertainty of inflation does not always result in estimates showing a stronger Fisher effect. In the case of South Africa, the coefficient of expected inflation is higher than

[3] For Tanzania, the effect in question has a *p* value of 0.063.

Table 15.2 *Interest rate equations allowing for effects of heterogeneity and uncertainty*

Country	α_0	α_1	α_2	α_3	$\bar{R}^2$	D.W.	Std. Err.
Kenya	−0.034	0.247	−0.348*	0.275	0.125	1.649	3.218
1988–2017	(0.581)	(0.186)	(0.170)	(0.246)			
Malawi	0.535	1.493*	−1.411**	0.801**	0.589	1.758	4.269
1982–2016	(0.728)	(0.690)	(0.426)	(0.176)			
Nigeria	0.230	−0.142*	−0.054	0.224*	0.177	2.115	2.768
1980–2017	(0.452)	(0.070)	(0.111)	(0.110)			
S. Africa	0.058	0.622	−0.049	−0.087	0.023	1.630	2.259
1962–2017	(0.302)	(0.334)	(0.380)	(0.459)			
Tanzania	−0.566	0.305	−0.931	0.925	0.212	1.465	2.473
1993–2016	(0.421)	(1.430)	(1.005)	(0.466)			
Zambia	−0.799	−2.096	2.057	0.386	0.533	2.142	5.065
1992–2017	(1.127)	(2.028)	(2.199)	(0.560)			

**, * indicate significance at the 1 percent and 5 percent level of significance, respectively.
Numbers in parentheses are White heteroskedasticity-consistent standard errors of estimated coefficients.

before, but only marginally significant. Further, the reported findings for South Africa tie in with a lively debate on the effects of expected inflation and its heterogeneity to which Nhlapo (2013), Kabundi and Schaling (2013), and Kabundi et al. (2015) have contributed. For Kenya, Malawi, and South Africa, the estimated α_1 coefficient is higher in Table 15.2 compared to Table 15.1. By contrast, for Nigeria and Zambia, the sign of the coefficient of expected inflation even turns negative in the new set of estimates.

Finally, Eq. (15.2) is also estimated using the instrumental variables method. As instruments, we use the lagged terms of the endogenous and the exogenous variables for the country considered

Table 15.3 *Instrumental variables estimates of interest rate equations*

Country	α_0	α_1	α_2	α_3	$\bar{R}^2$	D.W.	Std. Err.
Kenya 1988–2017	−0.100 (0.857)	−0.214 (0.318)	−0.412 (0.285)	0.084 (0.250)	0.000	1.970	4.683
Malawi 1982–2016	0.581 (0.792)	2.121* (0.957)	−1.962* (0.756)	0.727** (0.177)	0.538	1.896	4.594
Nigeria 1980–2017	0.236 (0.480)	−0.013 (0.245)	−0.102 (0.108)	0.237* (0.091)	0.120	2.105	2.903
S. Africa 1962–2017	0.060 (0.316)	0.616 (0.504)	0.084 (0.589)	−0.009 (0.400)	0.000	1.681	2.310
Tanzania 1993–2016	−0.583 (0.691)	0.793 (2.353)	−1.293 (1.995)	0.905 (0.546)	0.211	1.503	2.482
Zambia 1992–2017	−0.866 (1.159)	−2.847 (3.241)	2.934 (3.794)	0.165 (1.026)	0.530	2.105	5.085

**, * indicate significance at the 1 percent and 5 percent level of significance, respectively.
Numbers in parentheses are White heteroskedasticity-consistent standard errors of estimated coefficients.

as well as from one other major African economy, which here is Egypt. Table 15.3 documents that the instrumental variables method implies no major changes compared to the ordinary least squares results.

15.3   SUMMARY AND CONCLUSIONS

The findings for African economies are somewhat less informative concerning the Fisher effect compared to the results for the Asian economies. Nevertheless, applying the pattern-based approach to the quantification of inflation expectations helps to establish a number of results. First, there is evidence of a Fisher effect in lending rates for Malawi, South Africa, and Zambia. Further, a general tendency for higher heterogeneity of inflation expectations to lower interest rates can be reported. Finally, also for African economies, higher inflation uncertainty tends to raise lending rates. The expectations data reported here should be of interest for researchers studying the influence of expected inflation, its heterogeneity, and uncertainty in African economies.

APPENDIX 15.1   EXPECTED ONE-YEAR-AHEAD
    CPI-INFLATION (EXP), ITS HETEROGENEITY
    (HET), AND UNCERTAINTY (UNC) FOR SIX
    AFRICAN ECONOMIES

	Ken			Mal			Nig			SAf			Tan			Zam		
	Exp	Het	Unc	Exp	Het	Unc	Exp	Het	Unc	Exp	Het	Unc	Exp	Het	Unc	Exp	Het	Unc
1962	2.40	3.11	4.65				3.57	4.45	7.96	0.93	1.32	2.59						
1963	0.68	3.05	4.16				-0.56	8.91	6.74	1.14	1.41	2.32						
1964	0.08	1.25	1.38				0.33	5.50	4.03	2.12	2.98	3.73						
1965	2.01	6.90	6.50				2.67	6.67	6.76	3.17	4.36	5.73						
1966	3.68	4.90	6.91				6.28	8.97	10.97	2.53	3.15	5.59						
1967	1.48	2.44	4.81				-0.96	15.42	11.67	2.60	3.21	5.40	7.45	9.57	14.56			
1968	0.37	2.14	2.74				-0.42	5.88	6.87	1.38	1.99	3.95	9.14	11.81	17.73			
1969	-0.06	0.94	0.71				4.72	16.19	15.26	2.61	3.61	4.71	9.27	11.48	19.08			
1970	1.27	4.34	4.09				8.38	11.01	15.95	3.74	5.10	6.84	2.68	12.16	16.53			
1971	2.99	4.16	5.33				9.17	11.55	18.32	4.09	5.20	8.10	3.51	4.64	6.64			
1972	4.26	5.81	7.79				2.69	11.60	15.97	4.31	5.35	8.79	5.36	7.36	9.72			
1973	6.30	8.63	11.44				4.01	5.48	7.30	6.29	8.46	11.66	6.69	8.81	12.69			
1974	10.70	15.04	18.91				7.85	11.20	13.71	7.22	9.26	14.11	11.56	16.21	20.48			
1975	10.48	13.01	21.44				16.67	23.95	29.15	7.94	9.98	15.94	13.78	17.94	26.48			
1976	6.09	8.51	16.55				11.90	15.41	28.54	6.56	8.22	14.75	5.07	11.19	19.40			
1977	8.80	11.41	17.00				7.71	10.59	20.39	6.77	8.36	14.08	7.60	10.53	13.64			
1978	9.57	12.01	19.22				12.20	16.26	22.87	6.76	8.33	14.12	3.80	5.45	10.75			
1979	4.55	6.83	13.76				6.11	8.85	17.54	7.93	10.06	15.71	8.25	11.63	14.53			
1980	8.78	12.21	15.71				6.09	7.58	13.46	7.99	9.87	16.55	15.70	22.34	27.46			
1981	6.87	8.58	15.31				11.98	16.94	21.04	8.78	10.98	17.76	12.97	16.12	28.58			

(cont.)

	Ken			Mal			Nig			SAf			Tan			Zam		
	Exp	Het	Unc	Exp	Het	Unc	Exp	Het	Unc	Exp	Het	Unc	Exp	Het	Unc	Exp	Het	Unc
1982	12.08	16.82	21.57	5.99	7.48	13.38	4.89	7.71	15.50	8.42	10.38	17.81	14.50	18.14	29.30			
1983	5.99	8.61	17.01	8.29	10.94	15.70	12.05	17.75	21.33	7.22	9.00	16.04	13.64	16.81	29.06			
1984	6.29	7.77	13.60	11.54	15.51	21.42	9.52	12.10	22.06	6.93	8.54	14.77	17.62	22.92	33.92			
1985	7.88	10.15	15.33	5.60	8.18	16.29	4.49	6.90	13.95	9.70	12.89	18.24	15.95	19.66	34.11			
1986	1.90	11.88	14.98	8.49	11.11	16.24	3.73	4.77	8.72	10.34	12.98	20.76	15.69	19.33	32.99			
1987	5.24	8.38	9.76	14.08	19.60	25.14	7.37	10.40	12.98	9.04	11.21	19.81	14.73	18.16	31.49	20.39	25.32	44.83
1988	7.73	10.30	14.49	16.85	21.98	32.33	21.09	42.97	46.17	7.34	9.27	16.79	15.27	18.89	31.53	21.92	27.23	44.84
1989	8.10	10.14	16.35	7.16	11.22	22.61	21.61	26.64	46.08	8.57	10.78	17.16	13.00	16.21	28.92	41.80	59.04	73.52
1990	10.16	13.15	19.68	7.08	8.72	15.02	4.21	40.01	46.88	8.28	10.20	17.44	17.66	23.20	33.62	35.43	43.76	76.57
1991	10.94	13.70	22.06	7.51	9.31	15.38	8.34	11.63	14.88	8.79	10.91	17.99	13.99	17.56	31.57	33.57	41.38	71.65
1992	14.37	18.82	27.43	13.44	18.84	23.84	19.35	29.24	34.77	8.04	9.92	17.33	11.17	14.21	25.92	48.90	65.65	90.93
1993	21.95	30.09	39.87	11.96	14.73	25.28	24.21	31.02	47.38	5.61	7.39	13.84	13.12	16.50	26.29	48.70	60.46	99.70
1994	12.97	17.55	33.49	17.60	23.69	32.62	23.62	29.13	49.34	5.62	6.93	12.05	16.91	22.06	32.45	21.72	33.66	68.02
1995	1.89	30.15	33.23	32.54	46.11	57.06	28.46	36.36	55.92	5.50	6.78	11.59	13.53	16.97	30.47	15.16	20.28	38.40
1996	5.02	14.59	14.26	15.29	22.57	45.16	13.08	19.80	40.00	4.73	5.89	10.49	10.83	13.77	25.09	19.70	25.07	38.89
1997	7.08	9.17	13.71	6.45	15.86	26.32	5.90	10.80	20.33	5.53	6.99	11.02	8.77	11.16	20.35	11.09	15.60	30.45
1998	3.90	5.50	10.76	14.38	21.61	25.76	6.27	7.92	12.48	4.41	5.57	10.07	7.36	9.28	16.79	12.66	15.62	26.42
1999	3.85	4.79	8.51	21.15	28.32	39.43	3.98	5.37	10.24	3.41	4.39	8.07	4.50	6.25	12.10	13.64	16.98	27.78

2000	6.72	9.35	12.01	13.49	17.90	33.72	4.58	5.67	9.43	3.68	4.55	7.61	3.81	4.91	9.03	13.27	16.35	27.93
2001	3.40	4.85	9.55	11.54	14.65	26.65	10.47	15.14	18.35	3.89	4.83	7.97	3.52	4.37	7.73	11.20	14.00	25.05
2002	1.64	2.75	5.39	7.68	10.38	19.77	7.01	9.30	17.51	6.44	8.91	11.59	3.67	4.53	7.58	11.78	14.56	24.32
2003	5.52	14.15	14.26	5.38	7.30	13.96	8.19	10.20	16.68	3.39	4.77	9.32	3.65	4.50	7.63	11.39	14.04	24.06
2004	7.10	8.99	14.10	7.01	8.90	13.89	8.63	10.71	17.68	0.46	7.53	8.28	3.30	4.08	7.16	9.79	12.20	21.72
2005	6.30	7.79	13.69	9.17	12.02	17.49	10.04	12.72	19.93	0.92	3.05	3.42	3.51	4.35	7.19	10.11	12.48	20.98
2006	8.80	11.67	16.57	8.08	9.98	17.42	4.70	7.08	14.29	2.61	3.58	4.74	5.04	6.75	9.39	4.98	7.40	14.85
2007	5.55	7.41	14.02	4.46	6.37	12.55	3.33	4.52	8.65	4.49	6.32	7.92	4.61	5.68	9.73	6.61	8.37	13.14
2008	13.64	19.64	23.87	5.55	6.92	11.28	7.42	10.53	12.99	6.74	9.28	12.19	6.74	9.06	12.52	7.49	9.46	14.94
2009	5.79	9.24	18.50	5.36	6.61	11.32	6.96	8.58	14.54	4.46	5.81	10.81	7.36	9.31	14.62	7.88	9.80	16.11
2010	2.64	4.05	8.19	4.79	5.93	10.45	8.13	10.30	16.13	2.53	3.66	7.24	3.63	5.37	10.74	4.83	6.63	12.75
2011	7.75	12.61	14.59	4.95	6.12	10.25	6.41	8.11	14.69	3.57	4.58	6.98	8.07	11.41	14.17	4.10	5.26	9.65
2012	5.35	7.17	13.61	11.45	16.61	20.10	7.35	9.20	14.81	3.93	4.94	7.89	9.30	11.96	18.12	4.38	5.41	9.08
2013	3.43	4.79	9.31	14.15	18.25	27.52	4.99	6.60	12.40	3.92	4.84	8.17	4.46	6.63	13.31	4.61	5.71	9.45
2014	4.62	5.88	9.12	12.28	15.21	26.80	5.17	6.37	10.96	4.14	5.13	8.49	3.98	5.06	9.21	5.08	6.36	10.26
2015	4.37	5.38	9.25	11.56	14.25	24.76	5.72	7.15	11.55	3.00	3.90	7.23	3.80	4.69	8.18	6.46	8.38	12.45
2016	4.21	5.19	8.91	11.54	14.22	24.14	9.70	13.48	17.35	4.67	6.29	8.67	3.56	4.39	7.63	10.77	14.99	19.23
2017	5.30	6.85	10.28	6.33	9.04	17.81	9.32	11.55	19.17	3.46	4.39	7.98	3.67	4.53	7.59	4.31	6.84	13.73

16 Estimates of Expected Inflation for Major Economies

16.1 INTRODUCTION

In the following, estimates of expected inflation for 10 large economies will be presented. Due to space constraints, we have to limit the coverage to this relatively small set of countries. The economies selected are the largest according to their real GDP as documented by the World Bank in 2017: the USA, China, Japan, Germany, the United Kingdom, India, France, Brazil, Italy, and Canada. The main purpose of this project is to offer a service to fellow researchers and analysts. The estimates provide a starting point for those who do not want to compute pattern-based expectations by themselves. For those who need estimates for other countries or for higher frequency data, the spreadsheet files for the computation of pattern-based expectations are available for download from the website of this book.

16.2 EXPECTED INFLATION SERIES

The price-level measure used for the computations in this chapter is the CPI measure available from the World Bank.[1] For each country covered, annual series for the one-year- ahead expected inflation (Exp) as well as the associated measures of heterogeneity (Het) and uncertainty (Unc) are reported.[2] The series start in 1962 except for China and Brazil for which, due to the limited availability of data, the series

---

[1] All data used here are drawn from the World Bank's web portal under https://data .worldbank.org/indicator/.

[2] Note that for the heterogeneity measure, the same procedure as in Chapters 14 and 15 is used. This means that models for the upper limit (95 percent) and lower limit (5 percent) of the interquartile range are estimated. This contrasts with the more involved computations presented for the USA in Chapter 7 where the heterogeneity measure is based on specifying individual models for each subject.

start only in 1988 and 1982, respectively. Table 16.1 presents the expectations series for the USA, China, Japan, Germany, and the United Kingdom. Table 16.2 continues with the data for India, France, Brazil, Italy, and Canada. Finally, estimates for the long-term, that is, five-year-ahead, expected inflation for the 10 major economies are reported in Table 16.3. The final Chapter 17 will make use of pattern-based measures of expected inflation to compute ex ante real rates of interest for the countries covered here.

Table 16.1 *Expected one-year-ahead CPI inflation, its heterogeneity, and uncertainty for the USA, China, Japan, Germany, and the United Kingdom*

	USA			Chi			Jap			Ger			UK		
	Exp	Het	Unc	Exp	Het	Unc	Exp	Het	Unc	Exp	Het	Unc	Exp	Het	Unc
1962	1.04	1.30	2.10				4.65	6.02	9.01	2.21	2.84	4.31	3.06	3.91	6.01
1963	1.06	1.32	2.20				4.44	5.47	9.33	2.24	2.77	4.62	1.43	2.15	4.34
1964	1.09	1.35	2.26				2.40	3.45	6.81	1.76	2.24	4.07	2.64	3.65	4.77
1965	1.34	1.73	2.62				4.80	6.70	8.57	2.54	3.38	4.78	3.56	4.79	6.61
1966	2.45	3.45	4.32				3.34	4.29	7.88	2.61	3.25	5.30	2.76	3.47	6.23
1967	2.10	2.59	4.51				2.78	3.52	6.40	1.28	1.90	3.81	1.71	2.36	4.55
1968	3.28	4.48	6.00				3.83	5.03	7.30	1.20	1.51	2.71	3.57	5.02	6.30
1969	3.86	5.00	7.47				3.62	4.46	7.60	1.60	2.08	3.06	3.78	4.77	7.54
1970	3.97	4.93	8.13				4.74	6.20	9.09	2.76	3.87	4.90	4.31	5.45	8.59
1971	2.88	3.74	6.93				4.25	5.25	9.12	3.89	5.28	7.13	6.31	8.51	11.67
1972	2.32	2.98	5.46				3.23	4.14	7.62	3.76	4.66	7.75	4.42	5.69	10.48
1973	4.49	6.32	7.94				7.26	10.39	12.69	4.77	6.18	9.22	5.98	7.77	11.51
1974	7.31	10.21	13.00				13.14	18.51	23.15	4.60	5.67	9.62	9.88	13.74	17.67
1975	5.64	7.05	12.63				6.14	9.05	18.09	3.94	4.91	8.75	13.41	18.08	24.83
1976	3.47	4.79	9.25				5.71	7.20	13.01	2.83	3.70	6.91	8.61	11.38	21.39
1977	4.37	5.48	8.79				5.18	6.42	11.35	2.69	3.34	5.88	8.97	11.05	18.99
1978	5.02	6.34	9.98				2.62	3.87	7.76	1.95	2.54	4.72	4.60	6.74	13.45

Year															
1979	7.27	9.79	13.48				2.67	3.31	5.84	3.11	4.21	5.74	8.52	11.72	15.44
1980	8.06	10.25	15.94				5.36	7.60	9.40	3.90	5.13	7.42	10.34	13.52	19.78
1981	6.10	7.79	14.26				3.04	4.20	8.10	4.30	5.43	8.56	6.48	8.71	16.54
1982	3.61	5.09	9.96				1.82	2.63	5.21	3.54	4.44	7.96	5.14	6.68	12.42
1983	2.08	3.07	6.13				1.40	1.87	3.53	2.17	3.00	5.80	2.82	4.12	8.21
1984	3.20	4.20	6.09				1.80	2.29	3.57	1.76	2.29	4.25	3.47	4.31	7.08
1985	2.55	3.19	5.73				1.61	1.99	3.49	1.62	2.02	3.58	4.18	5.34	8.20
1986	1.33	1.95	3.89				0.63	1.31	2.33	0.20	3.29	3.62	2.20	3.16	6.25
1987	2.89	4.07	5.08				0.15	0.83	1.07	0.15	0.50	0.56	3.03	3.86	5.96
1988	2.95	3.69	5.96	10.55	15.18	18.46	0.57	1.62	1.59	0.98	2.66	2.64	2.82	3.47	6.00
1989	3.43	4.34	6.79	10.05	12.38	21.18	1.70	2.73	3.17	2.23	3.18	3.91	3.72	4.87	7.12
1990	3.73	4.67	7.54	2.04	18.12	21.44	2.42	3.19	4.58	2.06	2.54	4.34	4.84	6.38	9.18
1991	2.92	3.70	6.74	2.64	3.34	5.26	2.42	3.00	4.98	3.12	4.23	5.74	4.90	6.08	10.03
1992	2.12	2.78	5.20	4.62	6.46	8.21	1.25	1.82	3.63	3.60	4.63	7.02	2.65	3.80	7.50
1993	2.22	2.74	4.68	8.85	12.61	15.47	0.98	1.30	2.44	3.14	3.89	6.84	1.70	2.41	4.73
1994	1.99	2.46	4.33	13.64	18.76	24.68	0.56	0.81	1.62	1.80	2.54	4.97	1.50	1.92	3.50
1995	2.14	2.66	4.37	8.75	11.51	21.56	0.07	1.23	1.35	1.24	1.71	3.31	2.15	2.85	4.06
1996	2.22	2.75	4.57	4.65	6.91	13.86	0.05	0.36	0.40	1.20	1.49	2.65	1.90	2.34	4.07
1997	1.77	2.24	4.06	2.23	3.76	7.35	1.20	4.07	3.84	1.63	2.14	3.09	1.39	1.80	3.34
1998	1.16	1.57	3.01	-0.20	5.18	4.26	0.62	0.98	1.97	0.73	1.11	2.24	1.27	1.59	2.82
1999	1.83	2.44	3.42	-1.30	2.37	2.38	-0.10	1.53	1.16	0.50	0.68	1.32	1.13	1.40	2.48
2000	2.69	3.67	4.91	-0.08	2.37	2.52	-0.68	1.24	1.23	1.24	1.78	2.17	0.63	0.90	1.77
2001	2.11	2.63	4.71	0.71	1.01	1.24	-0.69	1.41	1.62	1.67	2.22	3.15	1.15	1.57	2.09

Table 16.1 (cont.)

	USA			Chi			Jap			Ger			UK		
	Exp	Het	Unc	Exp	Het	Unc	Exp	Het	Unc	Exp	Het	Unc	Exp	Het	Unc
2002	1.14	1.65	3.26	-0.22	2.16	1.74	-0.85	1.69	1.87	1.11	1.46	2.73	1.06	1.30	2.21
2003	1.89	2.54	3.52	0.55	1.82	2.04	-0.31	1.09	1.38	0.85	1.11	2.07	1.17	1.46	2.36
2004	2.08	2.64	4.13	2.64	4.27	4.95	-0.04	0.57	0.67	1.48	2.04	2.68	1.14	1.40	2.39
2005	2.58	3.34	5.00	1.30	1.97	3.98	-0.24	0.83	0.80	1.28	1.58	2.74	1.73	2.35	3.18
2006	2.39	2.95	5.08	1.35	1.67	2.89	0.10	0.71	0.79	1.31	1.61	2.71	1.94	2.48	3.82
2007	2.14	2.65	4.67	3.32	4.93	5.90	0.09	0.31	0.45	1.92	2.59	3.56	1.86	2.29	3.91
2008	2.91	3.83	5.53	4.10	5.25	8.03	0.95	3.25	3.07	2.04	2.56	4.08	2.77	3.73	5.11
2009	0.34	5.49	6.04	0.48	7.79	8.57	-0.39	3.77	3.05	0.29	4.20	4.68	1.37	1.98	3.92
2010	0.86	2.93	2.78	1.47	5.03	4.80	-0.58	1.53	1.96	0.91	1.53	1.75	1.99	2.57	3.85
2011	2.54	3.59	4.48	4.13	5.76	7.36	-0.29	0.81	1.04	1.79	2.51	3.15	3.01	4.11	5.50
2012	1.48	2.01	3.86	1.80	2.71	5.47	-0.06	0.52	0.62	1.60	1.97	3.38	1.79	2.42	4.62
2013	1.13	1.50	2.81	2.01	2.48	4.20	0.24	0.83	0.79	1.19	1.53	2.83	1.78	2.20	3.87
2014	1.35	1.68	2.72	1.45	1.89	3.51	1.83	6.05	5.74	0.71	1.00	1.96	1.08	1.49	2.88
2015	0.18	2.81	3.10	1.14	1.48	2.72	0.81	1.75	3.06	0.28	0.81	1.27	0.42	1.26	1.93
2016	0.92	3.10	2.93	1.69	2.24	3.17	0.09	1.39	1.53	0.50	0.72	0.88	0.89	1.30	1.57
2017	1.83	2.55	3.29	1.28	1.61	2.93	0.28	0.94	0.92	1.33	2.29	2.60	2.01	2.89	3.52

Table 16.2 Expected one-year-ahead CPI inflation, its heterogeneity, and uncertainty for India, France, Brazil, Italy, and Canada

	Ind			Fra			Bra			Ita			Can		
	Exp	Het	Unc	Exp	Het	Unc	Exp	Het	Unc	Exp	Het	Unc	Exp	Het	Unc
1962	2.81	4.00	4.92	3.86	5.50	6.75				3.44	4.92	6.02	0.93	1.15	1.92
1963	2.17	2.73	4.92	3.46	4.27	7.39				5.25	7.20	9.54	1.45	1.97	2.64
1964	7.17	15.91	16.67	2.13	2.93	5.64				3.88	4.91	8.90	1.56	1.98	3.1
1965	5.52	7.24	13.51	2.03	2.54	4.53				3.06	3.91	7.17	1.86	2.38	3.65
1966	6.65	8.35	13.36	2.00	2.46	4.22				1.60	2.36	4.73	3.00	4.15	5.42
1967	7.84	9.97	15.46	2.13	2.65	4.36				2.94	4.04	5.33	2.61	3.22	5.57
1968	2.68	7.69	12.05	3.48	4.80	6.28				1.14	1.92	3.76	2.94	3.69	5.91
1969	0.28	4.56	5.02	4.25	5.57	8.11				2.17	3.08	3.80	3.24	4.06	6.53
1970	2.49	8.55	8.06	3.61	4.48	7.91				3.75	5.27	6.62	2.33	3.03	5.62
1971	2.02	2.85	5.56	3.71	4.58	7.70				3.35	4.12	7.07	2.01	2.54	4.58
1972	4.58	6.50	8.03	4.12	5.16	8.30				3.98	5.06	7.85	3.76	5.28	6.66
1973	9.67	13.94	16.94	4.91	6.27	9.66				7.15	10.04	12.64	5.22	7.07	9.62
1974	15.49	21.35	27.97	8.66	12.14	15.36				11.38	15.84	20.32	7.13	9.59	13.23
1975	4.04	19.34	25.91	6.94	8.63	15.30				9.42	11.65	20.47	6.52	8.03	13.74
1976	-2.78	13.07	10.59	5.88	7.36	13.19				9.33	11.50	19.60	4.56	5.99	11.21
1977	1.76	12.52	14.04	5.93	7.30	12.43				9.58	11.84	19.83	5.15	6.38	10.57
1978	2.13	4.02	7.47	5.80	7.14	12.20				6.74	8.84	16.50	5.70	7.14	11.50

Table 16.2 (cont.)

	Ind			Fra			Bra			Ita			Can		
	Exp	Het	Unc	Exp	Het	Unc	Exp	Het	Unc	Exp	Het	Unc	Exp	Het	Unc
1979	4.32	6.20	7.55	6.58	8.28	13.18				8.68	11.08	17.08	5.75	7.11	11.94
1980	7.46	10.43	13.26	8.16	10.54	15.85				11.89	15.80	22.35	6.29	7.86	12.75
1981	7.80	9.83	15.62	7.81	9.63	16.40				9.82	12.20	21.64	7.57	9.69	14.86
1982	4.47	6.27	12.21	7.13	8.81	15.41	34.29	42.27	71.78	9.24	11.40	19.82	6.50	8.07	14.29
1983	7.62	10.31	14.06	5.73	7.25	13.15	41.90	53.72	81.98	8.38	10.36	18.19	3.45	5.01	9.95
1984	4.93	6.50	12.18	4.85	6.10	10.99	51.19	66.04	99.43	6.24	8.06	14.89	2.89	3.75	6.95
1985	3.45	4.64	8.83	3.78	4.84	8.89	54.46	67.99	110.3	5.70	7.09	12.60	2.84	3.51	6.10
1986	5.98	8.17	10.88	1.81	2.77	5.60	41.08	52.67	96.70	3.52	4.84	9.33	3.01	3.73	6.17
1987	5.57	6.88	11.61	2.53	3.29	4.86	56.61	74.07	108.3	3.25	4.08	7.35	3.10	3.84	6.40
1988	5.89	7.31	12.07	2.02	2.53	4.55	92.09	127.8	165.1	3.52	4.37	7.21	2.88	3.56	6.18
1989	4.43	5.69	10.46	2.66	3.46	5.12	117.1	155.3	220.8	4.30	5.51	8.40	3.55	4.55	6.94
1990	5.82	7.52	11.30	2.37	2.92	5.10	138.9	179.1	269.9	4.31	5.33	8.92	3.34	4.12	7.07
1991	8.69	11.83	15.93	2.39	2.95	4.99	64.80	97.25	196.0	4.18	5.16	8.83	3.89	4.93	7.73
1992	6.98	8.69	15.44	1.74	2.25	4.18	103.8	138.5	194.1	3.57	4.46	7.95	1.39	3.56	5.82
1993	3.68	5.36	10.67	1.66	2.05	3.60	125.1	162.4	241.5	3.22	4.00	7.05	1.55	1.99	3.01
1994	6.84	9.41	12.39	1.31	1.67	3.04	123.7	152.8	256.3	2.88	3.57	6.31	0.20	3.17	3.51
1995	6.30	7.77	13.17	1.47	1.82	2.98	22.42	236.3	272.8	3.74	4.86	7.20	1.43	4.85	4.58
1996	5.61	6.95	12.25	1.60	1.99	3.23	10.01	21.72	37.94	2.76	3.53	6.48	1.22	1.59	2.96

1997	4.56	5.76	10.42	0.91	1.28	2.50	4.15	6.31	12.77	1.43	2.12	4.25	1.34	1.65	2.77
1998	8.45	11.84	14.98	0.53	0.78	1.55	2.14	3.24	6.55	1.56	1.93	3.31	0.77	1.08	2.11
1999	3.33	5.40	10.75	0.51	0.64	1.14	3.65	4.96	6.69	1.35	1.68	2.98	1.54	2.15	2.74
2000	2.85	3.54	6.29	1.33	2.04	2.41	4.93	6.62	9.16	2.11	2.87	3.86	2.25	3.08	4.08
2001	2.74	3.37	5.83	1.34	1.66	2.83	4.51	5.56	9.51	2.13	2.66	4.32	1.94	2.39	4.16
2002	3.09	3.88	6.20	1.57	1.99	3.11	5.51	7.06	10.79	1.89	2.34	4.13	1.76	2.18	3.82
2003	2.74	3.39	5.96	1.67	2.09	3.40	9.22	12.82	16.49	2.06	2.56	4.19	2.15	2.75	4.21
2004	2.74	3.37	5.73	1.70	2.10	3.52	3.96	6.00	12.13	1.70	2.13	3.83	1.36	1.83	3.49
2005	3.05	3.83	6.15	1.39	1.75	3.15	4.54	5.62	9.37	1.58	1.95	3.42	1.77	2.25	3.50
2006	4.13	5.45	7.81	1.37	1.69	2.90	2.63	3.68	7.17	1.66	2.06	3.42	1.59	1.96	3.44
2007	4.28	5.34	8.69	1.23	1.52	2.68	2.63	3.26	5.77	1.47	1.82	3.21	1.70	2.11	3.47
2008	5.53	7.21	10.62	2.31	3.25	4.08	4.18	5.71	7.61	2.69	3.77	4.76	1.86	2.32	3.76
2009	6.87	8.93	13.22	0.27	4.45	4.90	3.37	4.19	7.42	0.76	3.03	4.27	0.28	3.82	4.27
2010	7.22	9.00	14.65	1.05	3.59	3.39	3.50	4.33	7.25	1.36	1.93	2.40	1.29	3.90	3.78
2011	5.31	6.85	12.66	1.76	2.34	3.32	4.58	5.98	8.77	2.30	3.22	4.07	2.39	3.30	4.31
2012	5.85	7.25	12.03	1.56	1.92	3.34	3.62	4.55	8.20	2.30	2.86	4.66	1.10	1.63	3.26
2013	6.73	8.50	13.41	0.72	1.10	2.22	4.21	5.30	8.43	1.01	1.58	3.18	0.74	1.03	2.00
2014	3.71	5.27	10.33	0.43	0.61	1.21	4.24	5.23	8.80	0.25	1.69	2.10	1.64	2.33	2.88
2015	3.96	4.89	8.49	0.07	1.04	1.15	6.03	8.05	11.27	0.05	0.50	0.58	0.85	1.21	2.38
2016	3.38	4.22	7.54	0.19	0.48	0.49	5.53	6.81	11.66	-0.07	0.29	0.23	1.24	1.60	2.39
2017	1.69	2.52	5.05	0.81	2.39	2.33	2.45	3.83	7.72	0.77	2.65	2.50	1.33	1.66	2.68

Table 16.3 *Expected five-year-ahead CPI inflation for the USA, China, Japan, Germany, the United Kingdom, India, France, Brazil, Italy, and Canada*

	USA	Chi	Jap	Ger	UK	Ind	Fra	Bra	Ita	Can
1962	0.76		2.92	1.49	2.01	1.70	2.27		2.04	0.69
1963	0.78		2.89	1.55	0.73	1.44	2.29		3.11	0.96
1964	0.80		1.27	1.18	1.65	3.83	1.24		2.43	1.1
1965	0.95		2.82	1.65	2.22	3.18	1.38		1.92	1.28
1966	1.51		2.07	1.77	1.8	4.14	1.39		0.83	1.86
1967	1.45		1.79	0.67	1.00	4.76	1.48		1.83	1.77
1968	2.03		2.42	0.84	2.13	1.38	2.12		0.57	1.97
1969	2.46		2.39	1.10	2.46	0.38	2.66		1.35	2.15
1970	2.60		2.95	1.70	2.78	1.38	2.35		2.23	1.47
1971	1.78		2.76	2.38	3.73	1.13	2.45		2.23	1.34
1972	1.49		2.01	2.48	2.67	2.66	2.68		2.57	2.24
1973	2.63		4.03	2.99	3.66	5.23	3.10		4.03	3.13
1974	4.13		6.99	2.98	5.46	8.29	4.81		6.20	4.18
1975	3.48		2.87	2.52	7.42	2.36	4.25		5.66	4.09
1976	1.91		3.47	1.73	4.70	−0.51	3.61		5.68	2.66
1977	2.82		3.27	1.80	5.47	1.20	3.76		5.82	3.30
1978	3.18		1.31	1.24	2.22	1.02	3.68		3.81	3.60
1979	4.25		1.79	1.95	4.82	2.51	4.09		5.22	3.66
1980	4.89		3.07	2.46	6.00	4.20	4.89		6.73	3.95

Year										
1981	3.62		1.70	2.77	3.53	4.78	4.83		5.83	4.60
1982	1.91		0.97	2.27	3.01	2.35	4.40	18.62	5.59	4.01
1983	1.07		0.89	1.24	1.43	4.42	3.47	21.84	5.09	1.74
1984	2.05		1.25	1.13	2.30	2.84	3.01	26.09	3.64	1.79
1985	1.68		1.13	1.13	2.67	1.98	2.33	28.26	3.55	1.91
1986	0.72		0.34	0.29	1.17	3.50	0.88	20.50	1.94	2.02
1987	1.75		0.12	0.11	2.00	3.55	1.67	28.28	2.09	2.08
1988	1.98	5.66	0.37	0.61	1.90	3.73	1.36	41.88	2.33	1.94
1989	2.25	6.07	1.06	1.38	2.36	2.68	1.75	54.30	2.74	2.30
1990	2.45	1.66	1.58	1.43	2.99	3.59	1.61	64.86	2.81	2.22
1991	1.86	1.78	1.66	1.95	3.15	4.95	1.64	23.73	2.73	2.52
1992	1.32	2.72	0.68	2.32	1.40	4.26	1.12	48.33	2.31	0.74
1993	1.54	4.84	0.65	2.07	0.95	1.83	1.16	58.68	2.12	1.07
1994	1.37	7.39	0.33	1.02	1.01	3.94	0.90	59.99	1.91	0.28
1995	1.48	4.80	0.12	0.75	1.42	3.97	1.05	16.17	2.39	0.83
1996	1.53	2.19	0.05	0.85	1.32	3.52	1.13	4.30	1.75	0.81
1997	1.19	1.05	0.71	1.11	0.92	2.83	0.54	1.90	0.75	0.97
1998	0.73	0.23	0.33	0.39	0.90	4.70	0.31	1.05	1.11	0.47
1999	1.21	-0.52	0.06	0.33	0.81	1.51	0.39	2.25	0.95	1.00
2000	1.70	0.06	-0.29	0.80	0.39	1.88	0.85	2.99	1.36	1.43
2001	1.42	0.49	-0.33	1.13	0.78	1.85	0.97	2.93	1.47	1.35
2002	0.64	0.03	-0.39	0.73	0.78	2.06	1.10	3.44	1.31	1.23
2003	1.25	0.35	-0.10	0.58	0.85	1.83	1.18	5.12	1.43	1.46

Table 16.3 (cont.)

	USA	Chi	Jap	Ger	UK	Ind	Fra	Bra	Ita	Can
2004	1.42	1.58	0.01	0.98	0.83	1.86	1.20	1.83	1.16	0.85
2005	1.71	0.66	-0.08	0.92	1.14	2.04	0.96	2.95	1.11	1.23
2006	1.64	0.97	0.09	0.95	1.33	2.58	0.99	1.45	1.18	1.12
2007	1.46	1.97	0.06	1.26	1.30	2.78	0.88	1.76	1.03	1.20
2008	1.88	2.62	0.57	1.41	1.75	3.40	1.44	2.53	1.65	1.30
2009	0.46	0.63	0.04	0.37	0.75	4.15	0.38	2.20	0.48	0.34
2010	0.52	0.85	-0.22	0.60	1.35	4.48	0.63	2.33	0.88	0.77
2011	1.56	2.46	-0.10	1.13	1.88	3.13	1.18	2.86	1.43	1.51
2012	0.90	0.90	-0.01	1.14	1.09	3.71	1.11	2.31	1.58	0.59
2013	0.74	1.40	0.16	0.80	1.24	4.17	0.38	2.72	0.51	0.46
2014	0.97	0.95	1.04	0.43	0.66	1.93	0.27	2.77	0.21	1.05
2015	0.25	0.77	0.43	0.18	0.26	2.59	0.10	3.61	0.06	0.50
2016	0.55	1.13	0.13	0.36	0.59	2.19	0.13	3.52	-0.02	0.87
2017	1.18	0.88	0.19	0.85	1.25	0.87	0.51	1.15	0.47	0.95

17 Estimates of Expected Real Interest Rates for Major Economies

17.1 INTRODUCTION

In the following, estimates of the real interest rate will be presented for the 10 largest economies according to the World Bank comparison for 2017. The countries included are the USA, China, Japan, Germany, United Kingdom, India, France, Brazil, Italy, and Canada. The interest rate used for this purpose is the nominal lending rate reported by the World Bank. Besides data on the nominal rates, the World Bank also reports real rates of interest. For these official calculations, inflation is measured as the percentage change of the GDP Deflator. For comparison and for the use by analysts and historians, we offer estimates of ex ante real rates based on the pattern approach. For this purpose, pattern-based expected inflation rates are computed (based on GDP-deflator data published by the World Bank) and used to correct the nominal lending rate for the expected inflation.[1] Evidently, the ex ante real rate of interest (i.e., neither the nominal rate nor the ex post real rate) appropriately characterizes the circumstances under which economic decisions, for example, by investing firms, are taken.

17.2 REAL INTEREST RATE SERIES

Since the lending rate refers to short- and medium-term loans, the one-year-ahead inflation expectations are used. Applying the short-term expected inflation matches the practice of the World Bank in the computation of the real rate. The World Bank computes the real rate of interest according to $i_t^r = [(1 + i_t)P_{t-1}/P_t] - 1$, where P_t is the GDP

---

[1] Data for lending rates and GDP deflators come from the World Bank's web portal under https://data.worldbank.org/indicator/.

deflator for the current year. This definition makes clear that this measure is not an ex post real rate of interest. An ex post measure would be computed according to $i_t^r = [(1 + i_t)P_t/P_{t+1}] - 1$ and would thus correct for the loss in purchasing power over the term (one year) of the loan. Hence, the World Bank measure of the real lending rate is best understood as an ex ante rate calculated on the assumption of static inflation expectations. The computation of the pattern-based measure of the real rate is done according to the formula $i_t^r = (i_t - \pi_t^e)/(1 + \pi_t^e)$. For this measure, the series of the one-year- ahead expected inflation (π_t^e) is computed for each country based on annual data. The procedure applied is the one outlined in Chapter 10.

Where price-level data are available from 1960, the first data point for expected inflation is 1962. Since lending rates go back as far as 1962 only for USA, Japan, France, and Canada, pattern-based real interest rates can be computed only for these countries. For China (in 1980), India (in 1978), Brazil (in 1997), and Italy (in 1989), the lending rate series start later but reach until 2017. Finally, for Germany (from 1977 to 2003), the United Kingdom (from 1967 to 2014), and France (from 1962 to 2005), the lending series does not cover recent years. Before tabulating the newly estimated series, the real interest rates based on the pattern-based approach are compared with the World Bank's numbers concerning real interest rates. Table 17.1 documents summary statistics of the two series for each of the 10 countries. The first notable finding pertains to the average real rate. Looking at averages, the pattern-based real rate is higher for each of the countries covered. The standard deviation of the pattern-based measure of the real interest rate is lower (higher) than the World Bank measure for China, Japan, Germany, the United Kingdom, India, France, and Canada (USA, Brazil, Italy). A marked difference between the two measures of real interest rates becomes apparent regarding the number of years of negative real interest rates. According to the pattern-based measure, the number of years of negative real rates is much lower. In fact, according to this measure, in 6 of the 10 countries, there is not a single year with a real interest rate below 0 percent.

Table 17.1 *Statistics for the pattern-based and World Bank measures of the real interest rate*

	USA	Chi	Jap	Ger	UK	Ind	Fra	Bra	Ita	Can
Pattern-based										
average real rate	4.74	3.73	3.20	8.18	3.42	8.67	4.62	45.59	5.86	4.51
(standard deviation)	2.49	1.98	1.88	1.30	2.91	2.17	2.50	14.8	3.02	2.72
World Bank										
average real rate	3.83	2.04	2.30	7.66	1.38	6.09	2.97	41.85	5.06	3.27
(standard deviation)	2.31	3.37	3.16	1.67	3.69	2.53	3.18	14.5	2.49	2.77
Years of negative value pattern-based	0	1	4	0	8	0	1	0	0	0
Years of negative value World Bank	1	10	5	0	17	2	9	0	0	5

Table 17.2 presents these series of the real interest rate based on the pattern approach for the 10 largest economies. These real rates should be informative for historians of the business cycle. To point just at one application, consider the level of the real rate of interest during some prominent episodes concerning monetary policy. To be more specific, consider the macroeconomic experience of three of the countries covered in fighting inflation. The USA, Germany, and the United Kingdom conducted monetary policies during the 1970s and 1980s aimed at bringing down inflation. In 1978, Paul Volcker became chairman of the Federal Reserve Board. Under his guidance, American monetary policy committed to end what became known as the "great inflation." Under a regime of money stock control, the rate of inflation gradually came down from its peak of 13.5 percent in 1980 to 3.15 percent in 1983. The ensuing recession went together with an increase in unemployment from 7.25 percent in 1980 to 9.86 percent in 1982. According to our estimates, the pattern-based real rate of interest over these years of monetary restraint was on average 10.67 percent, while the World Bank measure merely indicates an average level of 7.53 percent. The former number fits much better than the latter with an account of the US business cycle that focuses on the significant historical weakening of investment.[2]

---

[2] See Goodfriend and King (2005) for an account of the Volcker disinflation.

Table 17.2 *Real interest rates based on the pattern approach for the USA, China, Japan, Germany, the United Kingdom, India, France, Brazil, Italy, and Canada*

	USA	Chi	Jap	Ger	UK	Ind	Fra	Bra	Ita	Can
1962	3.44		5.60				0.05			4.55
1963	3.56		3.87				–0.96			4.00
1964	3.18		4.24				1.09			3.69
1965	2.94		4.25				1.53			3.20
1966	3.27		4.02				1.15			2.29
1967	3.27		3.53		3.52		0.96			2.82
1968	3.05		4.05		2.92		1.03			4.32
1969	4.47		4.29		2.76		2.15			4.70
1970	4.25		–3.26		1.21		3.44			3.90
1971	2.21		3.77		2.38		2.99			3.20
1972	2.21		3.20		2.81		1.85			1.92
1973	4.19		–0.73		2.55		3.41			1.10
1974	4.65		–2.98		–0.38		4.38			1.37
1975	2.05		4.32		–3.86		1.87			3.33
1976	3.55		3.07		3.50		2.71			4.16
1977	2.62		3.16	5.19	0.94		4.06			4.30
1978	4.40		3.45	5.38	2.29	11.74	3.28			5.31
1979	7.31		4.53	5.51	5.35	6.56	3.43			6.27
1980	9.55	2.29	4.33	8.14	5.08	9.94	5.46			8.02

Year										
1981	13.01	3.46	5.94	10.39	7.15	9.91	7.25			12.69
1982	11.09	6.98	6.07	9.96	7.61	11.56	6.39			10.34
1983	8.26	6.49	6.40	7.88	6.56	11.05	6.42			7.64
1984	9.46	4.04	5.42	8.06	6.19	11.41	7.77			9.78
1985	7.56	1.18	5.54	7.91	8.49	11.81	7.50			8.13
1986	6.91	4.96	4.65	8.55	7.89	12.02	6.41			8.23
1987	6.18	4.40	5.05	8.21	5.84	10.37	7.92			5.92
1988	6.61	1.48	4.68	7.35	5.95	11.27	6.95			7.63
1989	8.04	6.22	3.69	7.70	8.55	11.12	7.57		10.86	10.02
1990	7.32	5.83	4.81	9.53	9.68	9.79	8.58		8.88	11.70
1991	6.01	4.15	5.30	9.34	7.52	9.60	8.25		9.81	7.63
1992	4.62	3.27	4.96	9.99	7.40	13.81	8.49		13.82	6.37
1993	4.14	1.53	4.43	9.71	4.01	10.10	7.60		11.84	4.84
1994	5.47	−0.56	3.88	9.67	4.45	8.57	7.16		9.40	5.64
1995	7.17	4.78	3.80	9.71	0.95	9.78	7.10		9.62	6.73
1996	6.81	6.24	3.14	8.82	3.08	11.13	5.58		9.62	4.70
1997	7.05	7.16	2.29	7.50	5.68	9.57	5.64	73.56	8.77	4.07
1998	7.51	6.59	2.26	8.28	6.20	8.27	5.67	83.30	6.69	6.49
1999	6.65	7.01	3.07	8.31	4.66	10.29	6.11	74.86	5.16	5.33
2000	7.32	4.93	3.25	8.39	4.30	9.59	5.54	53.07	5.42	4.04
2001	5.13	4.22	2.91	8.34	4.39	9.71	5.30	52.06	4.87	4.47
2002	3.52	4.67	3.15	8.59	2.22	9.18	4.94	56.69	4.04	3.20
2003	2.47	3.48	3.18	8.76	1.81	8.65	5.11	58.41	3.46	2.24

Table 17.2 (cont.)

	USA	Chi	Jap	Ger	UK	Ind	Fra	Bra	Ita	Can
2004	2.13	0.96	2.65		2.44	6.75	5.24	50.57	3.62	1.56
2005	3.76	3.13	2.59		2.61	7.89	4.98	50.55	3.87	2.07
2006	5.66	3.28	2.45		2.34	6.58		46.35	4.09	3.84
2007	6.04	2.04	2.55		3.55	9.14		39.42	4.38	3.57
2008	3.61	0.25	2.83		2.52	7.42		41.43	4.92	1.79
2009	2.56	4.68	2.24		-0.46	8.41		39.96	3.24	2.83
2010	2.11	2.27	3.10		-0.80	2.28		34.57	3.75	1.99
2011	1.46	1.26	2.88		-1.16	4.75		38.58	3.48	0.57
2012	1.77	3.94	2.05		-0.75	5.51		31.54	4.06	1.96
2013	1.93	4.26	1.62		-1.07	6.29		22.53	4.11	1.64
2014	1.78	4.84	0.29		-0.89	8.11		26.94	4.04	1.38
2015	2.43	4.24	-0.59			8.55		39.05	3.29	3.03
2016	2.41	3.52	0.79			6.90		46.86	2.73	2.47
2017	2.35	1.60	1.09			7.22		44.45	2.44	1.03

Similarly, Germany started to seriously fight inflation in 1979. Inflation reacted sluggishly – declining from 5.8 percent in 1981 to 0.84 percent in 1986 – and the real interest rate reached a peak in 1981. According to the pattern-based measure, the average real rate over the first three years of this maneuver of monetary restraint was 9.14 percent. This contrasts with the World Bank measure of the real rate of 8.29 percent for this period. Finally, the example of the United Kingdom offers a particularly clear case for the new measure of the real rate. The changes in policy aimed at reducing the growth of the money supply brought UK's inflation down from a value of 18.23 percent in 1980 to 4.41 percent in 1983. During this period, unemployment almost doubled to reach a peak value of 11.77 percent in 1984. Against this background, the average value of the real rate of interest of 1.84 percent measured by the World Bank does not appear plausible. Arguably, the very strong contractionary impulse coming from the Bank of England is more accurately captured in the average of the newly computed measure of the real rate of interest which is 6.6 percent.[3]

---

[3] Analyses of these experiences of monetary policy are provided by Beyer et al. (2008) for Germany, and by Buiter and Miller (1983) for the United Kingdom.

Epilogue

The approach explored in this book poses a challenge to various notions of conducting economic research. First, the concept of rationality that is commonly used in economics is examined. Researchers who take it for granted that a theory of rational expectations should start from a normative standpoint find their assumption questioned. The work presented here documents a theory of bottom-up rationality. A second group of scholars find their beliefs questioned. The testing of hypotheses is not the only task to be addressed in the controlled environment of a laboratory. Instead, the economics laboratory can be fruitfully used for quantifying behavioral models. Such bottom-up models can serve as a basis for many forms of applied empirical work.

Finally, the institutions involved in regular surveys of expectations should be prepared for the arrival of a contender. There is indeed an alternative to the regular (monthly or quarterly) routine of questioning a large number of participants about their up-to-date forecasts. This alternative consists of devising questions or tasks for once-only types of surveys under laboratory conditions. This new form of surveying aims at quantifying time-invariant elements of behavior. The gains from this effort should be clear: behavior thus documented can help the testing of theoretical propositions, the formulation of new models, and the evaluation of policies.

References

Abiad, Abdul, Enrica, Detragiache, and Thierry Tressel (2010), A New Database of Financial Reforms, *IMF Staff Papers*, 57 (2), 281–302.

Adam, Klaus and Mario Padula (2011), Inflation Dynamics and Subjective Expectations in the United States, *Economic Inquiry*, 49 (2), 13–25.

Alter, Adam L. and Daniel M. Oppenheimer (2006), From a Fixation on Sports to an Exploration of Mechanism: The Past, Present, and Future of Hot Hand Research, *Thinking and Reasoning*, 12 (4), 431–444.

Altman, Morris (ed.) (2017), *Handbook of Behavioural Economics and Smart Decision-Making: Rational Decision-Making within the Bounds of Reason*, Cheltenham, Edward Elgar.

Andonov, Aleksandar and Joshua D. Rauh (2018), The Return Expectations of Institutional Investors, Stanford University, Graduate School of Business, Research Papers.

Ang, Andrew, Geert, Bekaert, and Min Wei (2007), Do Macro Variables, Asset Markets, or Surveys Forecast Inflation Better? *Journal of Monetary Economics*, Elsevier, 54 (4), 1163–1212.

Armstrong, J. Scott (2001), Extrapolation for Time-Series and Cross-Sectional Data, in J. Scott Armstrong (ed.), *Principles of Forecasting: A Handbook for Researchers and Practitioners*, Norwell, MA, Kluwer Academic Publishers, 217–243.

Arrau, Patricio, José De Gregorio, Reinhart, M. Carmen, and Peter Wickham (1995), The Demand for Money in Developing Countries: Assessing the Role of Financial Innovation, *Journal of Development Economics*, 46 (2), 317–340.

Balke, Nathan S. and Robert J. Gordon (1989), The Estimation of Prewar Gross National Product: Methodology and New Evidence, *Journal of Political Economy*, 97 (1), 38–92.

Balparda, Borja, Guglielmo M. Caporale, and Luis Alberiko Gil-Alana (2017), The Fisher Relationship in Nigeria, *Journal of Economics and Finance*, 41 (2), 343–353.

Banerjee, Ryan, Jonathan, Kearns, and Marco Lombardi (2015), (Why) Is Investment Weak? *BIS Quarterly Review*, March 2015, 67–82.

Barnea, Amir, Amihud, Dotan, and Josef Lakonishok (1979), The Effect of Price Level Uncertainty on the Determination of Nominal Interest Rates, *Southern Economic Journal*, 45, 609–614.

Barsky, Robert B. and J. Bradford DeLong (1991), Forecasting Pre-World War I Inflation: The Fisher Effect and the Gold Standard, *Quarterly Journal of Economics*, 106 (3), 815–836.

Barsky, Robert B. and J. Bradford DeLong (1993), Why Does the Stock Market Fluctuate? *Quarterly Journal of Economics*, 108 (2), 291–311.

Basu, Susanto and Brent Bundick (2017), Uncertainty Shocks in a Model of Effective Demand, *Econometrica*, 85 (3), 937–958.

Bauer, Michael D. and Erin McCarthy (2015), Can We Rely on Market-Based Inflation Forecasts? *Federal Reserve Bank of San Francisco Economic Letter*, September 21.

Berument, Hakan and Mohamed Mehdi Jelassi (2002), The Fisher Hypothesis: A Multi-Country Analysis, *Applied Economics*, 34 (13) 1645–1655.

Berument, Hakan, Zybeyir, KIlinc, and Umit Ozlale (2005), The Missing Link between Inflation Uncertainty and Interest Rates, *Scottish Journal of Political Economy*, 52 (2), 222–241.

Berument, Hakan, Nildag Ceylan, Basak, and Hasan Olgun (2007), Inflation Uncertainty and Interest Rates: Is the Fisher Relation Universal? *Applied Economics*, 39 (1), 53–68.

Beshears, John, James J. Choi, Andreas, Fuster, Laibson, David, and Brigitte C. Madrian (2013), What Goes Up Must Come Down? Experimental Evidence on Intuitive Forecasting, *American Economic Review*, 103 (3), 570–574.

Beyer, Andreas, Vitor, Gaspar, Christina, Gerberding, and Otmar Issing (2008), Opting Out of the Great Inflation: German Monetary Policy after the Break Down of Bretton Woods, NBER Working Paper No. 14596.

Bhatt, Ramesh S., Angela, Hayden, Andrea, Reed, Evelin, Bertin, and Jane Joseph (2006), Infants' Perception of Information along Object Boundaries: Concavities versus Convexities, *Journal of Experimental Child Psychology*, 94 (2), 91–113.

Binder, Carola C. (2015), Whose Expectations Augment the Philips Curve? *Economic Letters*, 136, 35–38.

Bloomfield, Robert and Jeffrey Hales (2002), Predicting the Next Step of a Random Walk: Experimental Evidence of Regime-Shifting Beliefs, *Journal of Financial Economics*, 65 (3), 397–414.

Boero, Gianna, Smith, Jeremy, and Kenneth F. Wallis (2008), Uncertainty and Disagreement in Economic Prediction: The Bank of England Survey of External Forecasters, *Economic Journal*, 118 (530), 1107–1127.

Bolle, Friedel (1988a), Testing for Rational Expectations in Experimental Predictions, in S. Maital (ed.), *Behavioral Economics*, Amsterdam, North Holland.

Bolle, Friedel (1988b), Learning to Make Good Predictions for the Following Value in a Time Series, in W. Albers, R. Selten, and R. Tietz (eds.), *Modeling Bounded*

Rational Behavior in Experimental Games and Markets, Berlin, Springer Lecture Notes 314.

Bomberger, William and William Frazer (1981), Interest Rates, Uncertainty, and the Livingston Data, *Journal of Finance*, 38, 661–676.

Bossons, John and Franco Modigliani (1960), The Source of Regressiveness in Surveys of Businessmen's Short-Run Expectations. NBER Chapters in *The Quality and Economic Significance of Anticipations Data*, Princeton, Princeton University Press.

Buiter, Willem and Marcus Miller (1983), Changing the Rules: Economic Consequences of the Thatcher Regime, *Brookings Papers on Economic Activity*, 2, 305–379.

Bullard, James and Kaushik Mitra (2002), Learning about Monetary Policy Rules, *Journal of Monetary Economics*, 49 (6), 1105–1129.

Byrne, Joseph P., Alexandros, Kontonikas, and Alberto Montagnoli (2013), International Evidence on the New Keynesian Phillips Curve Using Aggregate and Disaggregate Data, *Journal of Money, Credit and Banking*, 45 (5), 913–932.

Cagan, Phillip (1956), The Monetary Dynamics of Hyper-Inflation, in M. Friedman (ed.), *Studies in the Quantity Theory of Money*, Chicago, University of Chicago Press.

Caporale, Guglielmo M. and Luis A. Gil-Alana (2016), Interest Rate Dynamics in Kenya: Commercial Banks' Rates and the 91-Day Treasury Bill Rate, *Journal of International Development*, 28 (2), 214–232.

Cargill, Thomas F. (1976), Anticipated Price Changes and Nominal Interest Rates in the 1950's, *Review of Economics and Statistics*, 58 (3), 364–367.

Carlson, Kurt A. and Suzanne B. Shu (2007), The Rule of Three: How the Third Event Signals the Emergence of a Streak, *Organizational Behavior and Human Decision Processes*, 104 (1), 113–121.

Carrera, César (2016), Long-Run Money Demand in Latin American Countries: A Nonstationary Panel Data Approach, *Monetaria*, 4 (1), 121–152.

Carroll, Christopher D. (2003), Macroeconomic Expectations of Households and Professional Forecasters, *Quarterly Journal of Economics*, 118 (1), 269–298.

Cavallo, Alberto, Guillermo, Cruces, and Ricardo Perez-Truglia (2017), Inflation Expectations, Learning, and Supermarket Prices: Evidence from Survey Experiments, *American Economic Journal: Macroeconomics*, 9 (3), 1–35.

Chan, Joshua C. C. and Yong Song (2018), Measuring Inflation Expectations Uncertainty Using High-Frequency Data, *Journal of Money, Credit and Banking*, 50 (6), 1139–1166.

Chaomei, Chen and Mary P. Czerwinski (2000), Empirical Evaluation of Information Visualizations: An Introduction, *International Journal of Human-Computer Studies*, 53 (5), 631–635.

Chow, Gregory C. (1989), Rational versus Adaptive Expectations in Present Value Models, *Review of Economics and Statistics*, 71 (3), 376–384.

Christandl, Fabian and Detlef Fetchenhauer (2009), How Laypeople and Experts Misperceive the Effect of Economic Growth, *Journal of Economic Psychology*, 30 (3), 381–392.

Christiano, Lawrence J., Martin, Eichenbaum, and Charles L. Evans (2005), Nominal Rigidities and the Dynamic Effects of a Shock to Monetary Policy, *Journal of Political Economy*, 113 (1), 1–45.

Clements, Michael P. (2019), *Macroeconomic Survey Expectations*, Cham, Palgrave MacMillan.

Coibion, Olivier (2010), Testing the Sticky Information Phillips Curve, *Review of Economics and Statistics*, 92 (1), 87–101.

Coibion, Olivier, Gorodnichenko, Yuriy, and Rupal Kamdar (2018), The Formation of Expectations, Inflation, and the Phillips Curve, *Journal of Economic Literature*, 56 (4), 1447–1491.

Collins, Melissa A. and Elida V. Laski (2015), Preschoolers' Strategies for Solving Visual Pattern Tasks, *Early Childhood Research Quarterly*, 32 (3), 204–214.

Cooray, Arusha (2003), The Fisher Effect: A Survey, *Singapore Economic Review*, 48 (2), 135–150.

Coppock, Lee and Marc Poitras (2000), Evaluating the Fisher Effect in Long-Term Cross-Country Averages, *International Review of Economics and Finance*, 9 (2), 181–192.

Cozzi, Guido and Margaret Davenport (2017), Extrapolative Expectations and Capital Flows during Convergence, *Journal of International Economics*, 108 (6), 169–190.

Cukierman, Alex (1978), Heterogeneous Inflationary Expectations, Fisher's Theory of Interest and the Allocative Efficiency of the Bond Market, *Economics Letters*, 1 (2), 151–155.

Cukierman, Alex and Paul Wachtel (1982), Inflationary Expectations: Reply and Further Thoughts on Inflation Uncertainty, *American Economic Review*, 72 (3), 508–512.

Curtin, Richard T. (2019), *Consumer Expectations: Micro Foundations and Macro Impact*, Cambridge, Cambridge University Press.

De Bondt, Werner F. M. and Mary M. Bange (1992), Inflation Forecast Errors and Time Variation in Term Premia, *Journal of Financial and Quantitative Analysis*, 27 (4), 479–496.

De Bondt, Werner P. M. (1993), Betting on Trends: Intuitive Forecasts of Financial Risk and Return, *International Journal of Forecasting*, 9 (3), 355–371.

De Bruin, Wandi Bruine, Manski, Charles F., Topa, Giorgio, and Wilbert van der Klaauw (2011), Measuring Consumer Uncertainty about Future Inflation, *Journal of Applied Econometrics*, 26 (3), 454–478.

DeLong, J. Bradford and Konstantin Magin (2009), The U.S. Equity Return Premium: Past, Present, and Future, *Journal of Economic Perspectives*, 23 (1), 193–208.

De Nardi, Mariacristina, Eric, French, and David Benson (2012), Consumption and the Great Recession, *Federal Reserve Bank of Chicago Economic Perspectives*, 36 (1), 1–16.

D'Haultfoeuille, Xavier, Christophe, Gaillac, and Arnaud Maurel (2018), Rationalizing Rational Expectations? Tests and Deviations, NBER Working Paper No. 2527.

Dimsdale, Nicholas (2014), Monetary Trends in the U.K. since 1870, in M. Allen and D. Coffman (eds.), *Money, Prices and Wages: Essays in Honour of Professor Nicholas Mayhew*, Basingstoke, Palgrave Macmillan.

Dotsey, Michael, Lantz, Carl, and Brian Scholl (2003), The Behavior of the Real Rate of Interest, *Journal of Money, Credit, and Banking*, 35 (1), 91–110.

Ebersbach, Mirjam, Lehner, Wilma C. M. Resing, and Friedrich Wilkening (2008), Forecasting Exponential Growth and Exponential Decline: Similarities and Differences, *Acta Psychologica*, 127 (2), 247–257.

Edelman, Gerald M. and George N. Reeke, Jr. (1990), Is It Possible to Construct a Perception Machine? *Proceedings of the American Philosophical Society*, 134 (1), 36–73.

Eggleton, Ian R. C. (1982), Intuitive Time-Series Extrapolation, *Journal of Accounting Research*, 20 (1), 68–102.

Eichengreen, Barry (2004), The British Economy between the Wars, in R. Floud and P. Johnson (eds.), *The Cambridge Economic History of Modern Britain*, Cambridge, Cambridge University Press.

Fair, Ray C. (1991), Testing the Rational Expectations Hypothesis in Macroeconometric Models, *Oxford Economic Papers*, 45 (2), 169–190.

Feldman, Julian (1963), Simulation of Behavior in the Binary Choice Experiment, in E. A. Feigenbaum and J. Feldman (eds.), *Computers and Thought*, New York, McGraw-Hill, pp. 329–346.

Figlewski, Stephen and Paul Wachtel (1981), The Formation of Inflationary Expectations, *The Review of Economics and Statistics*, 63 (1), 1–10.

Fildes, Robert (1979), Quantitative Forecasting – The State of the Art: Extrapolative Models, *Journal of the Operational Research Society*, 30 (8), 691–710.

Fisher, Irving (1930), *The Theory of Interest*, New York, Macmillan.

Fitzenberger, Bernd, Wolfgang, Franz, and Oliver Bode (2008), The Phillips Curve and NAIRU Revisited: New Estimates for Germany, *Jahrbücher für Nationalökonomie und Statistik*, 228, 5–6.

French, Eric, Kelley, Taylor, and An Qi (2013), Expected Income Growth and the Great Recession, *Federal Reserve Bank of Chicago Economic Perspectives*, 37 (1), 14–29.

Frenkel, Jakob A. (1975), A Monetary Approach to the Exchange Rate: Doctrinal Aspects and Empirical Evidence, *Scandinavian Journal of Economics*, 78 (2), 200–224.

Friedman, Milton (1953), *Essays in Positive Economics*, Chicago, University of Chicago Press.

Friedman, Milton and Anna J. Schwartz (1982), Money and Interest Rates, in Milton Friedman and Anna J. Schwartz (eds.), *Monetary Trends in the United States and United Kingdom: Their Relation to Income, Prices, and Interest Rates, 1867–1975*, Chicago, University of Chicago Press, pp. 477–587.

Fuhrer, Jeffrey C. (2012), The Role of Expectations in Inflation Dynamics, *International Journal of Central Banking*, 8 (1), 137–166.

Galí, Jordi and Mark Gertler (1999), Inflation Dynamics: A Structural Econometric Analysis, *Journal of Monetary Economics*, 44 (2), 195–222.

Gefang, Deborah, Gary, Koop, and Simon M. Potter (2012), The Dynamics of UK and US Inflation Expectations, *Computational Statistics & Data Analysis*, 56 (11), 3120–3133.

Gennaioli, Nicola, Yueran, Ma, and Andrei Shleifer (2015), Expectations and Investment, *NBER Macroeconomics Annual*, 30, 379–431.

Gibson, William E. (1972), Interest Rates and Inflationary Expectations: New Evidence, *American Economic Review*, 62 (5), 854–865.

Gilovich, Thomas, Robert, Vallone, and Amos Tversky (1985), The Hot Hand in Basketball: On the Misperception of Random Sequences, *Cognitive Psychology*, 17 (3), 295–314.

Goldfeld, Stephen M. and Daniel E. Sichel (1990), The Demand for Money, in B. Friedman and F. Hahn (eds.), *Handbook of Monetary Economics*, Amsterdam, Elsevier, pp. 300–356.

Goodfriend, Marvin and Robert G. King (2005), The Incredible Volcker Disinflation, *Journal of Monetary Economics*, 52, 981–1015.

Gordon, Robert J. (2011), The History of the Phillips Curve: Consensus and Bifurcation, *Economica*, 78, (309), 10–50.

Granziera, Eleonora and Sharon Kozicki (2015), House Price Dynamics: Fundamentals and Expectations, *Journal of Economic Dynamics and Control*, 60 (November), 152–165.

Greenwood, Robin and Andrei Shleifer (2014), Expectations of Returns and Expected Returns, *Review of Financial Studies*, 27 (3), 714–746.

Grier, Kevin B. and Mark J. Perry (1996), Inflation, Inflation Uncertainty and Relative Price Dispersion: Evidence from Bivariate GARCH-M Models, *Journal of Monetary Economics*, 38 (2), 391–405.

Gürkaynak, Refet S., Eric, Swanson L, and Levin Andrew (2010), Does Inflation Targeting Anchor Long-Run Inflation Expectations? Evidence from the U.S., UK, and Sweden, *Journal of the European Economic Association*, 8 (6), 1208–1242.

Gylfason, Thorvaldur, Helgi, Tomasson, and Gylfi Zoega (2016), Around the World with Irving Fisher, *North American Journal of Economics and Finance*, 36 (2), 232–243.

Han, Weiwei, Xun, Wang, Fotois, Petropoulos, and Jing Wang (2018). Brain Imaging and Forecasting: Insights from Judgmental Model Selection. *Omega, The International Journal of Management Science*. https://doi.org/10.1016/j.omega.2018.11.015.

Haruvy, Ernan, Yaron, Lahav, and Charles N. Noussair (2007), Traders' Expectations in Asset Markets: Experimental Evidence, *American Economic Review*, 97 (5), 1901–1920.

Harvey, Nigel, Fergus, Bolger, and Alastair McClelland (1994), On the Nature of Expectations, *British Journal of Psychology*, 85 (2), 203–229.

Haubrich, Joseph, George, Pennacchi, and Peter Ritchken (2012), Inflation Expectations, Real Rates, and Risk Premia: Evidence from Inflation Swaps, *Review of Financial Studies*, 25 (5), 1588–1629.

Hendershott, Patrick (1984), Expectations, Surprises, and Treasury Bill Rates: 1960–82, *Journal of Finance*, 39 (3), 685–98.

Hey, John D. (1994), Expectations Formation: Rational or Adaptive or . . .? *Journal of Economic Behavior & Organization*, 25 (3), 329–349.

Hicks, John R. (1939), *Value and Capital*, Oxford, Clarendon Press.

Hirshleifer, David, Li, Jun, and Jianfeng Yu (2015), Asset Pricing in Production Economies with Extrapolative Expectations, *Journal of Monetary Economics*, 76 (November), 87–106.

Homer, Sidney and Richard Sylla (1991), *A History of Interest Rates*, 3rd edition, New Brunswick, NJ, Rutgers University Press.

Hong, Felix T. (2013), The Role of Pattern Recognition in Creative Problem Solving: A Case Study in Search of New Mathematics for Biology, *Progress in Biophysics and Molecular Biology*, 113 (1), 181–215.

Jones, Garett (2012), Cognitive Skill and Technology Diffusion: An Empirical Test, *Economic Systems*, 36 (3), 444–460.

Jurado, Kyle, Sydney C., Ludvigson, and Serena Ng (2015), Measuring Uncertainty, *American Economic Review*, 105 (3), 1177–1216.

Kabundi, Alain and Eric Schaling (2013), Inflation and Inflation Expectations in South Africa: An Attempt at Explanation, *South African Journal of Economic*, 81 (3), 346–355.

Kabundi, Alain, Eric, Schaling, and Modeste Some (2015), Monetary Policy and Heterogeneous Inflation Expectations in South Africa, *Economic Modelling*, 45 (2), 109–117.

Kahneman, Daniel (2003), Maps of Bounded Rationality: Psychology for Behavioral Economics, *American Economic Review*, 93 (5), 1449–1475.

Kaliva, Kasimir (2008), The Fisher Effect, Survey Data and Time-Varying Volatility, *Empirical Economics*, 35 (1), 1–10.

Kasman, Saadet, Adnan, Kasman, and Evrim Turgutlu (2006), Fisher Hypothesis Revisited: A Fractional Cointegration Analysis, *Emerging Markets Finance and Trade*, 42 (6), 59–76.

Keynes, John M. (1936), *The General Theory of Employment, Interest, and Money*, London, Macmillan.

Kim, Dong-Hyeon, Shu-Chin, Lin, Joyce, Hsieh, and Yu-Bo Suen (2018), The Fisher Equation: A Nonlinear Panel Data Approach, *Emerging Markets Finance and Trade*, 54 (1), 162–180.

Koustas, Zisimos and Apostolos Serletis (1999), On the Fisher Effect, *Journal of Monetary Economics*, 44 (1), 105–130.

Lahiri, Kajal, Christie, Teigland, and Mark Zaporowski (1988), Interest Rates and the Subjective Probability Distribution of Inflation Forecasts, *Journal of Money, Credit, and Banking*, 20 (2), 233–248.

Landier, Augustin, Yueran, Ma, and David Thesmar (2017), New Experimental Evidence on Expectations Formation, SSRN Working Paper.

Lawrence, Michael, Paul, Goodwin, Marcus, O'Connor, and Dilek Önkal (2006), Judgmental Forecasting: A Review of Progress over the Last 25 Years, *International Journal of Forecasting*, 22 (3), 493–518.

Lo, Andrew W. (2012), Reading about the Financial Crisis: A Twenty-One-Book Review, *Journal of Economic Literature*, 50 (1), 151–178.

Lovell, Michael C. (1986), Tests of the Rational Expectations Hypothesis, *American Economic Review*, 76 (1), 110–124.

Lucas, Robert E. Jr. (1972), Expectations and the Neutrality of Money, *Journal of Economic Theory*, 4 (2), 103–124.

Lund, Nick (2001), *Attention and Pattern Recognition*, London, Routledge.

Mankiw, N. Gregory and Ricardo Reis (2002), Sticky Information versus Sticky Prices: A Proposal to Replace the New Keynesian Phillips Curve, *Quarterly Journal of Economics*, 117 (4), 1295–1328.

Mankiw, N. Gregory, Ricardo, Reis, and Justin Wolfers (2003), Disagreement about Inflation Expectations, *NBER Macroeconomics Annual*, 18, 209–270.

Manski, Charles F. (2004), Measuring Expectations, *Econometrica*, 72 (5), 1329–1376.

Manski, Charles F. (2017), Survey Measurement of Probabilistic Macroeconomic Expectations: Progress and Promise, *NBER Macroeconomics Annual*, 32 (1), 411–471.

Matchaya, Greenwell C. (2011), The Nature of Inflation in Malawi up to the Early 2000s, *Journal of Economics and International Finance*, 3 (5), 289–304.

Mavroeidis, Sophocles, Mikkel, Plagborg-Møller, and James H. Stock (2014), Empirical Evidence on Inflation Expectations in the New Keynesian Phillips Curve, *Journal of Economic Literature*, 52 (1), 124–188.

Mazumder, Sandeep (2012), European Inflation and the New Keynesian Phillips Curve, *Southern Economic Journal*, 79 (2), 322–349.

Mishkin, Frederic S. (1992), Is the Fisher Effect for Real? A Reexamination of the Relationship between Inflation and Interest Rates, *Journal of Monetary Economics*, 30 (2), 195–215.

Mitchell-Innes, Henri A., Meshach J., Aziakpono, and Alexander P. Faure (2007), Inflation Targeting and the Fisher Effect in South Africa: An Empirical Investigation, *South African Journal of Economics*, 75 (4), 693–707.

Moerman, Gerard A. and Mathijs A. van Dijk (2010), Inflation Risk and International Asset Returns, *Journal of Banking & Finance*, 34 (4), 840–855.

Muth, John F. (1960), Optimal Properties of Exponentially Weighted Forecasts, *Journal of the American Statistical Association*, 55 (290), 299–306.

Muth, John F. (1961), Rational Expectations and the Theory of Price Movements, *Econometrica*, 29 (3), 315–335.

Nason, James M. and Gregor W. Smith (2008), Identifying the New Keynesian Phillips Curve, *Journal of Applied Econometrics*, 23 (5), 525–551.

Nerlove, Marc (1958), Adaptive Expectations and Cobweb Phenomena, *Quarterly Journal of Economics*, 72 (2), 227–240.

Nerlove, Marc (1983), Expectations, Plans, and Realizations in Theory and Practice, *Econometrica*, 51 (5), 1251–1280.

Ng, Serena and Jonathan H. Wright (2013), Facts and Challenges from the Great Recession for Forecasting and Macroeconomic Modeling, *Journal of Economic Literature*, 51 (4), 1120–1154.

Nhlapo, Nonhlanhla (2013), Assessing the Measurement of Inflation Expectations under South African Inflation Targeting, Working Paper South African Reserve Bank.

Norenzayan, Ara and Steven J. Heine (2005), Psychological Universals: What Are They and How Can We Know? *Psychological Bulletin*, 131 (5), 763–784.

Nunes, Ricardo (2010), Inflation Dynamics: The Role of Expectations, *Journal of Money, Credit and Banking*, 42 (6), 1161–1172.

Nusair, Salah A. (2008), Testing for the Fisher Hypothesis under Regime Shifts: An Application to Asian Countries, *International Economic Journal*, 22 (2), 273–284.

Oskarsson, Van Boven (2009), What's Next? Judging Sequences of Binary Events, *Psychological Bulletin*, 135 (2), 262–285.

Paunio, Jouko J. and Antti Suvanto (1977), Changes in Price Expectations: Some Tests Using Data on Indexed and Non-Indexed Bonds, *Economica*, 44 (173), 37–45.

Perez, Stephen J. and Mark V. Siegler (2003), Inflationary Expectations and the Fisher Effect Prior to World War I, *Journal of Money, Credit, and Banking*, 35 (6), 947–965.

Persson, Torsten and Guido Tabellini (1993), Designing Institutions for Monetary Stability, *Carnegie-Rochester Conference Series on Public Policy*, 39, 53–84.

Petropoulos, Fotios, Kourentzes, Nikolaos, Nikolopoulos, Konstantinos, and Enno Siemsen (2018), Judgmental Selection of Forecasting Models, *Journal of Operations Management*, 60, 34–46.

Pfajfar, Damjan and Emiliano Santoro (2013), News on Inflation and the Epidemiology of Inflation Expectations, *Journal of Money, Credit and Banking*, 45 (6), 1045–1067.

Pfajfar, Damjan and Blaz Zakelj (2014), Experimental Evidence on Inflation Expectation Formation, *Journal of Economic Dynamics and Control*, 44, 147–168.

Phiri, Andrew and Peter Lusanga (2011), Can Asymmetries Account for the Empirical Failure of the Fisher Effect in South Africa? *Economics Bulletin*, 31 (3), 1968–1979.

Phylaktis, Kate and David Blake (1993), The Fisher Hypothesis: Evidence from Three High Inflation Economies, *Review of World Economics*, 129 (3), 591–599.

Pistaferri, Luigi (2016), Why Has Consumption Remained Moderate after the Great Recession? Stanford University Working Paper.

Plott, Charles and Shyam Sunder (1988), Rational Expectations and the Aggregation of Diverse Information in Laboratory Security Markets, *Econometrica*, 56 (5), 1085–1118.

Posner, Michael I. (1989), *The Foundations of Cognitive Science*, Cambridge, MA, MIT Press.

Puccetti, Roland (1974), Pattern Recognition in Computers and the Human Brain: With Special Application to Chess Playing Machines, *British Journal for the Philosophy of Science*, 25 (2), 137–154.

Raab, Markus, Bartosz, Gula, and Gerd Gigerenzer (2012), The Hot Hand Exists in Volleyball and Is Used for Allocation Decisions, *Journal of Experimental Psychology*, 18 (1), 81–94.

Rabin, Matthew and Dimitri Vayanos (2010), The Gambler's and Hot-Hand Fallacies: Theory and Applications, *Review of Economic Studies*, 77 (2), 730–778.

Roos, Michael W. and Ulrich Schmidt (2011), The Importance of Time-Series Extrapolation for Macroeconomic Expectation, *German Economic Review*, 13 (2), 196–210.

Rötheli, Tobias F. (1998), Pattern Recognition and Procedurally Rational Expectations, *Journal of Economic Behavior and Organization*, 37 (1), 71–90.

Rötheli, Tobias F. (2007), *Expectations, Rationality and Economic Performance*, Cheltenham, UK, Edward Elgar.

Rötheli, Tobias F. (2011), Pattern-Based Expectations: International Experimental Evidence and Applications in Financial Economics, *Review of Economics and Statistics*, 93 (4), 1319–1330.

Rötheli, Tobias F. (2015), Sudden and Violent Changes in Long-Term Expectations: Keynes and Reality, in Helge Peukert (ed.), *Taking up the Challenge!*, Festschrift for Jürgen Backhaus, Marburg, Metropolis-Verlag, pp. 141–156.

Rudd, Jeremy and Karl Whelan (2007), Modeling Inflation Dynamics: A Critical Review of Recent Research, *Journal of Money, Credit and Banking*, 39 (1), 155–170.

Rumelhart, David E., James L., McClelland, and the PDP Research Group (1986), *Parallel Distributed Processing: Explorations in the Microstructure of Cognition, Volume 1: Foundations*, Cambridge, MA, MIT Press.

Said, Rasidah M. and Hwati Janor (2001), The Long-Run Relationship between Nominal Interest Rates and Inflation of the Asian Developing Countries, *Journal Ekonomi Malaysi*, 35, 3–11.

Sargent, Thomas J. (1973), Interest Rates and Prices in the Long Run: A Study of the Gibson Paradox, *Journal of Money, Credit and Banking*, 5 (1), 385–449.

Sargent, Thomas J. (1983), The Ends of Four Big Inflations, in Robert E. Hall (ed.), *Inflation: Causes and Effects*, Chicago, University of Chicago Press, pp. 41–97.

Scheufele, Rolf (2010), Evaluating the German (New Keynesian) Phillips Curve, *North American Journal of Economics and Finance*, 21 (2), 145–164.

Shafir, Eldar, Peter, Diamond, and Amos Tversky (1997), Money Illusion, *Quarterly Journal of Economics*, 112 (2), 341–374.

Shiller, Robert J. (1981), Do Stock Prices Move Too Much to Be Justified by Subsequent Changes in Dividends? *American Economic Review*, 71 (3), 421–436.

Simmons, Peter and Daniel Weiserbs (1992), Consumer Price Perceptions and Expectations, *Oxford Economic Papers, New Series*, 44 (1), 35–50.

Simon, Herbert A. (1959), Theories of Decision-Making in Economics and Behavioral Science, *American Economic Review*, 49 (3), 253–283.

Simon, Herbert A. (1972), Theories of Bounded Rationality, in C. B. McGuire and R. Radner (eds.), *Decision and Organization: A Volume in Honor of Jacob Marschak*, Amsterdam, North-Holland.

Sims, Christopher A. (2003), Implications of Rational Inattention. *Journal of Monetary Economics*, 50 (3), 665–690.

Smith, Vernon L. (2003), Constructivist and Ecological Rationality in Economics, *American Economic Review*, 93 (3), 465–508.

Söderlind, Paul (2011), Inflation Risk Premia and Survey Evidence on Macroeconomic Uncertainty, *International Journal of Central Banking*, 7 (2), 113–133.

Sosvilla-Rivero, Simón and Maria del Carmen Ramos-Herrera (2018) Inflation, Real Economic Growth and Unemployment Expectations: An Empirical Analysis Based on the ECB Survey of Professional Forecasters, *Applied Economics*, 50 (42), 4540–4555.

Spence, Ian (2006), William Playfair and the Psychology of Graphs. In: *2006 JSM Proceedings*, American Statistical Association, Alexandria, VA, pp. 2426–2436.

Stock, James H. and Mark W. Watson (2007), Why Has US Inflation Become Harder to Forecast? *Journal of Money, Credit, and Banking*, 39 (1), 3–33.

Summers, Lawrence (1983), The Nonadjustment of Nominal Interest Rates: A Study of the Fisher Effect, in James Tobin (ed.), *Macroeconomics, Prices and Quantities*, Washington, DC, Brookings Institute, pp. 201–241.

Symanzik, Jürgen, Fischetti, William, and Ian Spence (2009), Commemorating William Playfair's 250th Birthday, *Computational Statistic*, 24 (4), 551–566.

Thies, Clifford F. (1985), Interest Rates and Expected Inflation, 1831–1914: A Rational Expectations Approach, *Southern Economic Journal*, 51 (4), 1107–1120.

Tillmann, Peter (2010), A Note on the Stability of the New Keynesian Phillips Curve in Europe, *Applied Economics Letters*, 17 (3), 241–245.

Trehan, Bharat (2015), Survey Measures of Expected Inflation and the Inflation Process, *Journal of Money, Credit and Banking*, 47 (1), 207–222.

Tversky, Amos and Daniel Kahneman (1973), Availability: A Heuristic for Judging Frequency and Probability, *Cognitive Psychology*, 5 (2), 207–232.

Tversky, Amos and Daniel Kahneman (1974), Judgment under Uncertainty: Heuristics and Biases, *Science*, 185 (4157), 1124–1131.

Wagenaar, Willem A. and Sabato D. Sagaria (1975), Misperception of Exponential Growth, *Perception and Psychophysics*, 18 (6), 416–422.

Wagenaar, Willem A. and Han Timmers (1978), Extrapolation of Exponential Time Series Is Not Enhanced by Having More Data Points, *Perception and Psychophysics*, 24 (2), 182–184.

Wagenaar, Willem A. and Han Timmers (1979), The Pond-and-Duckweed Problem: Three Experiments on the Misperception of Exponential Growth, *Acta Psychologica*, 43 (3), 239–251.

Wallace, Myles S. and John T. Warner (1993), The Fisher Effect and the Term Structure of Interest Rates: Tests of Cointegration, *Review of Economics and Statistics*, 75 (2), 320–324.

Westerlund, Joakim (2008), Panel Cointegration Tests of the Fisher Effect, *Journal of Applied Econometrics*, 23 (2), 193–233.

Williams, Arlington W. (1987), The Formation of Price Forecasts in Experimental Markets, *Journal of Money, Credit and Banking*, 19 (1), 1–18.

Wright, Jonathan H. (2011), Term Premia and Inflation Uncertainty: Empirical Evidence from an International Panel Dataset, *American Economic Review*, 101 (4), 1514–1534.

Xu, Yingying, Hsu-Ling, Chang, Lobont, Oana-Ramona, and Chi-Wei Su (2015), Modeling Heterogeneous Inflation Expectations: Empirical Evidence from Demographic Data? *Economic Modelling*, 57 (6), 153–163.

Yaari, Gur and Shmuel Eisenmann (2011), The Hot (Invisible?) Hand: Can Time Sequence Patterns of Success/Failure in Sports Be Modeled as Repeated Random Independent Trials? *PLoS One*, 6 (10), 1–10.

Zarnowitz, Victor (1985), Rational Expectations and Macroeconomic Forecasts, *Journal of Business and Economic Statistics*, 3 (4), 293–311.

Zheng, Min, Hefei, Wang, Chengzhang, and Shouyang Wang (2017), Speculative Behavior in a Housing Market: Boom and Bust, *Economic Modelling*, 61 (February), 50–64.

Index

Abiad, Abdul, 171
accuracy in similarity matching, 56
Adam, Klaus, 86, 89
adaptive expectations, 2, 16, 20, 75
African economies, 15, 107, 179–181, 183
   Fisher effect in, 179–183
   inflation expectations in, 188
aggregate income, 133, 140, 163, *see also*
      GDP, gross domestic product
Alter, Adam, L., 18
Altman, Morris, 21
anchoring of inflation expectations, 89–92
Andonov, Aleksandar, 17
Ang, Andrew, 71
annual expectations data, 118–121, 128, 139,
      141, 188–198
Armstrong, J. Scott, 20
Arrau, Patricio, 166
Asian economies, 15, 107, 170, 181, 183
   Fisher effect in, 171–175
   inflation expectations in, 179
asset pricing, 17
automatic behavior, 3
availability heuristic, 18

Balke, Nathan S., 152
Balparda, Borja, 179
bands or ranges of possible developments, 34
Banerjee, Ryan, 137, 140
Bange, Mary M., 96
Bank of England
   as a source of data, 121–129
Barnea, Amir, 79
Barsky, Robert B., 17, 144
Basu, Susanto, 137
Bauer, Michael D., 11, 107
behavioral
   economics, 1, 3, 21, 95
   expectations data, 71
   foundation of expectations, 11
   macroeconomics, 1
   model of expectations, 8, 77
   tendencies, 7, 19, 83

Berlin. *see* Germany
Berument, Hakan, 101, 170, 172–173, 179
Beshears, John, 141
Beyer, Andreas, 205
Bhatt, Ramesh S., 3
binary time series
   experiments with, 23–24
Binder, Carola C., 112
Blake, David, 166
Bloomfield, Robert, 6, 22–24
Bolle, Friedel, 4
Bomberger, William, 79
Boero, Gianna, 79
Bossons, John, 16
bottom-up approach of modeling
     expectations, 1, 8, 112, 206
Brazil
   estimates of expected inflation for,
     188–198
   estimates of real interest rate for,
     199–204
Buiter, Willem, 205
Bullard, James, 89
Bundick, Brent, 137
business cycle, 14, 201, *see also* GDP
Byrne, Joseph P., 92

Cagan, Phillip, 2, 16, 94
Calcutta. *see* Inida
Canada
   estimates of expected inflation for,
     188–198
   estimates of real interest rate for,
     199–204
Caporale, Guglielmo M., 179
Cargill, Thomas F., 95
Carlson, Kurt A., 6, 24
Carrera, César, 166
Carroll, Christopher D., 5, 9, 71–73, 77–78
central bank communication. *see* anchoring
     of inflation expectations
central projection, 34
Chan, Joshua C.C., 83

Chaomei, Chen, 6, 22
China
    estimates of expected inflation for,
        188–198
    estimates of real interest rate for,
        199–204
Chow, Gregory C., 4
Christandl, Fabian, 19
Christiano, Lawrence J., 85
Clements, Michael P., 9
cognitive psychology, 1, 3, 8, 12
Coibion, Olivier, 72, 86
Collins, Melissa A., 3
comparison of expectations across
        treatments, 49–50
computations of inflation expectations,
        62–63
computer programs, 15, 66–68
conscious thinking. see reasoning
consumer price index, 22, 41–43, 56
context of expectations, 9, 13, 47–48, 52, 54,
        56, 111, 133, 140
Cooray, Arusha, 143
Coppock, Lee, 166
Costa Rica
    high inflation in, 162–168
Cozzi, Guido, 17
CPI, consumer price index
    as measure of the price level, 24
    comparison of short- and long-run
        expectations, 48
Cukierman, Alex, 82
Curtin, Richard T., 9
Czerwinski, Mary P., 6, 22

D'Haultfoeuille, Xavier, 4
Davenport, Margaret, 17
De Bondt, Werner F. M, 17, 96
De Bruin, Wandi Bruine, 34, 79, 82
De Nardi, Mariacristina, 140
deflation
    modeling expectations for, 110, 152
delayed updating. see sticky information
DeLong, J. Bradford, 109, 144
deviations from rational and optimal
        behavior, 21
Dimsdale, Nicholas, 128
disinflation
    episodes of, 201
Dotsey, Michael, 109

Ebersbach, Mirjam, 19
econometric analysis
    of German inflation, 92–93
    of historical interest rates, 154
    of interest rates and velocities in high
        inflation economies, 162–168
    of interest rates in African economies,
        179–183
    of interest rates in Asian economies,
        170–175
    of laboratory expectations data, 49–52,
        115–117
    of survey data, 69–77
    of UK inflation, 128–129
    of US inflation, 88–91
    of US interest rates, 94–109
econometric representation of expectations
    limitations of, 130–131
Edelman, Gerald M., 3
Eggleton, Jan, 3
Eichengreen, Barry, 128
Eisenmann, Shmuel, 18
elasticity of expectations, 116, 131,
        161, 169
eliciting expectations
    basic procedures and data, 22–33
    procedures for probability ranges, 34–41
encompassing set of circumstances, 6, 111
expected inflation. see inflation
        expectations
experts, role of, 4, 10, 71, 78
exponentially growing variable, 19
extrapolation, 2, 6–8, 13–14, 16–17, 20–23,
        47, 50–52, 71–72, 74–75, 79, 110–111,
        115–116, 133
    in economics, 17
    in forecasting, 20–21
    in psychology, 17–20
    linear model of, 7, 47, 115
    pattern-based versus linear, 50–52

Fair, Ray C., 4
Federal Reserve Bank of St. Louis
    as source of CPI and GDP data, 62, 69, 86
    as source of interest rate data, 103
Feldman, Julian, 3
Fetchenhauer, Detlef, 19
Figlewski, Stephen, 4, 75
Fildes, Robert, 20
financial economics, 15, 17

First World War, 14
Fisher effect, 13, 94–97, 109, 140, 143, 149,
        156, 163, 166, 170, 172–173, 175, 179,
        181, 183
    claim of long adjustment lags, 142–143,
        146, 150–151
    evidence for fast adjustment, 109,
        150–151, 156
    in African economies, 179–183
    in Asian economies, 171–175
    in high inflation countries, 166
    in historical times, 143–156
    strong form, 96, 109, 154, 166, 170–171,
        175, 180
    weak form, 96
Fisher, Irving, 1, 94, 143, 145, see Fisher effect
Fitzenberger, Bernd, 93
fixed pattern response, 6, 23
forecast performance
    of different measures of inflation
        expectations, 69–70
forecasting, 8, 10, 13, 17, 19–20, 77
four years of data, 6, 23, 41, 62
France
    estimates of expected inflation for,
        188–198
    estimates of real interest rate for,
        199–204
    Fisher effect in historical times, 143–156
Frazer, William, 79
FRED. see Federal Reserve Bank of St. Louis
French, Eric, 137, 140
Frenkel, Jakob A., 16
Friedman, Milton, 11, 94, 143
Fuhrer, Jeffrey C., 86

Galí, Jordi, 85
gambler's fallacy, 19, 21
GDP deflator
    as measure of the price level, 86
GDP, gross domestic product
    comparison of expectations with CPI
        inflation, 47
    comparison of short- and long-run
        expectations, 48
    expectations of, 8, 25, 27, 133–141
    pattern-based expectations in NKPC, 88
    role of optimistic and pessimistic
        expectations, 140

Gefang, Deborah, 90
generalized approach of modeling pattern-
        based expectations, 14, 110–120, 129,
        133, 138, 157
    key advantage of, 120
Gennaioli, Nicola, 17
Germany, 7–8, 24, 86, 110
    estimates of expected inflation for,
        188–198
    estimates of real interest rate for,
        199–204
Gertler, Mark, 85
Gibson, William E., 95
Gil-Alana, Luis A., 179
Gilovich, Thomas, 18
gold standard, 120
Goldfeld, Stephen M., 164
Goodfriend, Marvin, 201
Gordon, Robert J., 85, 152
Granziera, Eleonora, 17
great recession
    analysis of, 137–141
    contribution of income expectations, 140
Greenwood, Robin, 17
Grier, Kevin B., 78
Gürkaynak, Refet S., 90
Gylfason, Thorvaldur, 145–147

Hales, Jeffrey, 6, 22–24
Haruvy, Ernan, 4
Harvey, Nigel, 20
Haubrich, Joseph, 96
Heine, Steven J., 8
Hendershott, Patrick, 79
heterogeneity of expectations, 6, 27, 183
    comparison of alternative explanations,
        80–82
    concerning income, 34–41, 133–141
    concerning inflation, 78–84
    concerning inflation and its effect on
        interest rates, 95–109, 180–183
    of inflation in major economies, 193
heuristics, 3, 21
heuristics and biases research program, 18
Hey, John D., 4
Hicks, John R., 116
high inflation, 14, 63, 99, 140
    expectations for cases of, 157–168
higher-order expectations, 25, 27, 49, 63, 88

Hirshleifer, David, 17
Homer, Sidney, 107, 152
Honduras
    high inflation in, 162–168
Hong, Felix T., 12
hot hand phenomenon, 18, 21

India
    estimates of expected inflation for,
        188–198
    estimates of real interest rate for,
        199–204
    Fisher effect in historical times, 143–156
Indonesia, 170–178
inflation. *see* CPI and GDP deflator as basis,
    econometric analysis of
inflation expectations
    and historical interest rates, 143–156
    as determinant of nominal interest rate,
        94–109
    as driver of inflation, 91–93
    comparing pattern-based with survey-
        based version, 69–77
    eliciting data for the modeling of, 22–46
    in 10 large economies, 188–198
    in Asian and African economies, 170–178
    in times of high inflation, 157–169
    modeling heterogeneity and uncertainty
        of, 78–84
    modeling of, 68
inflation uncertainty. *see* uncertainty of
    inflation expectations
inflation-indexed bonds, 10, 107
instructions for experiment
    for similarity matching experiment,
        65–66
    for treatment (i), 41–42
    for treatment (iii), 43–46
international data set
    used by Irving Fisher, 144
interquartile range
    of expectations, 34, 79–80, 140, 188
Italy
    estimates of expected inflation for,
        188–198
    estimates of real interest rate for, 199–204

Jamaica
    high inflation in, 162–168
Janor, Hwati, 170

Japan
    estimates of expected inflation for,
        188–198
    estimates of real interest rate for,
        199–204
    Fisher effect in historical times, 143–156
Jelassi, Mohamed Mehdi, 170, 179
Jones, Garett, 3
judgmental forecasting, 21
Jurado, Kyle, 137

Kabundi, Alain, 182
Kahneman, Daniel, 3, 18, 91
Kaliva, Kasimir, 95–96
Kasman, Saadet, 179
Kenia, 179–187
Keynes, John M., 16
Kim, Dong-Hyeon, 170, 179
King, Robert G., 201
Koustas, Zisimos, 96
Kozicki, Sharon, 17

laboratory tasks, 23, *see also* treatments
lagged inflation
    as a proxy for expected inflation, 144
    in the NKPC, 85, 93, 128
Lahiri, Kajal, 105
Landier, Augustin, 4
Laski, Elida V., 3
Lawrence, Michael, 21
lending rate
    as measure of nominal interest rate, 163
Lo, Andrew W., 137
London. *see* UK
long-term expectations, xvii, 9, 16, 41, 52, 60,
        63, 82, 89–90, 92, 106, 121, 130, 133,
        136, 140, 179, 188
long-term expected inflation
    in the UK and the USA, 90–91
Lovell, Michael C., 4
Lund, Nick, 3
Lusanga, Peter, 179

Magin, Konstantin, 109
major economies. *see* USA, China, Japan,
        Germany, UK, Inidia, France, Brazil,
        Italy, Canada
Malawi, 179–187
Malaysia, 170–178
Mankiw, N. Gregory, 5, 78, 81, 88

Manski, Charles F., 9, 34
market-based measure of expected inflation.
    see inflation-indexed bonds
Matchaya, Greenwell C., 179
Mavroeidis, Sophocles, 128
Mazumder, Sandeep, 92
McCarthy, Erin, 11, 107
mean reversion
    of income, 141
mental resources, 3
Miller, Marcus, 205
Mishkin, Frederic S., 144
Mitchell-Innes, Henri A., 179
Mitra, Kaushik, 89
Modigliani, Franco, 16
Moerman, Gerard A., 102
monetary policy
    anchoring of inflation expectations, 89–92
    episodes of high real interest rates, 128
    similar real interest rates in specific
        historical periods, 205
money demand relationship, 162–166
money illusion, 95
monthly expectations, 118
Muth, John F., xvii, 2, 17
Muthian expectations. *see* rational
    expectations

Nason, James M., 129
Nerlove, Marc, 2, 9, 16, 215
New Keynesian Phillips curve, 13, 85–89, 91,
    128
    for Germany, 92–93
    for the UK, 128–129
Ng, Serena, 137
Nhlapo, Nonhlanhla, 182
Nigeria, 179–187
NKPC. *see* New Keynesian Phillips curve
nominal interest rate. *see* Fisher effect
    effect of heterogeneity of inflation
        expectations, 10, 101
    effect of uncertainty of inflation
        expectations, 6, 101, 103
Norenzayan, Ara, 8
Nunes, Ricardo, 86
Nusair, Salah A., 170

one-time survey of expectations, 23, 206
one-to-one effect. *see* Fisher effect, strong
    form

online material
    available from website of the book, 68
Oppenheimer, Daniel M., 18
opportunity costs of holding money, 164
Oskarsson, Van Boven, 18
overshooting
    of GDP expectations, 142

Padula, Mario, 86, 89
Paris. *see* France
parsimonious
    representation of expectations, 8, 115,
        136
participation fee, 25, 27
pattern recognition, 3, 12
pattern-based expectations
    as additional explanatory variable, 74
    comparing of data from subjects with
        different background, 129–130
    of aggregate income, 141
pattern-based extrapolation, xvii
patterns
    classes of, 51, 115, 131
    historically relevant, 24
    primary, 54, 59, 62
    trend versus no-trend, 50–51
Paunio, Jouko J., 10
Perez, Stephen J., 151–152, 154–155
periodicity of expectations. *see* monthly
    expectations
Perry, Mark J., 78
Persson, Torsten, 89
Petropoulos, Fotios, 20
Pfajfar, D., 4, 72
Philippines, 170–178
Phiri, Andrew, 179
Phylaktis, Kate, 166
pilot study
    of probabilistic version for higher-order
        expectations, 27
Pistaferri, Luigi, 137
Plott, Charles, 4
Poitras, Marc, 166
Posner, Michael I., 3
price level plateaus, 7, 115–116, 132
probabilistic treatment. *see* treatment (iii)
professional chartists. *see* technical analysis
professional forecasters
    role in formation of consumer
        expectations, 71–75

psychological universals, 8
psychology, 1, 3, 8, 13, 17
Puccetti, Roland, 3

Raab, Markus, 18
Rabin, Matthew, 18
Ramos-Herrera, Maria del Carmen, 4
range consistency of expectations data, 161
rational expectations, 2–4, 17, 78, 86, 144, 206
rational inattention. *see* sticky information
Rauh, Joshua D., 17
real interest rate, 15, 96, 200
    pattern-based measure of, 107, 127, 199, 204
reasoning, 3, 19, 21, 25
recent past of a series, 21
Reeke, George N., 3
regressive expectations, 16, 75
regressive tendency of expectations, 16, 116, 161, 169
regressiveness of expectations, 20, 131, 147
Roos, Michael, 74
Reis, Ricardo, 5, 88
Rötheli, Tobias F., 4, 6, 8, 22–24, 57, 140
Rudd, Jeremy, 86
Rumelhart, David E., 3

Sagaria, Sabato D., 19
Said, Rasidah M., 170
Santoro, E., 72
Sargent, Thomas, 4, 94, 143, 146
scaling law, 58–59
scaling of expectations, xvii, 53–54, 57–62
Schmidt, Ulrich, 74
Schaling, Eric, 182
Schwartz, Anna J., 94, 143
scientific method, 11
secular growth
    influence on GDP expectations, 141
Serletis, Apostolos, 96
Shafir, Eldar, 95
Shiller, Robert J., 17
Shleifer, Andrei, 17
short-run expectations. *see* short-term expectations
short-term expectations, 9, 41, 48, 52, 82, 107, 116, 119, 121, 127, 129, 136, 139, 152, 170, 179, 199
Shu, Suzanne B., 6, 24

Sichel, Daniel E., 164
Siegler, Mark V., 151–152, 154–155, 216
similarity matching, 13, 53–58, 62, 65, 88, 117–118, 132, 136
Simmons, Peter, 20
Simon, Herbert, 3
Sims, Christopher A., 5
Singapore, 170–178
small-sample bias
    in statistical reasoning, 19
Smith, Gregor W., 129
Smith, Vernon L., 21, 142
Söderlind, Paul, 96
Song, Yong, 83
Sosvilla-Rivero, Simón, 4
South Africa, 179–187
South Korea, 171–175
Spence, Ian, 14
sticky expectations. *see* sticky information
sticky information, 5, 71
Stock, James H., 78
stylized representative displays, 6–7, 14, 22, 53–54, 63
subjective expectations, 8, 49, 60, 63, 88, 133
Summers, Lawrence, 95, 144
Sunder, Shyam, 4
survey of consumer expectations, 69–76
survey of expectations, 4, 10, 34
    of households, 9, 12–13
    of professional forecasters, 9, 72–74, 86–87, 92
    under laboratory conditions, 22, 25, 47
Suvanto, Antti, 10
Sylla, Richard, 107, 152
Symanzik, Jürgen, 14
symmetry of expectations, 116–118, 136
system 1 and 2 of cognition, 3–4, 91

Tabellini, Guido, 89
Tanzania, 179–187
technical analysis, 22
Thailand, 170–178
theory building, 12
Thies, Clifford F., 143
Tillmann, Peter, 92
Timmers, Han, 19
Tokyo. *see* Japan
treatment (i), 41
    eliciting subjective point predictions, 25, 27–31, 34, 49, 51, 60, 66, 88

treatment (ii), 25, 27, 29, 32, 54
  eliciting higher-order expectations, 25
treatment (iii)
  eliciting point predictions and
    probability ranges, 27, 34–41, 49,
    60–66, 70–71, 82, 111, 133
treatments for high inflation experiment,
    157–158
treatments used in the laboratory, 11, 41
Trehan, Bharat, 20
trend versus no-trend patterns, 115
trending time series, 7, 20, 110, 116–118,
    131–132, 157
Tversky, Amos, 18

UK
  anchoring of inflation expectations,
    89–92
  estimates of expected inflation for,
    188–198
  estimates of real interest rate for, 199–204
  Fisher effect in historical times, 143–156
uncertainty of expectations
  concerning income, 34–41, 133–141
  concerning inflation, 78–79, 82–84
  concerning inflation and its effect on
    interest rates, 96–97, 101–109,
    172–175, 180–183
underestimation of future growth, 19
University of Michigan. see survey of
    expectations of households
USA, 7, 14, 24, 70, 79, 83, 86, 89, 110, 119,
    128, 138, 141
  anchoring of inflation expectations, 89–92
  estimates of expected inflation for,
    188–198
  estimates of real interest rate for, 199–204
  Fisher effect in historical times, 143–156

van Dijk, Mathijs A., 102
Vayanos, Dimitri, 18
velocity of money. see money demand
  in high inflation cases, 165
Venezuela
  high inflation in, 162–168
visual display. see visualization
visualization, 5, 22

Wachtel, Paul, 4, 75, 82
Wagenaar, Willem A., 19
Wallace, Myles S., 96
Warner, John T., 96
Watson, Mark W., 78
weighting of past observations
  depending on pattern, 2, 7, 21, 66, 94, 116
Weiserbs, Daniel, 20
Westerlund, Joakim, 96
Whelan, Karl, 86
Williams, Arlington W., 4
worksheet routine
  for computing series of expectations,
    63–68, 140
World Bank as a source of data
  for Asian and African economies, 183
  for high inflation economies, 157–168
  for major economies, 199
  of real interest rates, 199–205
Wright, Jonathan H., 78, 137

Xu, Yingying, 79

Yaari, Gur, 18

Zakelj, Blaz, 4
Zambia, 179–187
Zarnowitz, Victor, 4
Zheng, Min, 17

For EU product safety concerns, contact us at Calle de José Abascal, 56–1°,
28003 Madrid, Spain or eugpsr@cambridge.org.

www.ingramcontent.com/pod-product-compliance
Ingram Content Group UK Ltd.
Pitfield, Milton Keynes, MK11 3LW, UK
UKHW012200180425
457623UK00019B/302